READING GENESIS

Reading Genesis presents a panoramic view of the most vital ways that Genesis is approached in modern scholarship. Chapters by ten eminent scholars cover the perspectives of literature, gender, memory, sources, theology, and the reception of Genesis in Judaism and Christianity. Each contribution addresses the history and rationale of the method, insightfully explores particular texts of Genesis, and deepens the interpretive gain of the method in question. These ways of reading Genesis, which include its classic past readings, map out a pluralistic model for understanding Genesis in – and for – the modern age.

Ronald Hendel is Norma and Sam Dabby Professor of Hebrew Bible and Jewish Studies at the University of California, Berkeley. He is the editor-in-chief of the *Oxford Hebrew Bible*, a new critical edition of the Hebrew Bible, and, most recently, author of *Remembering Abraham: Culture, Memory, and History in the Hebrew Bible* (2005). Professor Hendel also serves as a columnist for the *Biblical Archaeology Review*.

Reading Genesis

Ten Methods

Edited by
RONALD HENDEL
University of California, Berkeley

CAMBRIDGE
UNIVERSITY PRESS

CAMBRIDGE UNIVERSITY PRESS
Cambridge, New York, Melbourne, Madrid, Cape Town, Singapore,
São Paulo, Delhi, Dubai, Tokyo, Mexico City

Cambridge University Press
32 Avenue of the Americas, New York, NY 10013-2473, USA

www.cambridge.org
Information on this title: www.cambridge.org/9780521732390

First published 2010

Printed in the United States of America

A catalog record for this publication is available from the British Library.

Library of Congress Cataloging in Publication data

Reading Genesis : ten methods / edited by Ronald Hendel.
p. cm.
Includes bibliographical references and index.
ISBN 978-0-521-51861-1 – ISBN 978-0-521-73239-0 (pbk.)
1. Bible. O.T. Genesis – Criticism, interpretation, etc. 2. Bible – Hermeneutics.
I. Hendel, Ronald S. II. Title.
BS1235.52.R43 2010
222′.110601–dc22 2010010043

ISBN 978-0-521-51861-1 Hardback
ISBN 978-0-521-73239-0 Paperback

A book like this, a problem like this, is in no hurry; we both, I just as much as my book, are friends of *slowness*. It is not for nothing that I have been a philologist, perhaps I am a philologist still, that is to say, a teacher of slow reading. . . . For philology is that venerable art which demands of its votaries one thing above all: to go aside, to take time, to become still, to become slow – it is a goldsmith's art and connoisseurship of the *word* which has nothing but delicate, cautious work to do and achieves nothing if it does not achieve it *slowly*. . . . [T]his art does not so easily get anything done, it teaches to read *well*, that is to say, to read slowly, deeply, looking cautiously before and aft, with reservations, with doors left open, with delicate eyes and fingers.

Friedrich Nietzsche, Daybreak

It is indeed this greater sense of possibility that moves us so deeply when we listen to those old and strangely simple stories.

Franz Kafka, "Investigations of a Dog"

Contents

Contributors

Robert Alter is the Class of 1937 Professor of Hebrew and Comparative Literature at the University of California, Berkeley. He is the author of *The Art of Biblical Narrative* and, most recently, *Pen of Iron: American Prose and the King James Bible*. He is a recipient of the Robert Kirsch Award (*Los Angeles Times*) for lifetime achievement in literature.

John J. Collins is the Holmes Professor of Old Testament Criticism and Interpretation at Yale Divinity School. His most recent books are *Encounters with Biblical Theology* and *The Bible after Babel: Historical Criticism in a Postmodern Age*. He is a past president of the Catholic Biblical Association and the Society of Biblical Literature.

Ronald Hendel is the Norma and Sam Dabby Professor of Hebrew Bible and Jewish Studies at the University of California, Berkeley. He is the author of *The Text of Genesis 1–11* and, most recently, *Remembering Abraham: Culture, Memory, and History in the Hebrew Bible*.

Robert S. Kawashima is Assistant Professor in the Department of Religion and the Center for Jewish Studies at the University of Florida. He is the author of *Biblical Narrative and the Death of the Rhapsode*.

Chana Kronfeld is Professor of Comparative Literature and Near Eastern Studies at the University of California, Berkeley. She is the author of *On the Margins of Modernism: Decentering Literary Dynamics* and translations of the poetry of Yehuda Amichai and Dahlia Ravikovitch.

Richard A. Layton is Associate Professor of Religion at the University of Chicago, Urbana–Champaign. He is the author of *Didymus the Blind and His Circle in Late-Antique Alexandria: Virtue and Narrative in Biblical Scholarship*.

Ilana Pardes is Professor of Comparative Literature at the Hebrew University of Jerusalem. She is the author of *Countertraditions in the Bible: A Feminist Approach* and, most recently, *Melville's Bibles*.

Naomi Seidman is the Koret Professor of Jewish Culture at the Graduate Theological Union. She is the author of *A Marriage Made in Heaven: The Sexual Politics of Hebrew and Yiddish* and, most recently, *Faithful Renderings: Jewish–Christian Difference and the Practice of Translation*.

Dina Stein is Assistant Professor of Hebrew and Comparative Literature at the University of Haifa. She is the author of *Maxims, Magic, Myth: A Folkloristic Perspective on Pirkei de Rabbi Eliezer* (in Hebrew).

Yair Zakovitch is the Father Takeji Otsuki Professor of Bible at the Hebrew University of Jerusalem. He is the author of *Introduction to Inner-Biblical Interpretation* (in Hebrew) and, most recently, *Inner-Biblical and Extra-Biblical Midrash and the Relationship between Them* (in Hebrew).

Acknowledgments

The making of this book has been surprisingly pleasant (with apologies to Qohelet), primarily due to the contributors' talents and good cheer. I thank them for their marvelous chapters, which exceeded my characteristically exaggerated expectations. We gathered to discuss an earlier round of drafts at a memorable Workshop on Reading Genesis, held at Berkeley in October 2008. I wish to acknowledge the Norma and Sam Dabby Chair of Hebrew Bible and Jewish Studies for funding this workshop and to thank my graduate students for their assistance: Danny Fisher, Rhiannon Graybill, Alison Joseph, Dale Loepp, and Yosefa Raz. The religion editor at Cambridge University Press, Andy Beck, initially enticed me with this book project, which soon outgrew the series that he was planning. His assistant at Cambridge, Jason Przybylski, was very helpful after Andy left. I extend my thanks to Janet Russell for her impeccable index.

Finally, I wish to thank Ann, Ed, and Nat for their bemused love as I grow old and wizened.

Reading Genesis

Ten Methods

Introduction

Ronald Hendel

This book attempts to do something new and old in biblical interpretation. The new involves three moves: (1) charting methods of reading Genesis that have become vital in recent years, including literary criticism, cultural memory, the history of sexuality, and inner-biblical interpretation; (2) renewing the practice of several older methods that retain their vitality, including source criticism and theology; and (3) expanding the horizons of the study of Genesis to encompass the reception and transformation of Genesis in Western culture, including rabbinic and patristic interpretation, translation, and modern literature. The family of methods presented in this book focuses on ways of reading Genesis *and* on ways of reading influential past readings of Genesis. To put it differently, we are engaged in studying a text and its effects in Western culture. This combination of perspectives is relatively new in biblical studies and represents a proposal about how Genesis can be read (and reread) in the university and the modern world.

At the same time, this book is a throwback to an older era – let us call it a pre-postmodern era – when texts were believed to have meanings and when it was the task of the interpreter to discuss those meanings with intelligence and insight. Each contributor to this volume practices what Nietzsche called "the incomparable art of reading well,"[1] which involves a commitment to the notion that texts and their interpretations are worth grappling with in our work and lives. This theoretical empiricism, which can have many flavors and intensities, necessarily includes an appreciation of the interdependence of various approaches to the text – including the historical, literary, philosophical, anthropological, and theological. It involves a pragmatic openness

---

[1] Friedrich Nietzsche, *The Twilight of the Idols and the Anti-Christ* (New York: Penguin, 1990), 194, §59.

1

to multiple converging and diverging paths of study for the simple reason that, as Wittgenstein says, "[I]t is possible to be interested in a phenomenon in a variety of ways."[2] There is no single authoritative – or authoritarian – method of reading Genesis.

A word about what we mean by "method." The subtitle of this book, *Ten Methods*, should not be taken to mean that there are fixed techniques or recipes for reading Genesis as there might be, for example, for operating heavy machinery or making onion soup. A method in humanistic scholarship is – as both the medieval schoolmen and Wittgenstein defined it – a "way of proceeding" (*modus procendi*), a bundle of insights and habits that seem to work. John Barton helpfully elucidates this sense of "method" in biblical studies:

> [W]e should see each of our "methods" as a codification of intuitions about the text which may occur to intelligent readers. Such intuitions can well arrive at truth; but it will not be the kind of truth familiar in the natural sciences. Reading the Old Testament, with whatever aim in view, belongs to the humanities and cannot operate with an idea of watertight, correct method.[3]

In other words, we should not reify our methods or pretend that they are scientific procedures. It is enough that they be, as the Germans say, *Wissenschaftlich*, which means, roughly, "intellectually rigorous." That is all we can ask of our scholarly efforts – and that is enough.

AFTER GUNKEL: ROADS NOT TAKEN

The classic treatment of Genesis in modern scholarship is Hermann Gunkel's commentary on Genesis, whose centennial we commemorate in 2010 (the third and final edition was published in 1910). As Ernest Nicholson rightly observed, "The influence of the methods pioneered by Gunkel upon subsequent Old Testament study can scarcely be overestimated."[4] Gunkel combined mastery of the older disciplines of source and textual criticism with a new focus on the history of traditions, comparative religion,

---

[2] Ludwig Wittgenstein, *Philosophical Investigations* (New York: Macmillan, 1958), 47.
[3] John Barton, *Reading the Old Testament: Method in Biblical Study* (2nd ed.; Louisville, KY: Westminster John Knox Press, 1996), 5.
[4] Ernest W. Nicholson, "Foreword: Hermann Gunkel as a Pioneer of Modern Old Testament Study," in Hermann Gunkel, *Genesis* (Macon, GA: Mercer University Press, 1997; German original, 3rd ed., 1910), 9.

folklore, and literary style. In his "Foreword," he posed two programmatic questions:

> How long until Old Testament scholars finally understand what a mighty task literary-historical problems present them, even in the realm of the narratives, and when will the testament of the great Herder finally be executed?[5]

Gunkel proceeded to unfold the historical and literary dimensions of the Genesis narratives. He showed how they originated in the folklore of Israelite and pre-Israelite cultures, tracing their transformation into larger narrative collections and, ultimately, into the literary documents of Genesis. This is literary history, the diachronic dimension of the stories and texts in their intricate evolution through time.

His evocation of Herder's "testimony" is a call for a close literary reading of Genesis, which Herder pioneered in *The Oldest Document of the Human Race* (1774) and *The Spirit of Hebrew Poetry* (1782).[6] Gunkel devoted a major section of his "Introduction" to "the artistic form of the legends of Genesis" (*Kunstform der Sagen der Genesis*), including issues such as prose style, genre, literary structure, character, description, speeches, motifs, keywords (*Stichwörter*), and other wordplay. Gunkel described this literary task in Herderian terms: "[O]ne who wants to do justice to such old accounts must have sufficient aesthetic sensibility to hear an account as it is and as it wants to be."[7] This requires empathy (what Herder called *Einfühlung*, literally, "feeling into") and sensibility to literary nuance. Gunkel embraced this literary task throughout his commentary, and he treated the variety of dimensions of Genesis – historical, folkloric, religious, and literary – with erudition and brilliance.

Gunkel's multilayered reading of Genesis displays a methodological pluralism that has largely been abandoned in recent biblical scholarship. After Gunkel, scholars have tended to be methodological monists: one is a historian, another is a source critic, a third is a redaction critic, and so forth. More recently, the degrees of specialization have proliferated: one is a feminist reader-response literary critic; another is a postcolonial Third World theologian. Each inhabits a single method (or a hybrid that functions as one method) and tends to regard other methods with hostility or suspicion.

---

[5] Gunkel, *Genesis*, v.
[6] See Christoph Bultmann, "Creation at the Beginning of History: Johann Gottfried Herder's Interpretation of Genesis 1," *Journal for the Study of the Old Testament* 68 (1995), 23–32. See also the excerpt from *The Oldest Document of the Human Race*, in J. G. Herder, *Against Pure Reason: Writings on Religion, Language, and History*, ed. Marcia Bunge (Minneapolis, MN: Fortress, 1992) 107–10; idem, *The Spirit of Hebrew Poetry* (2 vols.; Burlington, VT: Edward Smith, 1833).
[7] Gunkel, *Genesis*, xi.

Other scholars' methods are – in various measure – heretical, hegemonic, or narcissistic. There is a crisis of confidence in the field today – a fractured sectarianism – in which the terms of discourse are in constant contention. As Barton describes the current tension: "A great rift has opened . . . [with] each party on the whole regarding the other as largely worthless."[8]

Usually, the lines of fracture are drawn up as "history versus literature" or "diachronic versus synchronic"; sometimes the counterclaim is "objective versus subjective" or "empirical versus politically engaged." Each opposition, however, is overdrawn and based largely on portraying the other as a straw man or caricature. It is salutary to note that every intellectually responsible literary reading of Genesis relies on knowledge of an ancient language (i.e., biblical Hebrew, with a smattering of Aramaic, and – it is hoped – some Greek) and an awareness of ancient literary and cultural conventions. This is historical knowledge. And any historical reconstruction – of sources, redaction, or texts – that does not attend to the nuances of the literary text is merely incompetent. Reading the Bible is a multifarious task such that there are – to use Frank Kermode's term – many "forms of attention" appropriate for reading it.[9]

There are partisans on both sides of the battle lines of history versus literature and the related binary oppositions in the study of Genesis. Rather than posing simplistic oppositions, we should imagine and practice an interweaving dialectic. We should acknowledge that the task of richly reading Genesis involves both sides of each of these contrasts: history and literature, synchrony and diachrony, empirical data and ideology. The notion that one can read an ancient text *without* attention to its historicity or that one can reconstruct history *without* attention to the literary constituency of the text are equally symptomatic of sectarian illusions. As Wittgenstein says in another context, such "problems arise when language *goes on holiday.*"[10] We readily grant that Genesis is an ancient book – a discourse from the past – which necessarily entails the intertwining of history and literature.

An intelligent reading of any ancient literary text involves multiple skills and sensibilities. If we resist the seduction of sectarian rhetoric, it is easy to see that methodological pluralism – as exemplified by Gunkel's classic commentary – has virtues that offer a model for the present. This book resumes "the road not taken" by pursuing the path of multiple and complementary methods, which diverge and converge in illuminating ways.

---

[8] John Barton, *The Nature of Biblical Criticism* (Louisville, KY: Westminster John Knox Press, 2007), 187.

[9] Frank Kermode, *Forms of Attention* (Chicago: University of Chicago Press, 1985).

[10] Wittgenstein, *Philosophical Investigations*, 19.

This is not a lazy eclecticism but rather a methodological pluralism that befits the complex phenomenon that is the focus of our investigation: the task of reading Genesis in – and for – the modern age.

THE FATE OF TEXTS: LIFE AND AFTERLIFE

One of several new areas of biblical scholarship that we include in this book is the study of classic readings of Genesis in Western culture, from inner-biblical interpretation to postbiblical Jewish, Christian, and secular exegesis. The fate of Genesis in its reading publics has, in recent years, become a part of biblical scholarship. In some ways, this interest displays a new maturity in the field, which arose in part as a reaction to traditional interpretations of the Bible. Modern biblical scholarship is shaped by its formative era in Renaissance humanism with the admonition, *ad fontes* ("to the sources"), which the Reformation adapted to the Bible with the call for *sola scriptura* ("scripture alone"). The Protestant Reformers castigated traditional interpretation as the devil's (or the pope's) work, which had long ensured the "Babylonian captivity" of the church. Modern biblical scholarship defines itself in opposition to traditional church- and synagogue-based forms of interpretation; hence, it is both ironic and salutary that the study of "precritical" forms of reading has recently become part of the horizon of critical scholarship. The expansion of the guild of biblical scholarship to include Jews and Catholics has stimulated this new interest in the chain of interpretation, which complicates the focus on "scripture alone."[11]

In some respects, the attention to the fate of Genesis in postbiblical culture is entirely consonant with the long-standing epistemology of modern biblical criticism. Baruch Spinoza defined the "true method" of biblical interpretation as consisting of three interlocking steps: (1) mastery of biblical Hebrew, (2) careful discernment of the meanings of biblical texts, and (3) awareness of the history and transmission of the biblical books. The third step – what Spinoza called "the fate of each book"[12] – logically entails its reception and use in the chain of textual transmission, although Spinoza referred primarily to its editorial and scribal history. But the fate of Genesis is not limited to its material dissemination; it logically includes its cultural uses and effects – that is, its life in Western culture.

[11] See James L. Kugel, "The Bible in the University," in *The Hebrew Bible and Its Interpreters*, eds. W. H. Propp, B. Halpern, and D. N. Freedman (Winona Lake, IN: Eisenbrauns, 1990), 143–65.

[12] Baruch Spinoza, *Theological-Political Treatise*, ed. Jonathan Israel (Cambridge: Cambridge University Press, 2007; Latin original, 1670), 101.

Some pertinent remarks by Walter Benjamin illuminate this issue. He observed that the study of literature

> should struggle above all with the works. Their entire life and their effects should have the right to stand alongside the history of their composition. In other words, their fate, their reception by their contemporaries, their translations, their fame.[13]

Benjamin makes a valuable distinction between the "life" and the "effects" (*Wirkung*) or "afterlife" (*Überleben*; literally, "survival") of a literary work: "[I]n its afterlife – which could not be called that if it were not a transformation and a renewal of something living – the original undergoes a change."[14] Through its transformation – or, more precisely, its incessant variety of transformations – the text becomes a historical agent, a palimpsest of significant interpretations and uses through time. Hence, the plural task of reading Genesis should naturally include its life and afterlife, its meanings and effects.[15]

TEN METHODS

The family of methods treated in this book is not comprehensive. Our goal is to explore and expand illuminating ways of reading Genesis that are being actively pursued in contemporary scholarship. Other important methods are not included because they are not, strictly speaking, methods of reading – for example, textual criticism (although textual criticism has obvious implications for the concept of the text and for the parameters of any reading) and historical criticism (which, like textual criticism, is a necessary prolegomenon to an informed reading).[16] Other methods are not included because

[13] Walter Benjamin, "Literary History and the Study of Literature," in idem, *Selected Writings, Volume 2: 1927–1934* (Cambridge, MA: Harvard University Press, 1999), 464.

[14] Walter Benjamin, "The Task of the Translator," in idem, *Illuminations: Essays and Reflections*, ed. Hannah Arendt (New York: Schocken Books, 1968), 73; quoted in Naomi Seidman, *Faithful Renderings: Jewish-Christian Difference and the Politics of Translation* (Chicago: University of Chicago Press, 2006), 10. See also Chapter 8 in this volume.

[15] H.-G. Gadamer, among others, argued that these distinctions can hardly be made (*Truth and Method* [2nd ed.; New York: Continuum, 1984], 352–7); however, if one grants that sentences have semantic implicatures (a conversational sense based on grammar and culture), it is difficult to avoid such distinctions. See H. P. Grice, *Studies in the Way of Words* (Cambridge, MA: Harvard University Press, 1989). See further the distinction between *peshat* and *midrash* in Chapter 5 in this volume.

[16] See Ronald Hendel, *The Text of Genesis 1–11: Textual Studies and Critical Edition* (New York: Oxford University Press, 1998), 3–5; "Plural Texts and Literary Criticism: For Instance, 1 Samuel 17," *Textus* 23 (2007), 97–114; idem, "Historical Context," in *The Book of Genesis: Composition, Reception, and Interpretation*, eds. C. A. Evans, J. N. Lohr, and D. L. Petersen (Leiden, the Netherlands: Brill, forthcoming).

they are not yet "ripe" in the study of Genesis – for example, postcolonial criticism, which is still in a nascent phase (although I have made an attempt for Genesis).[17]

Also conspicuously absent are what Barton calls "advocacy" readings, which advance political agendas via robust personal or prescriptive readings. For example, many feminist readings are avowedly advocacy readings – even "prophetic" readings – following Phyllis Trible's programmatic call:

> As a critique of culture and faith in the light of misogyny, feminism is a prophetic movement, examining the status quo, pronouncing judgment, and calling for repentance.[18]

Laudable as such social criticism may be, there are problems and internal contradictions in scholarship with these aims. As Saba Mahmood observes, there is "a deeper tension within feminism attributable to its dual character as both an *analytical* and a *politically prescriptive* project."[19] The politically prescriptive part often tends to drive the analytical, which "impose[s] a teleology of progressive politics"[20] onto materials for which such categories are wholly foreign. This may be described as a form of "Orientalism," in which ancient Israelite texts and practices are accorded praise or blame depending on their relationship to modern progressive politics. Because of these issues, we have not included methods of advocacy scholarship. Chapter 4, "Gender and Sexuality," is analytical – not prescriptive – in its study of the representation of sex and gender in Genesis. But we agree that the expansion of scholarship to include this topic has real (and timely) ethical implications.

A partially overlapping category is postmodern readings, for which all texts – and any linguistic utterance – lack stable or determinative meanings. This position seems to be another instance when the critic's language "goes on holiday" – as if the act of reading were a solipsistic dance over the void. A key contradiction within this method is that a reading that views the text as meaningless must somehow exempt itself from this condition, or else it must embrace its own meaninglessness. As Bruno Latour argues, postmodernism is an "incomplete skepticism" rather than a coherent

---

[17] Ronald Hendel, "Genesis 1–11 and Its Mesopotamian Problem," *Cultural Borrowings and Ethnic Appropriations in Antiquity*, ed. Erich Gruen (Stuttgart: Franz Steiner Verlag, 2005), 23–36.

[18] Phyllis Trible, *Texts of Terror: Literary-Feminist Readings of Biblical Narratives* (Philadelphia, PA: Fortress Press, 1984), 3.

[19] Saba Mahmood, *Politics of Piety: The Islamic Revival and the Feminist Subject* (Princeton, NJ: Princeton University Press, 2004), 10.

[20] Ibid., 9.

position.[21] In postmodernism, "[n]othing has value; everything is a reflection, a simulacrum, a floating sign. . . . The empty world in which the postmoderns evolve is one they themselves, and they alone, have emptied."[22] When this book's contributors avail themselves of postmodern theory, we do so gingerly, without emptying our text – Genesis – of its life and meanings.

The first of our ten methods is "Literature." Robert Alter, the most consequential modern practitioner of this method, traces its history and transformations from Late Antiquity to modern times and provides a penetrating reading of the life of Jacob, who becomes a fully realized individual in the course of the narrative. Alter addresses how the Jacob story works as a realistic narrative and compellingly draws out the richness of his changing character. Alter's discussion elegantly demonstrates the rationale and interpretive gains of an informed literary reading of Genesis.

Chapter 2, "Cultural Memory," is my topic. This is a relatively recent method that blends insights from anthropology, history, and cultural studies. To approach Genesis in this way involves attention to a cluster of features: how collective memory serves as an agent of cultural identity, how the landscape and sacred sites revitalize ancestral memories, how social frameworks filter the collective past, and how narrative strategies make the past memorable. The stories of Jacob at Bethel and his journey to Mesopotamia are discussed as examples of biblical memory. This approach is arguably more illuminating than conventional historical inquiry and aptly supplements the literary perspective in Chapter 1.

Robert S. Kawashima provides a philosophically incisive treatment of the literary history of Genesis in Chapter 3, "Sources and Redaction." He shows how a discerning attention to the compositional history of Genesis entails a richer understanding of its literary and theological meanings. Through close readings of the features of the J and P sources in Genesis 1–11, the sources' large-scale literary structures, and their editorial combination, Kawashima constructs a compelling synthesis of the historical poetics of Genesis.

Chapter 4, "Gender and Sexuality," is a collaborative effort by Ilana Pardes, Chana Kronfeld, and myself. Here, we weave together the fruits of feminist biblical scholarship with recent perspectives from the history of sexuality. We focus on the culturally constructed character of sexual norms, particularly as shaped by the changing dynamics of public knowledge, legal power, and personal agency. Our narrative focus is the story of Sodom and Gomorrah, which involves conflicts of authority, honor, gender, and sexual

---

[21] Bruno Latour, *We Have Never Been Modern* (Cambridge, MA: Harvard University Press, 1993), 9.
[22] Ibid., 131.

behavior – including male and female sexual agents. Because the biblical system of knowledge, power, and agency is configured differently than our own, modern categories do not easily apply. How to understand the nuances of sexuality and gender in the Genesis narratives without anachronism is an important goal of this method.

Yair Zakovitch addresses the chain of interpretations *within* the Bible in Chapter 5, "Inner-Biblical Interpretation." He discusses how the senses of the text are affected by concentric circles of interpretation – within the story cycle, among different sources, and in later biblical writings. His narrative focus is Genesis 27, in which Jacob deceives his father Isaac and receives the blessing of the firstborn son. Various interpretations arise from this story, particularly as they depict the ethics of Jacob's character. Political, moral, historical, and hermeneutical aims color these interpretations. Zakovitch shows how the methods of inner-biblical interpretation serve to make Genesis a perennially relevant and multivalent text.

Dina Stein explores the life of Genesis in the postbiblical interpretive culture of Judaism in Chapter 6, "Rabbinic Interpretation." With the rise of the Bible as Holy Scripture, reading Genesis becomes an intricate art. The major method of rabbinic interpretation – Midrash – is, as Stein shows, rooted in the self-conscious citation of Scriptural authority. It is a self-reflexive method, conscious of its own meaning-producing activity. Midrash correspondingly portrays its biblical heroes – in this case, Abraham – as self-reflective individuals. By means of its chain of Scriptural citations, Midrash shows how God contemplated Abraham when He created the universe – thereby unifying the national and cosmic dimensions of Genesis – and depicts Abraham as a proto-rabbinic sage, citing Scripture himself. The rabbinic method of interpreting Scripture, in its own self-representation, is a mirror of God's creative acts of interpretation, as each contemplates the perfect and divine words of Genesis.

Richard A. Layton explores the formative period of Christian interpretive culture in Chapter 7, "Interpretation in the Early Church." To comprehend these reading practices as more than antiquarian curiosities, he develops a nuanced model of reception theory, melding together different strands of recent scholarship on this topic. With these interpretive tools in hand, he discusses the different ways that the "Call and Migration of Abraham" (Genesis 12) was understood and refashioned by postbiblical and early Christian interpreters: how they filled gaps, created communities of readers, and accommodated the story to their cultural and religious horizons, whether particularistic/national, universal/philosophical, or points in between. Layton persuasively shows how ancient interpretive practices – formulated by Paul, Philo, Augustine, Origen, and other luminaries – continue to inform

modern interpretive practices without our necessarily being aware of perpet-
uating them.

In Chapter 8, "Translation," Naomi Seidman addresses a method that
rarely receives attention but has important consequences. As she observes,
most readers over the millennia have only known the Bible through translation. There are many dimensions to translation: it entails loss of the original,
but it is also transformative because it creates new meanings – and new converts. The distinction between *original* and *translation* is complicated because
some "original" readings are only preserved in translation (e.g., in the Greek
Septuagint) and the Hebrew text of Genesis is sometimes distorted by scribal
error. Seidman shows that Christian and Jewish theories of translation –
and modern versions by Kafka, Derrida, and others – are often based on
Genesis stories, most memorably the Tower of Babel story, in which God
translates the original language into mutually conflicting local languages. In
Seidman's treatment, translation – which involves languages and cultures –
illuminates deep features in the life and afterlife of Genesis.

Ilana Pardes explores what she aptly calls "literary exegesis" in Chapter 9,
"Modern Literature." Novelists, poets, and writers of all kinds have interpreted
the stories of Genesis by refashioning them through literary imagination.
In her primary example, Melville's *Moby-Dick*, she shows how Melville –
through his narrator, a whaler by the name of Ishmael – presents a new
Bible and a reinvented Genesis for the new American world. A series of
"wild Ishmaels" populates the story and negotiate the dangers of the watery
wilderness, inverting the desert locale of Ishmael in Genesis 16 and 21. Melville
imagined these Ishmaels as virtuous outcasts, whereas the "chosen one" is an
Ahab, not an Isaac. The clash of characters and fates favors the rough Ishmael,
who alone survives when he is rescued by a wandering ship named *Rachel*, who
cries for her lost children as she grants our narrator new life. Pardes traces
the transformations of Ishmael – and Melville's biblical interpretations –
as complex, politically charged, and attuned to the complicated subtexts of
Genesis.

John J. Collins expertly treats the last of our family of methods, "Modern
Theology," in Chapter 10. He explores what it means to read Genesis theologically in the modern world, exposing the possibilities and pitfalls of this
method. Focused on the harrowing narrative of "The Binding of Isaac" in
Genesis 22, he offers penetrating critiques of influential modern theological
readings by Gerhard von Rad, Brevard Childs, Jon Levenson, and others.
Collins observes that theological interpretations tend to adopt an apologetic
stance toward the Bible and shirk the ethical problem at the heart of the story.

In his call for a critical biblical theology,[23] he makes a compelling case for theological readings that offer reasoned ethical engagement with the text rather than a pious defense of it. Collins's lucid treatment – both a critique and a program for theological method – demonstrates the continuing vitality of theological inquiry into the ethical implications of Genesis.

My hope is that these chapters find receptive readers. They offer a panoramic model of biblical studies as a truly interdisciplinary field, in which each method complements and complicates the others. As I have noted, the idea that methodological pluralism is desirable – or even possible – is contested in contemporary biblical scholarship. At a conference on Genesis a few years ago, an eminent biblical scholar cautioned me against such pluralism. "When you open one door," he warned, "you close another." This book is testimony to the possibility of opening multiple doors, with the aim of a multilayered understanding of Genesis and its legacy. Each door in this book opens a new vista that enables one to open the other doors with new perspectives and opened eyes.

A note on transliteration. We have adopted a simplified system, in which each Hebrew letter is represented by a single symbol (' ʿ) or English letter (including ḥ, ṭ, ṣ, and š). Vowel length is not indicated. The exception to the latter rule is vocal *šᵉwaʾ*, which is indicated by a raised *e*. Hebraists do not need a more elaborate system and nonspecialists need not be burdened by supererogatory notations (which are, in any case, linguistically questionable because they mix the phonology of different periods of Biblical Hebrew and its reading traditions).

A note on the cover art. The iconic Lucas Cranach painting of the Garden of Eden was chosen by the marketing department for the cover art, perhaps with the hope that the famous naked couple would catch the eye. I now see that the image, in a subtle way, expresses several themes of this volume. The forbidden fruit, which Eve nonchalantly gives to the puzzled Adam, is an apple. However, in Genesis the fruit is more esoteric – it is "knowledge of good and evil" fruit, which only grows on one tree in the middle of the Garden of Eden. This fruit cannot be found in any grocery store or fruit stand. But artists need an image to paint, and readers need a fruit to imagine, so a species was inferred from a close reading of the story – in the Latin translation (which was originally a translation of the Greek translation of the Hebrew). In Latin, "knowing good and evil" is "scientes bonum et malum." Malum, "evil,"

---

[23] See also John J. Collins, "Is a Critical Biblical Theology Possible?," in idem, *Encounters with Biblical Theology* (Minneapolis, MN: Fortress Press, 2005), 11–23.

is a homonym for "apple." And so the apple was naturally identified as the forbidden fruit. (This identification goes back at least as far as the mediocre Latin poet Commodian, ca. 3rd century C.E.) This interpretive motif, which found its way into all European cultures (including Yiddish), shows the rich and often unpredictable yield of reading Genesis.

1

ॐ

Literature

Robert Alter

Perceptions of the literary dimensions of the Hebrew Bible have a long pre-history, and they surely did not begin in America, England, Israel, and the Netherlands in the 1970s, as some have imagined. It is obviously true that the notion of Scripture as literal revelation, shared by Christians and Jews, to a large extent deflected interpreters over the centuries from explicitly consid-ering the literary shaping of the biblical texts, which were characteristically viewed as sources of theological truth and moral or spiritual instruction. Nevertheless, these texts had some very good readers from Late Antiquity onward who were by no means blind to the literary richness of the narra-tives and the poetry. Thus, the framers of rabbinic Midrash more than a millennium and a half ago, of course did not speak of recurrent motifs or mirroring episodes as a modern literary critic might do. Yet, *Genesis Rabbah* picked up the motif of deception through a garment, in each case linked with a kid, and the recurring keyword *recognize* (*haker*), which tied in Genesis 38 with Genesis 37. They equally identified the story of Jacob's switched brides as a measure-for-measure response to the story of his stealing the paternal blessing.

A finely imaginative sensitivity to the literary articulations of the biblical texts is registered in thousands of instances of allusions to the Bible in medieval Hebrew poetry, especially in its greatest age in eleventh- and twelfth-century Spain. Poets such as Samuel Hanagid, Solomon ibn Gabirol, Moses ibn Ezra, and Judah Halevi, although they were believing Jews who presumably saw the Bible as divine revelation, clearly were also reading both the narratives and the poems as literature because their responsiveness to the imagery of the biblical poems and to the complexities of the biblical stories is strongly registered in their own poetry. A paradigmatic case in point is the beginning of a poem by

Hanagid on the death of his beloved brother Yitzhak: "May God grant grace to you, my brother." This is a precise quotation of Joseph's words to Benjamin when his younger brother is first brought to him in Egypt (Genesis 43:29), except that Joseph says "my son," still concealing his true identity. Soon he will reveal himself and embrace his brother, weeping. Hanagid uses the term of true relationship that Joseph withholds, but he is keenly aware that in his case there can be no reunion with the brother now parted from him forever. His identification with the biblical figure is heightened by his awareness that he, too, is a Hebrew who has ascended to great power, as vizier of Granada. In all of this, he is brilliantly reading the narrative in Genesis as a moving story. At least in Hebrew tradition, the Bible maintained what I have called elsewhere a "double canonicity,"[1] literary as well as doctrinal.

An awareness of the literary power and subtlety of the biblical texts is also often manifested in the medieval Hebrew commentators. Rashi (1040–1105), whose commentary became virtually canonical, assumes that every word of Scripture is divinely dictated, but this often leads him, as a superb Hebraist, to make fine as well as fanciful discriminations about the use of one synonym in preference to another, about the repetition of terms, and much else. Abraham ibn Ezra (1089–1164) was himself an accomplished poet and a grammarian, and his commentary often affords acute insight into a range of literary phenomena from the links between consecutive passages and the thematic definition of space to chiastic patterns and the resonance of particular words.

The concrete experience, then, of reading Scripture in many instances could be thoroughly literary, but the conceptual framework with which these readers approached the Bible was not. The Bible was thought of as a set of divinely revealed texts framed to teach us the way in which we must go, to lay out the origins of the world and the people of Israel and the direction of history from creation to end-time. The Bible also was perceived to be what no large work of literature has ever been – a perfect, harmonious concordance of meaning and language from beginning to end, in which no word or linguistic particle was out of place, and in which – as the classical Midrash assumed – any phrase or word in Exodus or Numbers could find intricately answering words in Psalms, Job, or the Prophets. These texts, then, at least in ideological principle, were not meant to be read for the subtlety of their characterization or the power of their imagery, as one might read Homer or Chaucer or a modern novelist.

All this began to change with the advent of European Romanticism. J. G. Herder was a pivotal figure in effecting this change. He was an ideologue of

---

[1] Robert Alter, *Canon and Creativity* (New Haven, CT: Yale University Press, 2000), Chapter 1.

Romanticism but also a clergyman with knowledge of biblical Hebrew. His seminal work, *The Spirit of Hebrew Poetry* (1782), occasionally even makes philological comments on the Hebrew, although its main thrust is elsewhere. Herder's signal innovation was to shift the conceptual framework for thinking about the Bible from theology to literature. (It is noteworthy that he felt no conflict between making this shift and the religious faith that had brought him to the study of Scripture in the first place.) His points of reference as he discusses and rapturously celebrates the sundry biblical texts are the touchstones of classical – and, from time to time, modern German – literature: a reader who, as a matter of course, assumes poetic profundity in Homer or Sophocles is encouraged to look at Isaiah or Job with fresh eyes and to take in the brilliance of its poetry. Along the way, there is much Orientalist exaltation of the Hebrew national genius, but that view is part and parcel of the Romantic assumption that great literature in general is an expression of the distinctive genius of a particular people. The qualities of biblical writing that were paramount for Herder are its sublimity of expression, its musicality, and – perhaps above all else – its probing and powerful representation of human experience. These are terms that would have occurred intermittently at best, if at all, to the authors of the Midrash, the Church Fathers, Maimonides and Aquinas, Luther and Calvin. Herder's turn to the aesthetic and to the sheer representational power of Scripture has the effect of liberating the biblical texts from the predominantly didactic frame in which they were traditionally expounded.

Here is an exemplary passage from *The Spirit of Hebrew Poetry* that also conveniently reflects on the Jacob story, to which we presently turn. In the dialogue in which the book is cast, the character Euthyphron has been challenged by his interlocutor to justify the faults of the patriarchs evidenced in the narrative in Genesis:

> They are human failings, and the very fact, that they are recounted, that in their history nothing is kept back and concealed, makes their shepherd tale, considered as a pastoral narrative merely, invaluable. The timid Isaac, the crafty Jacob, stand forth in their doings; but you will not deny, that the craftiness of the latter was always recompensed with evil; and in his old age, like Ulysses, he exhibited among these patriarchal herdsmen a character well tried and approved. His history is an instructive mirror of the human heart.... [2]

---

[2] J. G. Herder, *The Spirit of Hebrew Poetry*, translated by Edward Marsh (Burlington, VT: Edward Smith, 1833), Vol. 1, 228.

The emphasis on "human" at both the beginning and the end of the excerpt is noteworthy. The patriarchal tales are referred to in relation to the literary genre of pastoral narrative, but they are judged to be more penetrating, more psychologically and morally true, than mere pastoral. The comparison between Jacob and Ulysses – Erich Auerbach will return to it a century and a half later – is even more revealing. (It would hardly have occurred to an exegete of Late Antiquity, even if he knew Homer, to mention the two in the same breath.) The defining phrase here is Herder's characterization of Jacob's story as "an instructive mirror of the human heart." Whatever Herder's Christian beliefs, he is clearly thinking of Scripture in humanistic and literary terms. This phrase, or its sundry close equivalents, had considerable currency in the literary criticism of the late eighteenth century: one was encouraged to read the novels of Richardson, Rousseau, and Goethe as instructive mirrors of the human heart, and that is how Herder invites us to read Genesis.

The book that marked a watershed in regard to setting the Bible in a literary context was Auerbach's *Mimesis* (1946). It is one of the few enduring masterworks of literary criticism written in the twentieth century and, at the same time, a study that squarely places the Bible alongside Homer at the source of the Western literary tradition. Indeed, in the famous comparison of the Odyssey with Genesis that takes up the first chapter, it is the Bible, not Homer, that emerges as the great forerunner of the representation of human life with existential seriousness in Western literature. As one follows Auerbach's chronological argument in the later chapters from Dante to Shakespeare to Balzac and Flaubert to the modernist novel, the ancient Hebrew writers' engagement with what Auerbach refers to as the problematic character of everyday life and the distinctive tenor of individual experience lays the ground more than any Greek counterpart for what is announced in the book's subtitle: the representation of reality in Western literature. What is generally remembered from the opening chapter of *Mimesis* is the productive idea of a narrative "fraught with background" – an idea that would bear fruit, for example, in the stress on filling in gaps in biblical narrative in the work of Menakhem Perry and Meir Sternberg – but Auerbach's placing the Bible in a fundamentally new context was still more momentous. He invited readers to think of the Bible not in relation to a tradition of exegesis and theology but rather in relation to major works of imaginative literature: Dante, Cervantes, Montaigne, and Stendhal, not the rabbis and the Church Fathers.

Auerbach, we may recall, draws a sharp contrast between Odysseus – who wakes up every morning of his life the same person, vivid but unchanging – and the figures of Jacob and David, who evolve through time and are changed by their experience (as, in fact, Herder hinted):

> But what a road, what a fate, lie between Jacob who cheated his father out of his blessing and the old man whose favorite son has been torn to pieces by a wild beast!. . . . The old man, of whom we know how he has become what he is, is more of an individual than the young man; for it is only during the course of an eventful life that men are differentiated into full individuality; and it is this history of a personality which the Old Testament presents to us as the formation undergone by those whom God has chosen to be examples. Fraught with their development, sometimes even aged to the verge of dissolution, they show a distinct stamp of individuality entirely foreign to the Homeric heroes.[3]

One could say that Auerbach is unpacking analytically what Herder referred to as an "instructive mirror of the human heart." The pronounced emphasis on individuality suggests that Auerbach ultimately has in view a long literary evolution that will lead to the realist novel. Like Levin in *Anna Karenina*, like Dorothea Brooke in *Middlemarch*, even like the aged Don Quixote on his deathbed, the biblical Jacob is imagined as learning by slow stages from the pressure of experience and all its pain, shedding illusions, sinking into "the final thought," as Saul Bellow strikingly says of the facial expression on the corpse seen at the end of *Seize the Day*. At the beginning of the 1980s, in a peremptory dismissal of literary approaches to the Bible, James Kugel declared that Abraham, Isaac, and Jacob were our forefathers, not characters,[4] but the persuasive weight of Auerbach's argument is that the seriousness expressed in them as representations of human life lies precisely in their being characters. To regard Jacob not as an eponymous prototype of national history or as a typological token of redemption history but rather as a fictional character fulfilling his individual destiny is a liberating perspective: transcending any doctrinal agenda, the full power of the biblical story is revealed as a representation of the tangled contradictions of living out a life through the cumulative vicissitudes of experience. I would add that this very power of fictional representation is inseparable from the religious seriousness of the story: these, we are invited to contemplate, are the tangled complexities of a human life; this is the quirky stuff of human nature itself, through which we are bidden to work out, however imperfectly, God's design on earth.

[3] Erich Auerbach, *Mimesis*, translated by Willard R. Trask (Princeton, NJ: Princeton University Press, 1953), 18.
[4] James Kugel, "On the Bible and Literary Criticism," *Prooftexts* 1 (September 1981), 217–36.

The final way station I want to cite in the emergence of literary redefinitions of the Bible is a pivotal book that – unlike Herder and Auerbach – does not propose a literary approach but rather a diagnosis of the cultural predicament that has marginalized literary readings. A generation after Auerbach, Hans Frei's *The Eclipse of Biblical Narrative* (1974) situates modern discussions of the Bible in a broad context of intellectual history of the eighteenth and nineteenth centuries. So far, I have singled out theological or devotional conceptions of the Bible as impediments over the centuries to engaging with its literary art. The modern academic study of the Bible – which became fully established in Europe (especially in Germany) during the nineteenth century – was, of course, neither chiefly theological nor devotional, whatever the faith commitments of many of its practitioners. Instead, these modern scholars, down to the present, have been consumed by the concern with history: the history of the often problematic texts of the Bible and the recovery of the real history of ancient Israel and its neighbors, which frequently has been exposed by archeology and other evidence to diverge sharply from what is reported in the Bible. There may be something intellectually admirable in any rigorous effort to establish what "really happened," but Frei argues at length that this effort has had the unfortunate consequence of creating a crisis in how the Bible is read. He makes a valuable distinction between what is historical and what is "history-like," a term he proposes as an equivalent of *realistic*. Biblical scholars, for example, have repeatedly addressed the question of whether there was a historical David and, if there was, whether he really fought a civil war against the house of Saul, established a mini-empire in trans-Jordan, contended with a rebellion by his son Absalom, and so forth. All such considerations, Frei proposes (not referring specifically to the David story), miss the point of these stories and deflect us from reading them as they were meant to be read.

What is important is not whether the David narrative as it appears in 1 and 2 Samuel matches the facts of history, to whatever extent they can be reconstructed, but rather how the narrative data create a compelling portrait of a man realizing his destiny in the realm of political power – himself manipulating power and transformed by it – living under the pressures and contradictions of the historical process. This "history-like" David, then, would not be different in kind from a character in a great political novel – say, Count Mosca in Stendhal's *The Charterhouse of Parma*. In fact, Frei often invokes the analogy of realist fiction, noting the paradox that at the very moment when the realist novel was emerging, historical scholarship was turning away from the possibility of recognizing in the Bible the imaginative authority of verisimilar narrative. Frei aptly summarizes this entire problematic development in the following terms:

> [T]he realistic or history-like quality of biblical narratives, acknowledged by all, instead of being examined for the bearing it had in its own right on meaning and interpretation was immediately transposed into the quite different issue of whether or not the realistic narrative was historical.[5]

In the next sentence, he speaks of a "simple transposition and logical confusion between two categories of meaning and interpretation" that continue to be an unresolved problem for reading the Bible. The new wave of literary studies of the Bible, which began more or less around the time of the appearance of Frei's book, has generally acted – whether by design or effect – to restore respect for the strong history-like character of biblical narrative.

One brief phrase in Frei's summary of the cultural predicament requires a gloss: "acknowledged by all." In what sense is the realistic or history-like character of Scripture universally acknowledged? I think that what Frei has in mind is that through the long age of faith, readers – even though they accorded the Bible unique status as the revealed word of God – quite naturally read the stories for their power as stories: for example, as Samuel Hanagid, elevated to the position of vizier of Granada, identified with Joseph and read the Joseph story, or as the writer in *Genesis Rabbah* read the tale of the switched brides. The introduction of questions of historicity created an obstacle for this type of reading: scholars who wanted to know whether the story of Joseph had the slightest grounding in historical fact were scarcely disposed – neither would they dispose the readers of their analyses and commentaries – to see in Joseph's struggle with his brothers one of the greatest representations of fraternal rivalry in our entire literary tradition.

Let me hasten to add that literary analysis of the Bible may sometimes incorporate the discoveries of historical scholarship – perhaps especially in regard to details of ancient Near Eastern life that appear in the stories – and it can scarcely ignore what scholarship has uncovered about the complex evolution of the texts. Literary readings of compact episodes, such as Auerbach's reading of the Binding of Isaac in Genesis 22, are probably the most comfortable to execute because they do not involve issues of possible continuities or discontinuities in a larger narrative sequence. As a methodological experiment, then, I will explore the viability of a literary reading of a sustained narrative. The story of Jacob – which, of course, also encompasses the story of Joseph and his

---

[5] Hans Frei, *The Eclipse of Biblical Narrative* (New Haven, CT: Yale University Press, 1974), 16.

brothers – takes up the entire second half of the Book of Genesis; in the Bible, it is exceeded in length only by the David story as a detailed narrative tracking of an individual life through many decades. I will address the question of how it works as a history-like or realistic narrative, an "instructive mirror of the human heart," and whether it coheres as a large narrative.

THE JACOB STORY

Biblical scholarship conventionally refers to the narrative sequence in which Jacob figures centrally as "the Jacob cycle."[6] The misleading implication of that designation is that what we have beginning in Genesis 25 is a collection of discrete stories – analogous, let us say, to the Paul Bunyan tales in American folklore – that hang together loosely and have limited sequential order among them. There is a confusion here between the inferred *origin* of the stories and how they work together as the literary composition in which they have been integrated. Analytic scholarship long ago demonstrated that Genesis is a composite text, assembled from different sources. Local contradictions sometimes ensue (perhaps most famously, the caravan that is Ishmaelite in one verse in Genesis 37 and Midianite in the next), and a few episodes may be suspected of being doublets of one another. The redactor of the final narrative, however, was far from being a mindless practitioner of cut-and-paste operations. We may conclude that he did not feel free to tamper extensively with the sources he brought together, but he also exhibits a strong sense of how to draw them into a coherent narrative that exhibits development of character with the continuities that necessarily accompany such development. Let us consider the principal lines of continuity and development.

A common technique in many literatures for pulling together the disparate parts of relatively lengthy narratives is the use of recurring motifs. Contemporary readers may be especially attuned to this technique because it often has been elaborately deployed in modern fiction, from the motif of the color blue in *Madame Bovary* to the dense cluster of motifs – melons, odalisks, the Promised Land, the messiah, and much else – in Joyce's *Ulysses*. Recurring motifs punctuate the continuities of the Jacob story. J. P. Fokkelman, in his early book *Narrative Art in Genesis*, aptly observed that stones are a defining motif for this character.[7] Jacob, in flight from his brother Esau, places a stone by his head when he goes to sleep at Bethel. After his nocturnal vision

---

[6] For example, Ronald Hendel, *The Epic of the Patriarch: The Jacob Cycle and the Narrative Traditions of Canaan and Israel* (Atlanta, GA: Scholars Press, 1987).

[7] J. P. Fokkelman, *Narrative Art in Genesis* (Assen and Amsterdam: Van Gorcum, 1975), 190–92.

there, he marks the place with a commemorative pile of stones. At the end of his journey to Mesopotamia, he rolls a heavy stone off the mouth of the well so that Rachel can water her flock – only in this particular version of the betrothal type–scene does a stone appear. On his return to Canaan many years later, he erects another pile of stones to indicate the border between him and Laban. These stones also symmetrically mark a narrative border because he sets up one stele as he is leaving Canaan and another now as he returns. It is worth noting that all of these stones do not necessarily derive from the same literary source: Jacob at the well is generally attributed to J, whereas the episodes of the two different stone markers appear to come from E, or from some intertwining of E with J; yet, the three together form a coherent sequence of motif.

It requires physical strength to push a huge stone off the mouth of a well. Thus, the stone motif naturally links up with the most salient motif of the Jacob story, which is wrestling. As everyone remembers, the wrestling with Esau begins in the womb, and Jacob emerges from the womb with a hold on his brother's heel, *'aqev*, from which he is given his name, *ya'aqov*. It is not the kind of hold that suggests pinning the adversary to the mat but rather tripping him up, pulling him down from below, which is largely what Jacob subsequently does to Esau. The contention between the twins and their future destiny had been defined in the oracle to the pregnant Rebekah. However, this poetic oracle – rather like its Delphic counterpart – is slyly ambiguous: its conclusion, "the elder, the younger's slave," *w'rav ya'avod ṣa'ir*, could also be read – given how biblical syntax works – the other way around as "the younger, the elder's slave." That is, the verb in the Hebrew between "elder" and "younger" could take either noun as object or subject.[8] This initial ambiguity is beautifully sustained some forty years later in narrative time when Jacob encounters Esau for the last time. Although Esau addresses Jacob as "my brother," Jacob on his part repeatedly prostrates himself before Esau and addresses him as "my lord," referring to himself as "your servant." The very last word that he pronounces to Esau in the story is *'adoni*, "my lord." We are not intended to doubt that Jacob has acquired both birthright and blessing; but a dialectic countermove is inscribed in the narrative: morally and historically, dominance is not a simple matter. Meanwhile, this last confrontation between Jacob and Esau immediately follows an episode of literal wrestling – Jacob's nocturnal struggle with the mysterious stranger. Having fought that match to a tie, he gets a new name that confers on him the identity of the one

[8] Richard Elliot Friedman, *Commentary on the Torah* (San Francisco, CA: HarperCollins, 2001), comment on Genesis 25:23.

who prevails. However, there is another consequence of his wrestling with the angle, to which we will return.

Wrestling leads to haggling, which is another form of contention: with words over objects of value instead of brute force to assert dominance. Jacob's role as haggler, of course, is most evident in his strained relationship with his sharp-dealing father-in-law, but it is also manifested in the first words he speaks in the story. As a rule, biblical narrative uses the first piece of dialogue assigned to a character to define the distinctive nature of the character, and Jacob's first words are a striking instance of this convention. Esau's crude and inarticulate expression of his hunger (his defining first words) have caught the attention of most readers, but Jacob's reply is equally worthy of scrutiny: "Sell now your birthright to me" (Genesis 25:31). This seems very terse and direct, but every word – and the place of every word in the syntactic chain – is carefully chosen: first, in the imperative, the crucial verb of the proposed transaction; then, the time of the proposed sale, not tonight or tomorrow, but now; then the prized object proposed for sale; and, finally, waiting to be revealed at the very end, "to me." Seen in his first words, Jacob is a careful man – indeed, a calculating man – and this is how he will continue to make his way in the world. We are reminded repeatedly – as Esau reminds us when he complains to Isaac about the stealing of the blessing – that the name "Jacob" suggests not only "heel" but also "to deal crookedly."

Jacob's predisposition to calculate terms and drive a hard bargain carries over from man to God. After the dream-vision at Bethel – which concludes with God's ringing promise to make Jacob the father of a great people – one might think that Jacob would be grateful, awestruck, dazzled by the destiny for which God has singled him out. Instead, he pronounces a vow that amounts to a stipulation of contractual conditions: "If God be with me and guard me on the way that I am going and give me bread to eat and clothing to wear, and I return safely to my father's house, then the LORD will be my God." The Israeli novelist Meir Shalev, in a recent Hebrew book on first occurrences in biblical narrative, shrewdly observes how Jacob picks up God's words and cannily reconfigures them. God had said, "I am with you and I will guard you wherever you go, and I will bring you back to this land." (The whole passage occurs in Genesis 28:13–16 and 20–21.) God appears to have made a grand promise of protection, but Jacob carefully stipulates not just return to the land but also safe return to his father's house and the provision of material goods.[9] It is an indication of how the patriarchs are conceived as individualized characters that none of the other forefathers speaks to God in

---

[9] Meir Shalev, *Beginning* [in Hebrew] (Tel Aviv: Am Oved, 2009), 39–41.

this fashion. Very much the man who carefully spelled out to his brother the terms of the sale of birthright, Jacob is prepared to be a loyal follower of the God who has so spectacularly revealed Himself at Bethel – on the condition that this God will deliver the goods for him in regard to nurture, wardrobe, and eventual safe conduct back home.

Yet, what makes the character of Jacob so deeply interesting is that the roles of the contender and bargainer reveal only one side of his personality. What might not have been anticipated in someone so given to self-interested calculation is that he is also a man of feeling – indeed, at times quite extravagant feeling. The first indication of this other side of Jacob is when he encounters Rachel at the well, kisses her, then raises his voice in weeping (Genesis 29:10–11). If the stone on the well is one differential marker of Jacob's betrothal type–scene, the weeping is another, for it occurs in none of the other meetings at a well between the young man and his future bride. At the end of a long solitary flight from hearth and home, uncertain when he will return, perhaps despairing over his hard fate, Jacob is surely overjoyed and also overwrought to discover a cousin at the very moment of his arrival in this foreign land. The fact that she is beautiful and that he is already, at first sight, falling head over heels in love with her no doubt heightens the intensity of his feelings. Rachel becomes the great love of his life, leading this calculating man to cast aside prudential calculation. Thus, memorably, the seven years of labor for Rachel in lieu of bride-price "seemed in his eyes but a few days in his love for her" (Genesis 29:20). The extravagance of that love, however, also has painful consequences that follow Jacob through the years all the way to his deathbed.

His great passion for Rachel is the ultimate cause for a chain of domestic disasters. It triggers Leah's jealousy and resentment, setting the stage for the hostility of her sons and the sons of the two slave girls toward Joseph. After Rachel's death, her firstborn son Joseph (who is beautiful like his mother) becomes the great object of his father's love – an emotional fixation that sows deadly dissension between Joseph and his brothers. One wonders, in fact, whether Jacob may unconsciously feminize his beloved son for he gives him a *kᵉtonet passim*, an ornamented tunic, which – as we learn in the story of the rape of Tamar in 2 Samuel 13 (an episode rich in allusions to the Joseph story) – is the customary garment of the daughters of kings. Jacob is obviously still thinking of his lost Rachel, even after having found Joseph, at the very end of his life. In what at first looks like a non sequitur, in the midst of explaining to Joseph how Ephraim and Manasseh are to be his heirs, Jacob suddenly says, "As for me, when I was coming from Paddan, Rachel died to my grief in the land of Canaan on the way, still some distance from Ephrath, and I buried her there on the way" (Genesis 48:7). This eruption of a seemingly unconnected memory carries psychological conviction: Jacob on his deathbed still feels the pain of a loss to which he never reconciled himself despite the passage of many decades. The biblical concern with memory, which often has a national and historical thrust, here has genuinely psychological weight – a phenomenon equally visible when Joseph beholds his brothers prostrate before him in the Egyptian court and remembers the dreams that predicted this moment (Genesis 42:9).

The great rule of Jacob's life – and a profound expression of its existential realism – is that he gets everything he aspired to have but not in the way he imagined and at a great cost to himself. He gets Rachel, whom he adores, but only after having had her older sister passed off on him first, which lays the ground for many years of rivalry between the co-wives. The long-barren Rachel is bitterly discontent and urgently entreats Jacob to give her "sons." The plural is perhaps ominous because she will die giving birth to the second one. Jacob fulfills the blessing he has obtained in deceit from his father by realizing the patriarchal consummation of multiple wives, twelve sons (and a daughter), and abundant wealth in livestock. But the sons cause him untold grief and, in the second half of his story, we see Jacob diminished by age, his physical powers waning, and the victim first of his sons' violent impulses in the massacre at Shechem and then of their cruel deception in the selling of Joseph into slavery. His words of impotent rebuke to his sons at the end of the Shechem story express the raw vulnerability of the man who seems to have everything: "You have stirred up trouble for me . . . when I am a handful of men. If they gather against me and strike me, I shall be destroyed, I and my household" (Genesis 34:30). On Joseph's disappearance, which Jacob is duped into thinking is Joseph's death, he seizes the role of prima donna of paternal grief, a far cry from the posture of wrestler that marked his early years. He has scarcely relinquished this role two decades later when his sons return from their first journey to Egypt. The verse-like language with which he responds to their request to take Benjamin down to Egypt – more threnody than dialogue – puts the grieving father at the head and the foot of the speech: "Me you have bereaved. Joseph is no more, and Simeon is no more, and Benjamin you would take! It is I who bear it all" (Genesis 42:36).

In the last movement of this riveting story, when Jacob stands, somber and proud, before the great king of Egypt, he responds in the following terms to Pharaoh's question about his age: "The days of the years of my sojournings are a hundred and thirty years. Few and evil have been the days of the years of my life, and they have not attained the days of the years of my fathers in the days of their sojournings" (Genesis 47:9). One senses here in the slow, studied repetition of "the days of the years" an old man looking back over a long span of lived experience. This constitutes, I think, a new moment in the representation of human life in literature, in which the character manifests a consciousness of having persisted through time and having been affected by it; it is a powerful argument for the narrative continuity of the entire Jacob story. Jacob refers twice to the lifespan as $m^e gurim$, "sojournings." This term for temporary residence is an apt one for nomadic pastoralists, but it also intimates something of the intrinsic transience of human life. It is, of course, an extravagant understatement to call 130 years "few," even if that makes literal sense in regard to the fabled longevity of Jacob's forefathers. But the existential truth it expresses is that any human life, whatever its length, is fleeting when looked at – as Jacob appears to do with his own life – under the aspect of eternity. The crucial thematic term in this speech is "evil." Jacob is the triumphant possessor of birthright and blessing and the divinely imparted name of Israel, and yet, in the ways we have seen, his triumphs have borne bitter fruit. Aged and infirm, battered on the anvil of experience, scarcely recovered from two decades of imagined bereavement, never to recover from the loss of his life's great love, he is prepared to sum up the days of the years of his life – perhaps even with some justice – as "evil."

This gesture of sad retrospection leads back to his nightlong struggle with the unnamed adversary in chapter 32. That mysterious encounter provides a compact image, or *mise-en-abîme*, of the Jacob story as a whole. By not yielding to the divine being with whom he wrestles, Jacob achieves a kind of victory, signally marked by the bestowal of a new name, Israel, that incorporates both lordliness ($\acute{s}^e rarah$, as Rashi aptly observes) and a theophoric suffix. Like his other triumphs, however, this one exacts a price. The angel strikes his hip socket and Jacob emerges from the struggle limping. The real point of this freighted detail is not the etiological explanation of why the future Israelites refrain from eating the sinew of the thigh but rather the maiming – the permanent maiming, one infers – of Jacob. There is an implicit generalization here about the nature of a person's life. A man inevitably contends with obstacles in the course of a long life, but the contention can be bruising. One may get what one desires, but there is very often pain to be suffered in the getting. It is the nature of the experience that we all encounter in the world to subject body and spirit to beatings, and the ensuing pain may never disappear, even on the brink of the grave. Finally, it is this unblinking sense of the arduous nature of an individual life that gives the Jacob story such weight.

In this analysis, I do not claim that the narrative reads exactly like a novel, although I do think it anticipates procedures for the representation of individual experience that would later be characteristic of the novel. That claim points to the general direction of Robert Kawashima's recent study, *Biblical*

Narrative and the Death of the Rhapsode, which argues in persuasive analytic detail that biblical narrative – as a set of compositions formulated in writing and, hence, free of the limitations imposed by oral composition – created a new access to consciousness and the experience of time that adumbrated novelistic narration.[10] The most salient difference of the biblical material from the novel, of course, is its composite character. Instead of a single writer following the work through successive drafts – scrutinizing the galleys and perhaps making changes and additions on them – and so fully responsible for the final product, the long biblical narrative we are considering is a splicing of the work of three different writers (and perhaps, at least in the case of P, a group of writers), with a high likelihood that snippets from other sources have been introduced in the process. The writers, moreover, are concerned not only with the fate of individual characters but also with establishing a schema with which to read future national history and a set of etiologies for explaining certain everyday practices and political constellations of the writers' own era.

The composite character of the text, at least in the Jacob story, poses less difficulty than one might imagine. Most of the passages I have cited can confidently be attributed to J, although any interventions of E and P do not seem to contradict the general tenor of the story. Although there are often marked disparities of detail and terminology among the three principal sources of Genesis, it may be that the differences in the fundamental conception of the character of the once-independent narratives were not so significant. In any case, I assume that the redactors gave pride of place to J because that writer's vision of Jacob was so powerfully persuasive, as well as because of the authority of temporal precedence it carried. As to the purpose of fashioning the story – although there were aims (e.g., cultic, theological, and political) that were not at all novelistic and perhaps did not in themselves require a long sustained narrative – the evidence of the story itself attests to an absorbing interest on the part of the writer, or even the writers, in how an individual fate plays out in time. Here is a man, singled out in the womb by an oracle (if somewhat ambiguously) for a great destiny, then determined (with a little help from his mother) to realize it through his own initiative; struggling, in this era before any national state, in the challenging arena of the family to take what he deems his; knowing love's consuming power and its galling discontents; with the passage of time experiencing the loss of loved ones, physical vigor,

---

[10] Robert S. Kawashima, *Biblical Narrative and the Death of the Rhapsode* (Bloomington: University of Indiana Press, 2004).

and control over his own family. All of this, I argue, makes a story that holds together strongly. As Auerbach says, "It is only in the course of an eventful life that men are differentiated into full individuality." Such individuality is palpably consummated in the Jacob story from womb to grave, perhaps for the first time in Western literature.

2

༧

Cultural Memory

Ronald Hendel

Memory, wrote Augustine in his *Confessions*, is "the present of things past."[1] The past exists only in our present memories and is mediated by places, objects, texts, and customs. As individuals, our past selves and relationships persist only to the extent that we remember them. However, individual memories also can be of events that never happened or that did not happen in quite the way we remember them. Memories recall the past in a way that re-creates the past, foregrounding and embellishing certain parts and suppressing others. No one has total recall; our memories are always partial, meaning that they are both incomplete and biased, colored in various ways. Memory is unreliable, but it is also the foundation of our sense of self.

Cultures also have what we can call memories. Often, these are memories of the formative past when an ancestral group underwent crucial transitions. Children are initiated into cultural memories as part of the process of acculturation, and these shared memories comprise an essential ingredient and causal agent of group identity. The shared memories of a culture are subject to the same types of changes as individual memory. They are a blend of historical details and imaginative embellishments, blending and crystallizing differently according to the concerns and experiences of each generation.

Maurice Halbwachs, who first systematically addressed the topic of cultural memory, observed that "collective memory . . . reconstruct[s] an image of the past which is in accord, in each epoch, with the predominant thoughts of the society."[2] The representations of cultural memory are not the past of the historian and neither are they wholly fictive. They are versions of the past that serve as foundations for collective practices and identity; as such,

[1] Augustine, *Confessions* 9.20.
[2] Maurice Halbwachs, "The Social Frameworks of Memory" (1925), in idem, *On Collective Memory*, ed. Lewis A. Coser (Chicago: University of Chicago Press, 1992), 40. Among recent studies of cultural memory, see particularly Jan Assmann, *Das kulturelle Gedächtnis: Schrift,*

they are true existentially and morally, if only intermittently true historically. However, there are constraints on how far cultural memory can swerve from history. A culture's memory is always built on previous representations of the past, and revisions are constrained by practices that persist in the present. In this sense, cultural memory is a reconstruction of the past in which the old and the new are melded together into a complex whole, even as disharmonies persist between old memories and their revisions.

Genesis is a book of cultural memory in at least two senses. First, it is a complex textual amalgam of the cultural memories of ancient Israel concerning the ancestral past. It is, in the diction of the Palestinian Targums, a "Book of Memories." Second, it has served as a repository of cultural memories for Jews and Christians (and, indirectly, for Muslims) for millennia. Until relatively recently, the book of Genesis was *the* authoritative cultural memory of the most distant past for Western cultures; for some Jewish and Christian groups, it remains so today. The latter sense – that is, Genesis as the cultural memory of the West – is treated in subsequent chapters of this book. The first sense – that is, Genesis as the cultural memory of ancient Israel – is the topic that I pursue here. To approach Genesis as a canvas of ancient cultural memories allows us to attend at the same time to many of its dimensions: its literary resonances; its compositional complexity; its political and religious claims; its links with landscape, ritual, and everyday practices; and its relationship to historical events.[3] Like the scope of memory itself, the method of attending to cultural memory in Genesis is multifaceted.

The following discussion focuses on the theory and practice of reading Genesis as a book of cultural memory. I first turn to salient theories of cultural memory, with an aim to highlight the stakes and interpretive gains of reading Genesis in this mode. Then I turn to a perspicuous narrative sequence in Genesis: the stories of Jacob's dream and his journey to Mesopotamia.

THEORIES OF CULTURAL MEMORY

Of the many facets and theories of cultural memory,[4] I address three that are most relevant for biblical scholarship: social frameworks, mnemohistory, and poetics. These correspond roughly to the complementary disciplines of sociology, history, and literature.

Erinnerung und politische Identität in frühen Hochkulturen (Munich: Beck, 1992); idem, *Religion and Cultural Memory* (Stanford, CA: Stanford University Press, 2006); and Barbara A. Misztal, *Theories of Social Remembering* (Maidenhead, UK: Open University Press, 2003).

[3] See my previous efforts in *Remembering Abraham: Culture, Memory, and History in the Hebrew Bible* (New York: Oxford University Press, 2005).

[4] See Misztal, *Theories*, passim.

Social Frameworks

Halbwachs argued that in our everyday lives, the past is perceived and filtered through various "social frameworks" (*cadres sociaux*) of memory. These
frameworks pertain to the multiple social groups to which an individual
belongs, including nation, religion, ethnic group, social class, profession, and
family: "[E]ach group . . . compose[s], either definitively or in accordance
with a set method, a fixed framework within which to enclose and retrieve its
remembrances."[5] The frameworks of memory provide a filter and template
that determine which details pertaining to the past are memorable and which
are irrelevant and, hence, forgotten. Cultural memory, as mediated by the
social frameworks, yields a past with present relevance.

For each group, cultural memory provides a sense of identity, stability, and
cohesion. By revising the past to suit the group's present concerns, the group
overcomes the problem of historical change: it "gives us an illusion of not having changed through time and of retrieving the past in the present."[6] Because
the noncorresponding parts are filtered out, the structures of contemporary
life are authorized by the authority of the past.

However, because the groups to which people belong are plural and because
some groups are inevitably in conflict, cultural memories are always plural
and in potential conflict. Halbwachs observes, "[J]ust as people are members of many different groups at the same time, so the memory of the same
fact can be placed within many frameworks, which result from distinct collective memories."[7] Different groups may contest one another's memories,
producing what we may call countermemories.[8]

In his monograph on the "legendary topography" (*topographie légendaire*)
of the Holy Land, Halbwachs explored how the social frameworks of memory
organize perceptions of the landscape of Israel. He writes: "[C]ontact with
these localities refreshed and revitalized memories . . . just as we come back to
places where we have spent a part of our life to relive and rediscover details that
had vanished."[9] In the biblical landscape, details of cultural memory come
alive for each pilgrim, creating a living presence for the sacred past. Individual
memory and collective memory blend in the revitalizing experience available
at these sacred sites. As a source of personal and collective subjectivity, the

[5] Halbwachs, *The Collective Memory* (New York: Harper & Row, 1980; French original, 1950),
    156–7.
[6] Ibid., 157.
[7] Halbwachs, "Social Frameworks," 52.
[8] On countermemory, see Hendel, *Remembering Abraham*, 41–2 and n. 43.
[9] Halbwachs, "The Legendary Topography of the Gospels in the Holy Land" (1941), in idem,
    On Collective Memory, 199–200.

biblical landscape is "a work of the mind," as Simon Schama writes in *Landscape and Memory*: "Its scenery is built up as much from strata of memory as from layers of rock."[10]

The social frameworks of memory take us to the things of this world – places, events, objects – and superimpose on them commitments and beliefs of a conceptual order. It binds the physical plane with the symbolic and spiritual:

> [C]ollective remembrance has a double focus – a physical object, a material reality such as a statue, a monument, a place in space, and also a symbol, or something of spiritual significance, something shared by the group that adheres to and is superimposed on this physical reality.[11]

Hence, for the pilgrims in the Holy Land, "its visible facts are the symbols of invisible truths."[12] As we will see in Genesis, the sensible world is refracted through the frameworks of memory.

Mnemohistory

Halbwachs's theory has been described as "presentist" – that is, oriented toward the uses of the past in the present.[13] The art historian Aby Warburg (a contemporary of Halbwachs) articulated an approach to cultural memory that focused on its diachronic or historical dimension.[14] Warburg focused on the continuities and transformations of symbols through time, particularly motifs from Classical Antiquity that were appropriated in the Renaissance. He defined such motifs as *mnemes* – that is, cultural forms that objectify and transmit social memory. He was particularly concerned with how artists "enter into critical engagement with the world of pre-established forms"[15] – that is, how they receive and transform the social memories embedded in inherited symbols. Warburg regarded cultural symbols as an "archive of memory" (*Archiv des Gedächtnisses*) that is subject to the interpretations and transformations of individuals and cultures.[16] The study of such transformations of

---

[10] Simon Schama, *Landscape and Memory* (New York: Random House, 1995), 7.

[11] Halbwachs, "Legendary Topography," 204.

[12] Ibid., 224.

[13] Lewis A. Coser, "Introduction: Maurice Halbwachs 1877–1945," in Halbwachs, *On Collective Memory*, 26.

[14] See Aby Warburg, *The Renewal of Pagan Antiquity* (Los Angeles, CA: Getty Research Institute, 1999); idem, *Der Bilderatlas Mnemosyne*, eds. M. Warnke and C. Brink (2nd ed.; Berlin: Akademie Verlag, 2003).

[15] Warburg, *Mnemosyne*, 4; trans. in Matthew Rampley, *The Remembrance of Things Past: On Aby M. Warburg and Walter Benjamin* (Wiesbaden, Germany: Harrassowitz, 2000), 89.

[16] Kurt W. Forster, "Introduction," in Warburg, *Renewal of Pagan Antiquity*, 31 and n. 103.

memory belong to the larger task of what Warburg called cultural history (*Kulturhistorie*).[17]

The Egyptologist Jan Assmann has advanced an approach to the history of cultural memory, building on Warburg's legacy, that he calls mnemohistory. Assmann writes:

> Unlike history proper, mnemohistory is concerned not with the past as such, but only with the past as it is remembered. It surveys the story-lines of tradition, the webs of intertextuality, the diachronic continuities and discontinuities of reading the past. Mnemohistory is not the opposite of history, but rather is one of its branches or subdisciplines.[18]

The interconnections between the remembered past and the historical past – what Warburg called the "wandering roads" (*Wanderstrassen*) of cultural memory – are the focus of this type of inquiry. It is the diachronic axis of the study of cultural memory, which provides an important complement and correction to the synchronic axis of Halbwachs's approach.

Poetics

Cultural memories, although mediated by social frameworks, places, and symbols, necessarily rely on the narration of those memories. Recounting the past involves the forms and practices of narrative, which dramatize the details and events of cultural memory. Paul Ricoeur explored the nexus between memory and narrative, proposing that "time becomes human time to the extent that it is organized after the manner of a narrative."[19] That is, narrative is a fundamental form of memory, both personal and collective.

In an article on "Distortion in Collective Memory," Michael Schudson discusses how the process of narration shapes cultural memory. Narratives simplify complex events; they foreground individual protagonists and antagonists rather than general processes; they impose temporal plots of conflict and resolution; and they make the past knowable: "The past that comes to be known best or known at all is ... the one made into stories."[20] Through their

---

[17] Warburg, *Mnemosyne*, 5; see also Felix Gilbert, "From Art History to the History of Civilization: Gombrich's Biography of Aby Warburg," *The Journal of Modern History* 44 (1972), 383.

[18] Jan Assmann, *Moses the Egyptian: The Memory of Egypt in Western Monotheism* (Cambridge, MA: Harvard University Press, 1997), 8–9.

[19] Paul Ricoeur, *Time and Narrative, Volume 1* (Chicago: University of Chicago Press, 1990), 3.

[20] Michael Schudson, "Dynamics of Distortion in Collective Memory," in *Memory Distortion: How Minds, Brains, and Societies Reconstruct the Past*, ed. D. L. Schacter (Cambridge, MA: Harvard University Press, 1995), 358.

authoritative stories, social groups assert their ownership over the relevant past.

The poetics of memory focuses on the literary forms and strategies whereby the text transforms the remembered past into narrative discourse. As Robert Alter describes the poetics of Deuteronomy, "The resources of rhetoric are marshaled to create through a written text the memory of a foundational national event."[21] Similarly, the rhetoric of memory is deeply woven into the Genesis narratives. The stories recount memories but, in a sense, they also constitute memories, for they organize the past in narrative temporality and form, which makes the past memorable.

These three theories of cultural memory – social frameworks, mnemohistory, and poetics – illuminate complementary and interlinked dimensions of Genesis as a book of memory. In my view, these theories represent an advance over the common practices of biblical scholarship regarding the biblical representation of the past, which usually revolve around issues of referential truth or falsity or theological relevance. These standard scholarly practices radically simplify the manifold senses of biblical memory. In the discussion of Jacob's dream and his journey to Mesopotamia, I address literary features, social and conceptual frameworks, supplements and countermemories, and mnemohistory as aspects of the method of cultural memory, which forms a loose and multilayered mode of inquiry.

JACOB'S DREAM (GENESIS 28:10–20)

When Jacob comes on the site that he will name Bethel ("House of God"), he finds only rocks and earth and a place to sleep. After his dream, these will form a sacred landscape:

> [Jacob] came to a place and spent the night there, for the sun had set. He took some stones of the place, and set them as his headrest, and he lay down in that place. He had a dream, and behold, a staircase was standing on earth and its top reached to heaven. And behold, angels of God were going up and down on it. . . . Jacob woke from his sleep . . . and he was frightened. He said, "How fearsome is this place. It is none other than the house of God, and this is the gate of heaven." Jacob arose in the morning and took the stone that he had set as a headrest, and he set it up as a standing stone, and he poured oil on its top. . . . Jacob made a vow, saying, "If God will be with me and guard me on this path that I am going, and if he gives me bread to eat and clothes to wear, and if he returns me in peace to the house of my father, then Yahweh

---

[21] Robert Alter, *The Five Books of Moses: A Translation with Commentary* (New York: W. W. Norton, 2004), 870.

will be my God. And this stone, which I have set up as a standing stone, will
be the house of God, and of everything that you give to me, I will give a tithe
to you." (Genesis 28:10–20)

As Hermann Gunkel observed, in their essence and origin, the stories of the
sacred sites founded by the patriarchs are collective memories:

> Again and again on such occasions we hear of specific locales – of Bethel,
> Penuel, Shechem, Beersheba, Lahai-roi... and of the trees, springs, and
> memorial stones at these sites. These are the most ancient sanctuaries of
> Israel's tribes and clans.... [A later period] raised the question as to why
> precisely this place and this sacred sign are so particularly sacred? The
> consistent response was, "Because the deity appeared to the patriarch at
> this site. In memory of this fundamental revelation, we worship God at this
> place."[22]

Gunkel did not pursue the implications of his insight into the public and
authoritative quality of the foundation legends as collective memory ("in
memory of this... we worship God at this place"). Guided by the romantic
presuppositions of his day, he viewed the stories as primitive etiologies – that
is, as naïve explanations of contemporary phenomena. He viewed these stories
as "the beginnings of human knowledge, of course only minor beginnings,
but as beginnings still worthy of our respect."[23] To view these texts as simple
"just-so stories," however, is to underestimate their multilayered effects.

As Gunkel observed, this story answers the question, "Why are this place
and this pillar so sacred?" However, as a cultural memory, the story has deeper
resonance. It informs the ancient Israelites about their collective identity and
religious destiny, rooted in the formative events of the ancestral past, and
it binds this knowledge into the landscape and into everyday practices. As
Halbwachs observes, such stories have a double focus, infusing the physical
world with spiritual and social meanings. The story of Jacob at Bethel creates
a "legendary topography," or "ethnoscape" – a sacred landscape of national
memory.[24]

Bethel was a strategic Israelite site in that it was located near important
routes along and through the central highlands. It is remembered in the Bible
as an important religious shrine from the patriarchal era until the seventh
century B.C.E. According to one source, Bethel was the site of the Ark of the

---

[22] Hermann Gunkel, *Genesis* (Macon, GA: Mercer University Press, 1997; German 3rd ed., 1910),
xxi.

[23] Gunkel, *Genesis*, xviii. On Gunkel's romantic view of folklore, see Sean M. Warner, "Primitive
Saga Men," *Vetus Testamentum* 29 (1979), 325–35.

[24] Anthony D. Smith, "Nation and Ethnoscape," in idem, *Myths and Memories of the Nation*
(New York: Oxford University Press, 1999), 149–59.

Covenant in premonarchical times (Judges 20:27). After the establishment of the Northern Kingdom, it became a royal shrine and is said to have been destroyed during King Josiah's reforms (2 Kings 23:15). For hundreds of years – according to these various sources – Bethel was a major site of Israelite worship.

At this site, Israelite worshipers encountered a place where cultural memory is palpable, where one encounters the presence of the collective past. The literary representation of this memory in Genesis 28 makes the concreteness of the place emphatic through its rhetoric, particularly by repetitions and deictic particles that highlight the site's tangible presence:

> He came to a *place* and spent the night *there*.
> He took from the stones of *the place*... and he lay down in *that place*.
> *This* is the gate of heaven.
> *This* stone that I have set up.

These words express a sense of immediacy, of being there at a particular place, with its hard stones and peculiar visions. Note how the deictic pronouns change their focus from far to near as the narrative voice shifts from the narrator's to Jacob's own: "*there*... *that* place.... *This* is the gate.... *This* stone." In the rhetoric of the story, the proximity of Bethel becomes incrementally closer until Jacob is *here*, in *this* place. Through this rhetoric, the memorable past becomes a subjectively felt presence.

The repetition of *wᵉhinneh*, a deictic particle that has the effect of allowing the reader to see through the eyes of the character,[25] intensifies the immediacy of the scene: "He had a dream, and behold (*wᵉhinneh*), a staircase was standing on earth and its top reached to heaven. And behold (*wᵉhinneh*), angels of God were going up and down on it" (v. 12). The doubled emphasis on the progressive vision – first the staircase and then angels – brings the scene into sharp experiential focus. The divine things are placed squarely in the reader's imagination as the reader sees the vision through Jacob's eyes. This rhetoric of memory makes the reader a witness to the revelation, reviving the past with the pragmatic effects of "presentative" language.

When worshipers entered the sacred site of Bethel, they saw the standing stone and the place where Jacob slept, dreamt, and vowed. Through the material landscape, invested with sacred memory, the experience of Jacob at Bethel – his fear and amazement, his new awareness, the heavenly staircase and the ascending angels, his vow concerning his future bond with God – became

---

[25] This usage occurs with verbs or situations of perception; see Bruce K. Waltke and Michael O'Connor, *An Introduction to Biblical Hebrew Syntax* (Winona Lake, IN: Eisenbrauns, 1990), 676; and on these verses, see J. P. Fokkelman, *Narrative Art in Genesis* (2nd ed.; Sheffield, UK: Sheffield Academic Press, 1991), 50–3.

part of the Israelite experience and practice of worship. Jacob vows that if God protects and preserves him, "This stone that I set up as a standing stone will be the house of God," which serves – by anticipation and synecdoche – to name the place Bethel, the "House [or Temple] of God."

For the worshiper, to enter Bethel is to traverse a liminal threshold into the House of God, the holy place where heaven and earth meet. This is an *axis mundi*, a point of legendary topography, where the metaphysical and mundane worlds come together in a single space. When one sees and touches "this stone," one may sense the unseen presence of the traversing angels and the revitalized hope that "God will be with me and guard me on this path that I am going." At Bethel, the worshiper enters into a sacred geography and sacred time where the collective past becomes a palpable presence, merging cultural memory with personal experience and overcoming the problems and contingencies of mundane history.

SUPPLEMENTS AND COUNTERMEMORY

The story of Jacob's dream and vow has its conclusion in his return to Bethel when he returns to Canaan nearly two decades later: "God said to Jacob, 'Arise and go up to Bethel and dwell there. And make there an altar to the God who appeared to you when you were fleeing from your brother Esau'" (Genesis 35:1). Jacob obeys, recalling that God has fulfilled the terms of his vow at Bethel. Jacob says to his family, "Let us arise and go up to Bethel, so that I may make there a standing stone to God who answered me in my day of distress, for He has been with me on the path that I have gone" (Genesis 35:3). At Bethel, Jacob constructs the altar and formally names the place El Bethel ("God of Bethel"; Genesis 35:7).

In addition to the paired stories of Jacob's dream and his formal establishment of the cultic site of Bethel, there are other versions and supplements to the story. To express it differently, there are other cultural memories that pertain to this remembered past and that complement or contest the story I have quoted. The alert reader will notice three ellipses in the text of Genesis 28:10–20 previously cited. The ellipses are the supplements to this text, which belong to a different source or sources (the portion quoted is from the E source). The supplements are as follows:

> And behold, Yahweh was standing by him, and he said, "I am Yahweh, the God of Abraham your father and the God of Isaac. The land on which you lie I shall give to you and to your seed. Your seed shall be like the dust of the earth, and you shall spread westward and eastward and northward and

southward, and all the families of the earth shall be blessed through you and your seed. And behold, I am with you, and I will guard you wherever you go, and I will return you to this land. For I will not leave you until I have done what I have told you.". . . And [Jacob] said, "Indeed, Yahweh is in this place, and I did not know it.". . . And he called the name of that place Bethel, but Luz was the name of the city previously. (Genesis 28:12–15, 16b, 19)

It is not clear whether these supplements are from the J source or from a redactor who used language from J in order to harmonize the composite JE text. What is clear is that the supplements bring into the story the theme of the patriarchal promises, recapitulating the promises that Yahweh had given to Abraham. Note the parallels in words and phrasing between divine promises in Genesis 28:13–14 and the earlier promises to Abraham (a.k.a. Abram, prior to his name change in Genesis 17):

The land on which you [Jacob] lie I shall give to you and to your seed. Your seed shall be like the dust of the earth. (Genesis 28:13–14)

All the land which you [Abram] see I shall give to you and to your seed forever. I will make your seed like the dust of the earth. (Genesis 13:15)

. . . and you [Jacob] shall spread westward and eastward and northward and southward. (Genesis 28:14)

Lift your [Abram's] eyes and look . . . northward and southward and eastward and westward. (Genesis 13:14)

. . . and all the families of the earth shall be blessed through you [Jacob]. (Genesis 28:14)

. . . and all the families of the earth shall be blessed through you [Abram]. (Genesis 12:3)

This textual supplement serves to bind Yahweh's revelation to Jacob at Bethel with his previous revelations to Abraham, thereby enriching this story with the theme of the patriarchal promises. This creates an additional layer of continuity within the patriarchal stories, pointing backward and forward in time to the transmission of the blessings across the patriarchal generations and highlighting Jacob's status as the divinely chosen heir to the promises. It also points to the future fulfillment of the promises in the descendants of Jacob/Israel who live in the Promised Land. That is, this layer emphasizes the teleological orientation of the stories, which implicates their Israelite audience. This supplement makes the remembered past point forward to the present in a relationship of promise and fulfillment. It colors the collective identity of Israel as the product of God's promises and as a medium of God's blessing to all the earth. This is a powerful memory supplement to the surrounding story of Jacob at Bethel.

Another version of the story of Jacob at Bethel – from the P source – may best be characterized as a countermemory. That is, the story does not add a supplementary layer to the other stories of the remembered past but rather implicitly contests those stories. It is often argued that the P source deliberately transforms earlier traditions to suit its own theological perspective.[26] In so doing, it produces a countermemory, a representation of the past that revises and seeks to replace previous memories. In this case, the P representation of Jacob at Bethel synthesizes two previous stories, concerning the sacred sites of Bethel and Penuel (Genesis 32:23–33), while omitting all details that clash with P's theology of a transcendent and omnipotent God:

> God appeared to Jacob again when he came from Padan Aram, and He blessed him. God said to him, "As for your name Jacob, your name shall no longer be called Jacob, but Israel shall be your name." And he called his name Israel. And God said to him, "I am El Shaddai. Be fruitful and multiply. A nation and an assembly of nations shall come from you, and kings shall come from your loins. The land which I gave to Abraham and to Isaac, I shall give to you, and I shall give the land to your seed after you." God went up from him at the place where he had spoken to him, and Jacob set up a standing stone at the place where He had spoken with him, a pillar of stone. He poured a libation on it and anointed it with oil. Jacob called the name of the place where God had spoken with him Bethel. (Genesis 35:9–15)

The immediate effect of this divine revelation at Bethel is to revise the memories of the previous stories about Bethel and Penuel, both from the E source. In the P version, there is no indication of any previous revelations at Bethel – no dreams of angels or celestial stairways or gates of heaven. Neither is there any sense of a previous dangerous encounter at Penuel, where in the E version Jacob wrestles with a divine being (perhaps God himself) and receives from him the name Israel: "Your name shall no longer be called Jacob, but Israel, for you have striven with God (or gods) and humans and have prevailed" (Genesis 32:29). In the countermemory of P, God changes Jacob's name to Israel at Bethel – not Penuel – and the divine revelation consists only of God's speech. There is no visual aspect to the divine revelation, no wrestling with divine beings, and no angels. According to P's theology, God is immaterial and transcendent without anthropomorphic qualities other than speech. Even his speech is transcendent in power – he makes statements like

---

[26] See Richard E. Friedman, *Who Wrote the Bible?* (New York: Simon & Schuster, 1987), 188–206; David M. Carr, *Reading the Fractures of Genesis: Historical and Literary Approaches* (Louisville, KY: Westminster John Knox Press, 1996), 125–9.

"kings shall come from you," which are accomplished solely by virtue of his words (cf. "Let there be light"). As here, when God speaks, his human subjects do not reply; they need only obey.

The content of God's speech draws a line of continuity from earlier epochs of creation to the time of Jacob. The command to "be fruitful and multiply" hearkens back to God's creation of humans in Genesis 1 and to the covenants with Noah (in Genesis 9) and Abraham (in Genesis 17). A dense pattern of echoes links this scene with the Abrahamic covenant in particular, where God says to his chosen one:

> Your name shall no longer be called Abram. Your name shall be Abraham, for I shall make you the father of many nations. And I shall make you exceedingly fruitful, and I shall make you into a nation, and kings shall come from you. (Genesis 17:5–6)

Each of these statements has a counterpart in God's speech to Jacob at Bethel: the name change, the promise that his descendants will become many nations, the blessing of fruitfulness, and even the promise that "kings shall come from you." By means of these repetitions, the P text represents Jacob as Abraham's legitimate heir, to whom God grants the patriarchal promises.

This countermemory of Jacob at Bethel bypasses the strange events in the earlier biblical memories. It makes Jacob a more refined figure, no longer bargaining with God for protection and blessing. God and the divine world are also remembered differently – now, one only hears a majestic voice rather than recalling a mysterious deity wrestling with the patriarch or angels ascending and descending the cosmic staircase.

It is a textual irony that this countermemory of Bethel is juxtaposed in our text of Genesis with the prior memories of Bethel and Penuel. Rather than supplanting these memories, the revised version of the revelation at Bethel seems now to supplement them. Yet, it still seems to achieve its ends as an alternative memory. Because it comes last in the sequence, it has the final word and, to that extent, may revise our impressions of the significance of Jacob's divine encounters. It is, after all, P's transcendental God that becomes normative in the cultural memory of Judaism and Christianity. The countermemory better suits the postbiblical frameworks and, hence, effectively overwrites the earlier memories.

RETURN TO MESOPOTAMIA

Jacob's encounters at Bethel are a frame around his journey to Haran, his family's ancestral homeland. The reasons for the journey are twofold. First, he is fleeing from Esau's wrath. As his mother Rebekah commands him: "Rise and flee to Laban, my brother, in Haran, and dwell with him for some time until your brother's wrath subsides" (Genesis 27:44–45). Second, he needs to find a wife among his kinsfolk. As his father Isaac commands him: "You shall not take a wife from the daughters of Canaan. Rise and go to Paddan Aram, to the house of Bethuel, your mother's father, and take there a wife from the daughters of Laban, your mother's brother" (Genesis 28:2). These two motives – from the J and P sources, respectively – neatly combine as Jacob flees from his brother and journeys toward his relatives and future wives.

Each motive for the journey presents Haran as the place of patriarchal origins, the ancestral homeland, where one can marry within the tribe. There is a deep attachment to the region of Haran; it is part of the legendary topography of Genesis. Why should this be so? This question leads to the domain of mnemohistory. The interconnections between the remembered past and the historical past are the focus of this type of inquiry.

In the case of the biblical memory of the patriarchal homeland, we may be able to trace a chain of memory and cultural tradition that long predates the biblical text. Haran (Akkadian *Ḫarrānu*) was a strategically located site in the Upper Euphrates region of Mesopotamia and was a station along important trade routes. During the Middle Bronze Age (ca. 1800–1500 B.C.E.), it was a central meeting place for a major confederation of tribes whose grazing land extended from the Haran region all the way to western Syria. This confederation was called the Yaminites (*banu-yamina*), meaning "Southerners" (literally, "sons of the right [hand]"). As Daniel Fleming observed, Haran was in the heart of Yaminite territory and, as a prominent site with a famous temple, it was well suited to be a tribal center.[27]

The chiefs and elders of the Yaminite tribes came to Haran to create alliances, as in the following reference from a Mari letter: "Asdi-takim and the kings of Zalmaqum, with the chiefs and elders of the Yaminites, have slain the ass together in the Sin temple of Ḫarrān."[28] To "slay the ass together" refers to a ceremony in which the parties swear mutual allegiance, with the slain ass as an implicit warning not to violate their treaty. This is similar to the ceremony in Genesis 15 where Abraham cuts various animals in two to confirm his covenant with Yahweh. This ancient rite is probably the source of the biblical formula, "to cut a covenant" (*karat bᵉrit*). The point here is that the ceremony of alliance takes place at Haran, in the heartland of tribal memory.

---

[27] Daniel E. Fleming, "Mari and the Possibilities of Biblical Memory," *Revue d'Assyriologie* 92 (1998), 69.

[28] *Archives royals de Mari* XXVI.24, trans. Fleming, "Mari," 69; see also Fleming, *Democracy's Ancient Ancestors: Mari and Early Collective Governance* (Cambridge: Cambridge University Press, 2004), 199–200.

As William F. Albright long ago observed, there are other sites in the region of Haran that also seem to resonate in biblical memory.[29] Several of the names of Abraham's kin are place-names in this region: Teraḥ (i.e., Abraham's father) corresponds to *Til Turaḥi* ("hill of the ibex"), known from Neo-Assyrian texts. Naḥor (i.e., Abraham's grandfather and brother) corresponds to *Naḥur*, known from Old Assyrian texts. Serug (i.e., great-grandfather) corresponds to *Sarugi*, known from Neo-Assyrian texts. Place-names tend to persist for a long time, so we may assume that they are not restricted to a particular period.

These sites in the region around Haran – the remembered patriarchal homeland – seem to populate Abraham's genealogy. These patriarchal names seem to be memory-traces from the tribal lands of the Upper Euphrates, although they have been "frozen" into personal names. These names seem to be a forgotten testimony to the memories of Haran as the ancestral homeland, where Abraham sends his servant to find a wife for Isaac (Genesis 24) and where Jacob meets his wives.

Some scholars argue that the references to Haran as the patriarchal homeland are late, invented memories, perhaps stemming from the exilic or postexilic period when Jews lived in Babylonia.[30] However, I aver that memories of ancestral homelands are not so easily invented and that such tribal memories of migrations from the homeland tend to be long-lived, particularly in the Near East. For example, the prophet Amos in the eighth century B.C.E. seems to know that the ancestral homeland of the Philistines was Caphtor (Crete) and that of the Arameans was Qir (probably in the Middle Euphrates region): "Thus says Yahweh: 'Did I not bring up Israel from the land of Egypt, and the Philistines from Caphtor, and Aram from Qir?'" (Amos 9:7). The Philistines did indeed come from Caphtor and other Aegean islands in the early twelfth century B.C.E.,[31] which means that this cultural memory was more than four hundred years old when Amos recited it. The Aramean memory of migration from Qir also may be historically reliable, although this is less clear.[32] By analogy with these and other cultural traditions, it is plausible that the

---

[29] William F. Albright, *From the Stone Age to Christianity: Monotheism and the Historical Process* (2nd ed.; Garden City, NY: Doubleday, 1957), 236–7; and recent bibliography in Hendel, *Remembering Abraham*, 52.

[30] See John Van Seters, *Abraham in History and Tradition* (New Haven, CT: Yale University Press, 1975), 34, with Hendel, *Remembering Abraham*, 138, n. 39.

[31] See Lawrence E. Stager, "The Impact of the Sea Peoples in Canaan (1185–1050 BCE)," in *The Archaeology of Society in the Holy Land*, ed. Thomas E. Levy (2nd ed.; London: Leicester University Press, 1995), 332–48.

[32] See Ran Zadok, "Elements of Aramean Pre-History," in *Ah, Assyria: Studies in Assyrian History and Ancient Near Eastern Historiography Presented to Hayim Tadmor*, eds. Mordechai Cogan and Israel Eph'al (Jerusalem: Magnes Press, 1991), 114.

biblical memories of the patriarchal homeland – both explicit (i.e., Haran) and implicit (i.e., the names of Abraham's kin) – preserve a chain of memory that stems from hundreds of years prior to the composition of the Genesis texts.

Jacob's journey to Haran, I suggest, seems to preserve traces of archaic tribal memories that reach back to the Amorite tribal culture of the early- to mid-second millennium B.C.E. However, the task of mnemohistory does not end with isolating the historical background of cultural memory. We need to trace the back-and-forth, the *Wanderstrassen*, of historical and cultural changes in the subsequent reception of these cultural memories. What are the diachronic turns and discontinuities in the chain of ancestral tradition?

During the transition to the Late Bronze Age (ca. 1500–1200), the major sites in the region of Haran became largely depopulated.[33] Toward the end of the Late Bronze Age, the region saw the rise of Aramean tribal culture. In the Bible, the Arameans are generally depicted as enemies and rivals of Israel, a relationship that came to a climax in the ninth century when Aramean kings conquered broad swaths of Israelite territory.[34] The portrait of Laban, called "the Aramean," reflects the mistrust and rivalry between Israel and Aram in this period. However, whereas the Arameans are seen as rivals and enemies, they are also relatives – and Laban's family lives in Haran, the patriarchal homeland. This is a curious juncture: the enemy is also our kin, and he dwells in our ancestral home.

The overlay of Aramean ethnicity on older tribal memories accounts for this curious circle. In the terms of mnemohistory, it explains why the rival Arameans are at the same time the patriarchal ancestors. By this confluence of cultural memory and contemporary revision, the second-millennium homeland takes on a first-millennium ethnic coloring. Hence, the Israelite worshiper at the festival of the first fruits proclaims, "My father was a perishing [?] Aramean." In Hebrew, this ritual formula has assonance and rhythm: *'arammi 'oved 'avi*. Each word links with the next as the chain of memories draws the cultural identity of Israel into the contemporary model of its ancestral memories. In the remembered past, the patriarchal homeland must – in the Iron Age – become an Aramean land. Mnemohistory reveals a palimpsest

---

[33] T. J. Wilkinson, "Water and Human Settlement in the Balikh Valley, Syria: Investigations from 1992–1995," *Journal of Field Archaeology* 25 (1998), 63–87.

[34] See 1 Kings 20, 22; 2 Kings 8–13; and the recently discovered ninth-century Old Aramaic royal inscription from Tel Dan, probably written by King Hazael; see Nadav Na'aman, "Three Notes on the Aramaic Inscription from Tel Dan," in idem, *Ancient Israel's History and Historiography: The First Temple Period* (Winona Lake, IN: Eisenbrauns, 2006), 173–86.

in which old details are revised to conform to the present while retaining the inherited symbolism of the ancestral archive of memory.

MEMORY AND FORGETTING

The nineteenth-century historian Ernest Renan emphasized the importance of collective memory in the formation of national identity. An essential ground of a nation, he observed, is "the possession in common of a rich legacy of memories." Yet, at the same time, there are aspects of the past that must be forgotten in order for a nation to have a coherent collective identity: "Forgetting, I would even go so far as to say historical error, is a crucial factor in the creation of a nation."[35] Some things must be forgotten – among them the contingencies involved in the origins of a nation. Cultural memories of national origins tend to affirm the unique destiny and "chosenness" of a people – and none more so than Genesis. Beginning with the call of Abraham, Israel is God's chosen people, and the stories largely consist of various threats, turning points, and resolutions in this divinely ordained destiny. Anything that obscures or conflicts with this deeper plot and its values and institutions is liable to be forgotten, perhaps necessarily so.

It is illuminating to consider what is forgotten for the sake of the nation and institution in the biblical memories of Bethel and related sites. We have seen that the countermemory in P suppresses the dream-vision of angels on the heavenly staircase at Bethel and the divine wrestling match at Penuel. The priestly institution with its intensified view of Israelite monotheism required certain features of past memories to be forgotten, contested, or anathematized. This type of revision of cultural memory occurs with every religious reformation, when past forms become the object of calumny and erasure. In the memory framework of P, God is a transcendent, omnipotent, and nonembodied being who has no need of angels or other aid. Like the priestly authority "to proclaim to the Israelites the laws" (Leviticus 10:11), God's word is authoritative. The memory of Bethel in P supports the social order and religious claims of the priests.

The earlier memories have no problem with Jacob's dream-vision of angels at Bethel or with his divine wrestling match at Penuel. The place-name *Penuel* can mean either "Face of God" or "Face of *a god*," and the story takes advantage of this ambiguity by obscuring whether Jacob's wrestling opponent is God or a lesser deity. This ambiguity, as Mark Smith observed, may be a

---

[35] Ernest Renan, "What Is a Nation?" (1882), in *Nation and Narration*, ed. Homi Bhabha (London: Routledge, 1990), 19, 11.

strategic moment of "cultural amnesia" that involves the forgetting of an older, non-Yahwistic deity.[36] This amnesia may illustrate Renan's point about the necessity of forgetting particular details in the formation of a nation. The memory of Jacob's divine encounter is implicated in his new name, Israel, which is taken to mean "Striven with God (or gods)." But which god? For the nation of Israel to exist, the god who strives with Jacob must be compatible with the Israelite framework of memory. Hence, if not Yahweh, it must be Yahweh's angel – and not a night demon or river-god or any other non-Yahwistic deity.

Yet, whereas some gods are forgotten, the memories of the E source include the detail that Jacob's family worshiped foreign gods at Haran. When Jacob returns to Canaan but before he arrives at Bethel, "Jacob said to his household and to all who were with him, 'Put aside the foreign gods that are in your midst'... and Jacob buried them under the terebinth near Shechem" (Genesis 35:2, 4). Jacob's family had served foreign gods, but now they turn their religious worship solely to the God who revealed himself at Bethel. This scene fulfills Jacob's earlier vow, "If God will be with me... and if he returns me in peace to the house of my father, then Yahweh will be my God" (Genesis 28:20–21). This story recalls a scene of transition from the worship of other gods to the exclusive worship of one God – from an ancestral polytheism to Israelite monotheism. The fulfillment of Jacob's vow, in this sense, is a complement to God's call of Abraham; now, both parties – God and Israel – have chosen each other.

However, this version too has forgotten some details about the God of Bethel. The name that Jacob gives to this place, "God (El) of Bethel," suggests an earlier memory of the founding of Bethel in which the god was El, the high god of pre-Israelite Canaan. According to customary usage, the name "El of Bethel" refers to the manifestation of El at this particular site, just as the term "Yahweh of Samaria" refers to the manifestation of Yahweh at the religious site of Samaria (compare other Near Eastern divine titles: e.g., Dagan of Tuttul, Ishtar of Arbela, and Baal of Ugarit). Furthermore, the place-name *Bethel* refers to El because it means "House (or Temple) of El" (compare other Israelite place-names of this type with other divine names: e.g., Beth-Dagon, Beth-Anat, and Beth-Shemesh). This original meaning – pertaining to El, the high god of the Canaanites – has been forgotten in biblical memory and survives in frozen form in the place-name and the divine epithet, "El of Bethel."

[36] Mark S. Smith, "Remembering God: Collective Memory in Israelite Religion," *Catholic Biblical Quarterly* 64 (2002), 640–4, 649–51.

A key factor to this collective forgetting is that El is one of the names of Yahweh in the Bible. As Frank Cross observed, "El is rarely if ever used in the Bible as the proper name of a non-Israelite, Canaanite deity in the full consciousness of a distinction between El and Yahweh, god of Israel."[37] That is, the historical distinction between El and Yahweh has been forgotten in Israel, perhaps necessarily so. The El of Bethel is Israel's God, not a Canaanite god from a past epoch. In other words, the boundary between Israel and Canaan is where cultural forgetting takes place.

As Freud would say, some repression of memory is necessary for a healthy life. Renan anticipates this Freudian insight, but for the collective memory of a nation. Ancient Israel repressed aspects of older cultural memory to create space for its own national and religious life. Modern scholarship has reconstituted some of these repressed memories, including the features of ancient Israelite culture and religion that are shared with the wider family of Canaanite and West Semitic civilizations. The biblical memories of Jacob at Bethel seem to implicate this wider cultural world, but they just as clearly have forgotten the particular details of its historical past. The memory-traces of the forgotten past survive in the names of places, people, and God and in the vestiges of older stories. As Smith describes these remnants of Canaanite polytheism, "Here cultural amnesia seems to result from long tradition, which included a process of interpreting older traditions no longer fully understood."[38] So, the stories must forget some threads of history while retaining and transforming others. Cultural memory in Genesis moves in a cycle of remembering and forgetting, of shifting and self-authenticating versions of the past.

CONCLUSIONS

The method of reading Genesis as a book of cultural memory is a relatively recent innovation. Yet, it has roots in previous subfields of modern biblical scholarship. The work of Hermann Gunkel, particularly in his focus on folklore, social context, and history of traditions, laid the groundwork for an approach to cultural memory in the Bible. Halbwachs, Assmann, and others developed the critical instruments of this method and demonstrated its relevance for the Bible. Several recent books by biblical scholars have begun to

---

[37] Frank Moore Cross, *Canaanite Myth and Hebrew Epic: Essays on the History of the Religion of Israel* (Cambridge, MA: Harvard University Press, 1973), 44.

[38] Mark S. Smith, *The Memoirs of God: History, Memory, and the Experience of the Divine in Ancient Israel* (Minneapolis, MN: Fortress Press, 2004), 153.

domesticate this method, joining it to the philological, historical, and literary skills that are native to biblical scholarship.[39]

There are many levels and byways of cultural memory in Genesis. Focusing on the stories of Jacob at Bethel and his journey to Mesopotamia, I have addressed legendary topography and the cultic retrieval of memory; the rhetoric of memory; the textual dialectic of memories, supplements, and countermemories; the mnemohistory of the patriarchal homeland; and the necessity of collective forgetting. These are distinct aspects of the method of cultural memory.

Cultural memory is an approach that encompasses several areas of inquiry that sometimes seem resistant to one another: it includes literature, history, culture, and religion in a way that crosses disciplinary boundaries. It also extends to the reception of Genesis in postbiblical Jewish and Christian cultures because the Bible has long provided a point of departure for the West's memory of its formative past. The study of cultural memory includes modern concepts of the past – and even the scholarly study of Genesis, which has its own complicated relationship to the cultural memories that are its object of inquiry. Genesis remains a part of our collective past, our archive of memory, which continues to shadow us in the present.

[39] See Hendel, *Remembering Abraham*; Smith, *Memoirs of God*; and Adriane Leveen, *Memory and Tradition in the Book of Numbers* (Cambridge: Cambridge University Press, 2008).

3

~

Sources and Redaction

Robert S. Kawashima

PHILOLOGY

The modern discipline of biblical studies was born when the Bible became the object of modern (as opposed to traditional) knowledge – that is, knowledge governed by the ideal of formalized science.[1] True, certain premodern commentators had already expressed doubts about various traditional claims regarding the Bible's authorship.[2] How likely is it, for example, that Moses – the author of the Torah ("the Five Books of Moses") according to venerable tradition – wrote the account of his own death in Deuteronomy 34:1–8? But it was only after the advent of Renaissance Humanism in the fourteenth and fifteenth centuries – the period that witnessed the rediscovery of classical Greek and Latin texts and the invention of the printing press – that the Bible, along with other ancient texts, began to be subjected to systematic scrutiny. Criticism, as the modern analysis of texts came to be called, attempted not only to establish critical editions of the Bible and other ancient works out of the welter of available manuscripts (lower or textual criticism) but also to determine those works' provenance on the basis of various linguistic and literary criteria (higher criticism).

Common to both tasks is the desire for what Jean-Claude Milner refers to as "precision"[3] – a symptom, Roland Barthes would have added, exhibited by

---

[1] See Jean-Claude Milner, "Lacan and the Ideal of Science," in *Lacan and the Human Sciences*, ed. Alexandre Leupin (Lincoln: University of Nebraska, 1991), 27–42.

[2] Richard Elliott Friedman, *Who Wrote the Bible?* (New York: Summit Books, 1987), 15–21.

[3] See Milner, *L'Oeuvre claire: Lacan, la science, la philosophie* (Paris: Seuil, 1995), 33–76, esp. 43–6; English translation: "The Doctrine of Science," in Slavoj Žižek, ed., *Jacques Lacan: Critical Evaluations in Cultural Theory* (London: Routledge, 2003), 1.264–94. Milner seems to view the ideal of "precision" as a type of a transition between ancient and modern science. One might arguably situate this term in relation to Lacan's well-known distinction between the "exact sciences" and the "conjectural sciences" – physics versus psychoanalysis.

those who "love," are "obsessed by," the text.[4] Not coincidentally, criticism also came to be known as philology. Such were its accomplishments that Galileo himself, Milner reminds us, took it as his ideal: "In the eyes of Galileo, mathematics and measure were the means – some of the means, it will subsequently be revealed – that would permit humble physics to one day equal what prestigious philology, through the science of language (through grammar) and through the science of written documents, had long ago accomplished."[5] This "love of words" would eventually beget the first "exact science" of language – viz., comparative philology or historical linguistics – as well as the modern discipline of literary studies.

It should come as no surprise, then, that humanism, in giving birth to biblical criticism, also produced a new mode of biblical interpretation. If Christian readings of both scripture and history, from Paul to Dante, generally took the form of what Erich Auerbach calls "figural interpretation" – episodes from the "Old Testament," for example, being "interpreted as figures or phenomenal prophecies of the events of the New Testament"[6] – by the end of the eighteenth century, Hans Frei informs us, "belief in the layers of meaning in a single text – literal, typological, and spiritual or mystical had virtually disappeared as a major force."[7] This century was instead "the period of the direct reading of the 'plain' text, the one common ground among all the differing hermeneutical schools."[8] As his subsequent discussion makes clear, debates about modern (philological, critical) interpretation all revolved around the figure of the author, whether it was a question of "literal meaning," that is, the author's "intention," or "historical understanding," namely, seeking "to understand how the ancient writers had experienced and thought, in their own distinctive, culturally or historically conditioned consciousness."[9] If philological criticism made it possible to ask that peculiarly modern question, "Who wrote the Bible?," modern interpretation made the answer to that question relevant.

Unfortunately, the passage from criticism to interpretation was for a long time obstructed in biblical studies by the debris of the history of its scholarship – an historical accident touched on by Robert Alter in Chapter 1. In fact, however, criticism is not only historically connected to the modern study of literature, it is also essentially related to interpretation as such.

---

[4] Roland Barthes, *The Pleasure of the Text* (New York: Hill and Wang, 1975), 21.
[5] Milner, *L'Oeuvre claire*, 45.
[6] Auerbach, *Mimesis* (Princeton, NJ: Princeton University Press, 1953), 73.
[7] Frei, *The Eclipse of Biblical Narrative* (New Haven, CT: Yale University Press, 1974), 56.
[8] Ibid., 55.
[9] Ibid., 63–4.

Consider Auerbach's philological approach to literary interpretation. If his philology little resembles that of biblicists, it is only because criticism, in its encounter with the Bible, necessarily came to specialize in the analysis (in the narrow sense) of a composite text into its constituent sources. Both biblical and Romance philology, however, are animated by the same desire: namely, the desire for a precise knowledge of the text. Thus, in "Figura," Auerbach carefully analyzes this Latin word's variegated uses in a dozen authors in order to trace its semantic evolution, from ideas inherited from Hellenic thought to its "strangely new meaning... in the Christian world."[10] Starting from a single word precisely understood, he is able to explicate an entire mode of interpretation, "or to put it more completely, the figural view of history," which helped shape medieval art. It is on the basis of this critical semantic history that he finally constructs his conceptual framework for interpreting Dante's *Divine Comedy*. As Auerbach makes clear in *Mimesis*, this method is centered on the author. True, the literary work as an object in the world inevitably "dissociates itself from its author's intention [*Absicht*] and leads a life of its own" and the "transforming and transcendent interpretations" deriving from this post-authorial history of reception are "often fertile."[11] No matter how cherished and entrenched such misreadings become, however, it is the duty of "philological criticism," Auerbach insists, to reconstruct what the author originally "inten[ded]" (*besabsichtigte*): "Yet the historian – whose task it is to define the place of a given work in a historical continuity – must endeavor insofar as that is still possible, to attain a clear understanding of what the work meant [*bedeutete*] to its author and his contemporaries" – that is, his "aesthetic intention [*Kunstabsicht*]."[12]

Ultimately, higher and lower criticism as well as modern interpretation all belong to a single "research program," to borrow Imre Lakatos's phrase,[13] in which the text is conceptualized in relation to the figure of the author – not simply a proper noun attached to an individual biography but rather, more abstractly, a point of intersection of certain crucial factors: linguistic, historical, and so forth. They all presuppose, in other words, a particular, specifically modern concept of meaning, one constituted in terms of authorial intention. Note, however, that I do not offer here a positive substantial definition of

---

[10] Auerbach, *Scenes from the Drama of European Literature* (Minneapolis: University of Minnesota Press, 1984), 28.

[11] Auerbach, *Mimesis*, 353.

[12] Ibid., 343, 353–4.

[13] See Lakatos, "Falsification and the Methodology of Scientific Research Programmes," in *Criticism and the Growth of Knowledge*, eds. Imre Lakatos and Alan Musgrave (Cambridge: Cambridge University Press, 1970), 91–196; he criticizes Thomas Kuhn's related but problematic notion of scientific "paradigms."

"authorial intention" but rather a negative relational definition. To use the language of geometry, the figure of the author constitutes a type of ideal point, whose relation to the text – let us call this relation "intention" – determines its meaning. It is this necessary reference to provenance – namely, to the author – that distinguishes modern, critical interpretation from premodern interpretation: allegorical, figural, and so forth. In fact, it reflects a profound shift in thought that takes place in the early Renaissance, whose "attempt to get closer to the classical spirit and to relive and rethink the past in terms of the present completely transcends the medieval approach to ancient letters."[14] Conversely, to the extent that some now deny the relevance of the author, they have embarked on a post-philological (i.e., postmodern) research program of textual analysis; to be consistent, then, they can and should reject philology in all of its forms.

The precise intention of the author in all of its plenitude, strictly speaking, may be irrecoverable, but every act of criticism is nonetheless an attempt to attain it – like an asymptote one forever approaches but never reaches.[15] Thus, the enterprise of producing critical lexicons – those storehouses of philological learning – is already an acknowledgment that all languages evolve over time. It attests to the conviction that the modern interpretation of a work must therefore locate it as precisely as possible within the history (not to mention the dialectal range) of its language, a point defined with respect to the author. For precisely this reason, modern scholars – whether or not they recognize

[14] L. D. Reynolds and N. G. Wilson, *Scribes and Scholars: A Guide to the Transmission of Greek and Latin Literature* (3d ed.; Oxford: Clarendon Press, 1991), 124. Thus, if modern criticism descends from scribal traditions stretching back to antiquity – from the first gloss to the medieval compilations of *scholia* – a veritable "Copernican Revolution" separates it from the premodern study of texts (see the discussion of the *scholia* in 10–18) – analogous, one might add, to the difference between medieval and generative grammar.

[15] Two objections inevitably will be raised: "the intentional fallacy" and "the death of the author." In fact, neither affects my argument because I merely claim to describe meaning as it is defined by philology. Whether philology can or should accommodate these more recent concerns is an entirely separate question that I do not address here. However, *doxa* has sadly reduced these important notions into clichés, so a few remarks are in order. The actual point of William K. Wimsatt and Monroe C. Beardsley's oft-cited, infrequently read, rarely grasped essay, "The Intentional Fallacy" (in Wimsatt, *The Verbal Icon* [University of Kentucky Press, 1954], 3–18), is to reject any interpretation or judgment based on "consulting the oracle" (18); i.e., the "criticism of poetry" must emphasize "evidence" that is "internal" rather than "external" to the poem (10–11). Similarly, Barthes's 1968 announcement of "The Death of the Author" (in *The Rustle of Language* [Berkeley: University of California Press, 1989], 49–55), far from espousing a literary atheism vis-à-vis the author, registers an event in the history of literature (viz., the birth of the *nouveau roman*). Barthes summarizes this history in terms of the succession of three figures: the "mediator" of "the narrative code" found in "ethnographic societies" (49); the "author" of "the work" (53) of "literature" (54), a strictly "modern character" (49) who functions as the point of origin of "his book" (52); and, finally, the "modern scriptor" of "the new writing" (54), who unlike the author "is born *at the same time* as his text" (52).

it – consult lexicons of biblical Hebrew, as opposed to some stage of post-biblical Hebrew, when studying a text like Genesis. Relatedly, what Frei calls "historical understanding" amounts to reconstructing the thought world of author and audience, thus placing intention within a particular horizon of possibility. For example, it is not enough to translate *t*͏*ᵉhom* in Genesis 1:2 (in consultation with an appropriate lexicon) as "deep." To understand more fully how the ancient writer thought about this idea, it helps to know that according to ancient Near Eastern myths such as *Enuma Elish*, the cosmos evolved out of a primordial sea and that Tiamat, the name of the Mesopotamian *ur*-goddess personifying this sea, is cognate with *t*͏*ᵉhom*. To turn to criticism proper, the ideal *Urtext* that textual criticism seeks to establish is nothing but the objective correlate of authorial intention, so that one is simply meaningless without the other. For example, when scholars restore to Genesis 4:8 the words Cain spoke to his brother – "Let us go out to the field," a sentence missing in the traditional Hebrew text (i.e., the Masoretic Text, or MT) but preserved in other manuscript traditions – they are hypothesizing that the latter approximate more closely the text originally produced by the biblical writer.[16] If this reconstruction is correct, attempts to make sense of MT here, however well intentioned and ingenious, must be rejected as incorrect.[17] Similarly, higher criticism is by definition a search for the author – that is, the time and place of a work's composition. To reject Moses as the author of Torah is to recognize that critically determining who actually wrote the Pentateuch is crucial to its study, whether one is evaluating it as an historical document or interpreting it as a literary work of art. No philology, then, without the author.

SOURCES

One of the great and enduring achievements of philology is the Documentary Hypothesis. Although numerous scholars contributed to it – from Hobbes and Spinoza to Jean Astruc, J. G. Eichhorn, K. H. Graf, and W. M. L. De Wette – it was Julius Wellhausen who synthesized these various insights (including his own) into a single compelling argument in his foundational study, *Prolegomena to the History of Israel*.[18] In its mature form, the theory contends that the Pentateuch (i.e., Genesis – Deuteronomy) consists almost entirely of four originally independent "sources," which were combined in two primary

---

[16] For details, see Ronald S. Hendel, *The Text of Genesis 1–11* (New York: Oxford University Press, 1998), 46–7.

[17] For example, Albert Ehrman ("What Did Cain Say to Abel?," *JQR* 53 [1962]: 164–7) defends MT by interpreting "said to" without a reported speech as "was angry with."

[18] New York: Meridian Books, 1957; first published in 1878 as Volume 1 of *Geschichte Israels*. Broadly speaking, I adopt here Friedman's analyses.

stages of "redaction" by two principal redactors, or editors. According to the conventions established by German scholarship, biblicists generally refer to these sources as J (the Yahwist), who consistently refers to God as Yahweh; E (the Elohist), who generally refers to God as Elohim; P (the Priestly source), which reflects the interests of the Aaronid priesthood; and D (the Deuteronomic source), which is confined to Deuteronomy and is related to another important philological discovery, the Deuteronomistic History (which spans Deuteronomy, Joshua, Judges, 1–2 Samuel, and 1–2 Kings).

Although dating remains a rather conjectural and highly contested issue, one plausible view maintains, broadly speaking, that J and E were composed during the Divided Monarchy (922–722 B.C.E.), the former reflecting the perspective of the Southern Kingdom (Judah), the latter that of the Northern Kingdom (Israel); they were combined by R_{JE} (the redactor of J and E) in the aftermath of the Assyrian conquest of the North (722); P was written in response to JE, perhaps in two primary stages,[19] before the Babylonian Exile (586); D, also a response to JE, was composed in the period leading up to Josiah's (Deuteronomistic) religious reforms (622); and finally, a Priestly redactor, R, combined P with JE and D in the mid-fifth century during the restoration of Judah under Persian rule.

As the name suggests, strictly speaking, the Documentary Hypothesis is only a theory; that is, it is not impervious to empirical falsification because unless archeologists miraculously uncover an ancient parchment containing J or E or P, demonstrating the existence of this or that source, they must remain hypothetical reconstructions. However, one should not be misled by the adverbial "only" into underestimating the epistemological status of this or any other modern "theory." Newtonian mechanics – still taught in introductory physics courses – was "only" a theory; Einstein's theory of relativity, which replaced it, is "only" a theory; and it remains to be seen whether relativity will be supplanted by a unified field theory, which would be "only" a theory. Likewise, it is not inconceivable – but neither is it inevitable – that the Documentary Hypothesis might someday be superseded. For this to happen, however, scholars will not only have to identify weaknesses in the current theory but also formulate a more powerful and elegant – as opposed to more "nuanced," "complicating," or "supple" – counter-theory. Given the explanatory power of the Documentary Hypothesis, this counter-theory would most likely need to incorporate its predecessor – as Einstein's theory does Newton's – rather than simply dismiss it. One should be highly suspicious of any newer

[19]   See Israel Knohl, *The Sanctuary of Silence* (Minneapolis, MN: Fortress Press, 1994).

theory that did so. The research program of modern philology will likely remain intact.

In fact, a number of scholars claim to have moved beyond the Documentary Hypothesis.[20] Although I do not share their optimism – and the need for brevity precludes detailed consideration of their positions – they at least continue to operate in the mode of modern criticism; whether they do so convincingly is another matter entirely. Others, however, effectively reject the project of philology, dismissing the Documentary Hypothesis by retreating behind facile notions of the "unity" of the traditional text.[21] Such approaches should be rejected as regressions into premodern knowledge. This is not to say that all biblical scholars should and need to practice source criticism. Any modern approach to the Bible, however, in principle must be able to reconcile itself with philological criticism.[22] Having "tasted the fruit" of modern knowledge – sweet or bitter according to the individual's palate – the critical scholar cannot return to the blissful ignorance of prelapsarian tradition.

To demonstrate what is at stake in the Documentary Hypothesis, let us briefly consider the two creation stories found in Genesis 1:1–2:4a (P) and Genesis 2:4b-3:24 (J). Together, they constitute an example of what scholars call "doublets" – namely, repetitions found throughout the Pentateuch (and beyond) pointing to the presence of multiple underlying sources. Like most doublets, they employ distinct terminology, most notably (but not solely) different names for God: in P's account, "God" (*'elohim*) creates "the heaven and the earth" (Genesis 1:1); in J's account, "Yahweh God" (*yhwh 'elohim*) makes "earth and heaven" (Genesis 2:4b). They exhibit striking narrative inconsistencies: according to P, humans – both male and female – are created last and at the same time (Genesis 1:27); according to J, the man is made first, then the animals, and finally the woman (Genesis 2:18–21).[23] More broadly, they portray distinct views of reality, including the divine: P has God simply speak the world into being; J has Yahweh plant the garden and form the man with his bare hands. Finally, when these criteria are applied throughout the

---

[20] For a critical discussion of these, see Ernest Nicholson, *The Pentateuch in the Twentieth Century: The Legacy of Julius Wellhausen* (Oxford: Clarendon Press, 1998).

[21] See, e.g., Umberto Cassuto, *The Documentary Hypothesis and the Composition of the Pentateuch* (Jerusalem: Magness Press, 1961). He was, to be sure, an accomplished philologist, but he was not consistently modern.

[22] Robert Alter's literary approach to the Bible, in contrast to certain contemporary alternatives, is thus modern; see *The Art of Biblical Narrative* (New York: Basic Books, 1981), 131–54. Relatedly, one should not overestimate the resemblance between modern literary approaches such as Alter's and traditional modes of close reading (e.g., rabbinic), however much one can still learn from these masters of tradition.

[23] Against the feminist re-reading of this story, see Robert S. Kawashima, "A Revisionist Reading Revisited: On the Creation of Adam and Then Eve," *Vetus Testamentum* 56 (2006), 46–57.

Tetrateuch (i.e., Genesis – Numbers), the passages attributed, respectively, to
J, E, and P are found to cohere as larger continuous documents – D being
already (i.e., still) intact. Thus, according to P's flood story (now combined
with J's in Genesis 6–9), "the fountains of the great deep and the windows of
heaven were opened" by God (7:11), invoking the diagram of the world drawn
up in Genesis 1, according to which the primordial ocean was divided in half
and confined to the marginal spaces above and below the vault of heaven
(Genesis 1:6–8). According to J's version, the flood results from overabundant
rain (Genesis 7:12), which J subtly anticipates by establishing the total absence
of rain at the time of Creation (Genesis 2:5). In this way, several independent
lines of evidence, each consisting of numerous examples, converge to form a
remarkably coherent picture of the formation of the Pentateuch.

The question, then, is how to interpret the Pentateuch in a manner that is
consistent with philology in general and with the Documentary Hypothesis in
particular. As biblical scholars recognized early on, the modern critic cannot
naïvely read the Pentateuch as a single integral text but rather must isolate
J and E and P and D. The determinative relation of provenance to meaning
requires that each source be interpreted individually with respect to its own
particular author. It bears repeating that source criticism is not inimical to
interpretation, but the critical interpreter must first be thoroughly disabused
of modern assumptions about the book, most notably that it is the integral
work of a single author.[24] It then becomes clear that identifying and resolving
(when appropriate and possible) tensions and contradictions within the text
by disentangling the text's underlying sources constitutes a crucial preparatory
step to precise literary perception. The details and, therefore, the meaning of
each source reveal themselves most fully to the philologist's critical gaze.

To return to the Creation accounts, P's version, when read carefully on
its own terms and not merely as J's less interesting rival, reveals a strangely
placid world. Strictly speaking, it does not have a plot: there is no tension to be
resolved, no opponent to be overcome by the protagonist, no dynamic internal
to the sequence of events such that event would lead unto event as cause to
effect. Rather, each action springs forth solely and freely from the Creator, the
pure inscription of divine will on the material world, transforming a formless
void into a coherent whole that is in the end "very good" (Genesis 1:31). Mythic
traditions about a cosmic battle between the Creator and the primordial sea
have been utterly denatured here, although knowing about these traditions
still helps one appreciate the decidedly undramatic effect achieved by P. If

---

[24] In this regard, Karel van der Toorn's recent book is indispensable: *Scribal Culture and the
Making of the Hebrew Bible* (Cambridge, MA: Harvard University Press, 2007).

an intelligible logic nonetheless emerges from the order of days, it is spatial rather than temporal. Thus, God establishes in the first three days three zones of existence: (1) light and dark, (2) sky and ocean, and (3) dry land with its plant life. In the next three days, God creates beings that correspond, respectively, to each zone: (4) the heavenly luminaries, (5) birds and fish, and (6) land animals and, ultimately, humans. P's creation, in effect, is the projection of a two-dimensional synchronic structure into a quasitemporal sequence, a static vision of the chain of being, preformed within the mind of God and thus bearing no traces of an historical becoming. P's understanding of Creation, in turn, reflects his broader understanding of the nature of God in relation to the world. Already in Genesis 1, P shows God to be an abstract, transcendent, absolute Being. God may speak to (i.e., command and bless) Creation, but it does not speak in response. Rather, P ascribes to the created order, both animate and inanimate, only a minimal activity – namely, passive obedience. Thus, the historical process in P, if process it is, is wholly determined by divine will. In other words, it entirely operates according to the principle of divine intervention and revelation.

Nothing is further from P's vision than J's. Whereas God systematically judges each stage of Creation to be "good" in Genesis 1, Yahweh is forced to admit in Genesis 2 that the man's solitude is "not good" (2:18). Thus, whereas Genesis 1 recounts the sequential realization of a preordained perfection, Genesis 2–3 proceeds in ad hoc fashion, from an initial flaw to a trial-and-error search for a suitable companion for the man, out of which the animals accidentally emerge as mere by-products. It is only fitting, then, that Adam – not Yahweh – decides when this search is over: "This is the one, bone of my bones and flesh of my flesh" (Genesis 2:23). In fact, the humans in J's story not only speak and act but also disobey. The fruit of their ostensible sin, however – viz., "the knowledge of good and evil" – does not bring about "the Fall" of later tradition but rather the completion of humankind.[25] To be wanting in this knowledge is to be a mere child (Deuteronomy 1:39). Contrary to later misreadings, then, Eve's defiant act, bravely risked under the threat of death (Genesis 2:17), makes humanity fully human – which is to say, autonomous from (or external to) the divine realm (i.e., the garden). In other words, the etiological intent of the story is not to mourn what was and therefore never meant to be but rather to describe what now irrevocably is, namely, the human condition. For J, to be human is to be no mere passive recipient of divine revelation but rather an active, creative participant in history – that is,

---

[25] See Tikva Frymer-Kensky, *In the Wake of the Goddesses* (New York: Free Press, 1992), 108–17; Kawashima, "*Homo Faber* in J's Primeval History," *ZAW* 116 (2004), 483–501.

"like God." J's history, accordingly, is the gradual unfolding of the resultant dialectic between Yahweh and the sons of Adam.

By extension, the sources, when viewed as integral wholes, each exhibit a distinctive, carefully ordered design. Just as no literary critic would dream of interpreting a passage from a novel without in some way considering the work as a whole – not to mention, for example, the *oeuvre* of its author – so too should the biblical sources be read and interpreted in their entirety. In fact, more than twenty years ago, Richard Friedman issued a challenge to the field of source criticism to contribute to the "synthesis, and not merely division, of the text."[26] This critical synthesis, however, has yet to take place. The labor of philology must continue, then, if we are to fully recover and appreciate these ancient works of literature. Let us continue our analysis of J and P as coherent narrative wholes.

P divides history into four distinct dispensations, which one might usefully conceive of in relation to four emblematic figures: Adam, Noah, Abraham, and Moses. As Frank Moore Cross showed, the latter three periods are marked by three covenants, each more exclusive than the last and each associated with a particular name of God and a different covenantal "sign" (*'ot*): the Noahic covenant between Elohim and "all flesh" (i.e., humans and animals), signified by the rainbow (Genesis 9:1–17); the Abrahamic covenant between El Shadday and Abraham and his "seed" (Ishmael as well as Isaac), signified by circumcision (Genesis 17:1–14); and the Mosaic covenant between Yahweh and Israel (Exodus 6:2–8), signified by the Sabbath (Exodus 31:12–17).[27] The succession of covenants thus traces the progressive revelation of law: bloodguilt; circumcision; and, finally, the Sabbath and priestly observances. One should also note the careful progression of the signs themselves: from the natural and public sign of the rainbow to the cultural and private sign of circumcision to the esoteric sign of the Sabbath, which subsists not in concrete substance but rather in abstract ritual observance. Furthermore, each new dispensation begins in an historical rupture, each precisely located by the repeated phrase "in that very day" (*bᵉ'eṣem hayyom hazzeh*): when Noah enters the ark (Genesis 7:13); when Abraham circumcises himself and the males of his household (Genesis 17:23, 26); and when God rescues the Israelites from slavery in Egypt (Exodus 12:17, 41, 51). Each break is accompanied by divine judgment: the flood, the destruction of the cities of the plain, and the plagues of Egypt. In each case,

---

[26] "The Recession of Biblical Source Criticism," in *The Future of Biblical Studies*, eds. Richard Elliott Friedman and H. G. M. Williamson (Atlanta, GA: Scholars Press, 1987), 99.

[27] Cross, *Canaanite Myth and Hebrew Epic* (Cambridge, MA: Harvard University Press, 1973), 295–300. N.B., the blood of the Passover sacrifice also functions as a "sign" in P (Exodus 12:13).

God remembers (*wayyizkor 'elohim*) his covenant partner and thus rescues some chosen party: "God remembered" Noah and thus ends the flood, saving those in the ark (Genesis 8:1; see also 9:16); "God remembered" Abraham and thus spares Lot and his family (Genesis 19:29); and "God remembered" his covenant with Abraham, Isaac, and Jacob and thus redeems Israel from slavery (Exodus 2:24). There is arguably a fifth dispensation embedded within the Mosaic one – namely, the "covenant of peace" and "eternal priesthood" that God establishes with Phinehas (Numbers 25:12–13).[28] Although God does not reserve for the Aaronid priests a second esoteric name alongside Yahweh, He does grant them a "sign" (*'ot*) of their prerogatives: namely, the censers rescued from divine fire – God's judgment on Korah and company – and hammered into bronze plating for the altar by his father, Eleazar, son of Aaron, a "reminder" (*zikkaron*) – this time to the Israelites – that only those "from the seed of Aaron" may approach God with incense (Numbers 17:2–5 [16:37–40]).

In other words, P propounds a revolutionary view of history. Consistent with what is already evident in Genesis 1, however, P's revolutions are wholly theological rather than political affairs: part divine intervention, part sacred revelation. Each dispensation consists of God's imposition of a new order on the earth, with which creation – humans in particular – simply must comply. Conversely, so little happens between these revolutionary moments – or, more precisely, what happens in between does not generally interest P – that one might almost characterize Priestly thought as a weak version of deism,[29] at least in the limited sense that P's Creator is too abstract and impersonal to maintain any ongoing interactions with mundane reality. Thus, after establishing each dispensation, God simply allows the world to run its course as a more or less self-sustaining system – like the proverbial cosmic clock.

As befits a history that comprises four more-or-less static dispensations, the "plot" of P's overall narrative – like that of its account of the creation of the world – is more spatial than temporal. That is, the succession of ages traces a logical structure rather than a causal sequence – what one might characterize as four concentric circles corresponding to four levels of purity. The age of Adam proceeds from a primary cut between the order of the secular world and the chaos of the primordial deep. The Noahic covenant carves out within this ordered reality a clean realm comprising those species that do not consume blood; this will later function as one of the criteria of P's dietary restrictions, so that predators and scavengers will be pronounced unclean and therefore deemed unfit for consumption by the holy nation of

---

[28] My thanks to Yair Zakovitch for making this suggestion to me.
[29] See related remarks in Kawashima, "The Jubilee Year and the Return of Cosmic Purity," *Catholic Biblical Quarterly* 65 (2003), 388–9.

Israel (Leviticus 11). Under the Abrahamic covenant, the sons of Abraham, in effect, will purify themselves through circumcision and thus mark themselves off from the rest of humankind. Finally, the children of Israel, by observing the Priestly stipulations of the Mosaic covenant, will sanctify themselves to God. By virtue of their holiness, maintained by the eternal priesthood of Phinehas and his sons, they will finally be permitted to house the very presence of God – the "glory of Yahweh" – in their midst: namely, in Jerusalem, in the temple (Exodus 40:34–38), in the "holy of holies" at its very center (Exodus 26:31–37). Ultimately, then, a minimal plot does take shape: the transcendent God of Israel, external to the very world He creates, overcomes this divide through a logical series of dispensations, making possible the construction of a sacred space fit for receiving Yahweh's numinous presence.[30]

J, not unlike P, divides history into discrete ages. Let us similarly name these after three emblematic figures: Cain, Ham, and Israel. In the age of Cain, the eldest son of Adam and his descendants invent the basic forms of civilization: agriculture and animal husbandry (Genesis 3:17–19; 4:2–4, 20); music and metalworking (Genesis 4:21–22); and, finally, Yahwism itself, from the first offerings (Genesis 4:3–4) to the first prayer (Genesis 4:26b).[31] This age comes to an end in the flood. The age that follows belongs instead to the lineage of Ham, which includes the likes of Nimrod (viz., Mesopotamia), Egypt, and the various "native" cultures of Canaan, most notably Sodom and Gomorrah (Genesis 10:8–19). This is the age, in other words, of the ancient empires – next to which Israel will be a mere child – and their heroic–monumental culture. In response to the relatively short lifespan imposed by Yahweh on humanity, this culture is dedicated to the pursuit of "name" (i.e., epic glory or fame), which functions as a compensation for death (Genesis 6:1–4). This glory is achieved either by feats of strength such as those undertaken by the Nephilim (i.e., giants) – also known as "the mighty ones (*haggibborim*) . . . the men of name" (Genesis 6:4) – or by the construction of enduring monuments such as the Tower of Babel, also a bid for "name" (Genesis 11:4). Nimrod exemplifies this culture (Genesis 10:8–12). He is the first "mighty hunter" (*gibbor ṣayid*) – thus, by implication one of the Nephilim[32] – whose exploits earn him the heroic

---

[30]   See Kawashima, "The Priestly Tent of Meeting and the Problem of Divine Transcendence: An 'Archaeology' of the Sacred," *Journal of Religion* 86 (2006), 226–57.

[31]   Partly summarizing Kawashima, "*Homo Faber.*" N.B., following Knohl ("Cain: The Forefather of Humanity," in *Sefer Moshe*, eds. Chaim Cohen, Avi Hurvitz, and Shalom M. Paul [Winona Lake, IN: Eisenbrauns, 2004], 63–7), I attribute the report of Noah's birth (5:29) to J, where it was originally located at the end of the Cainite genealogy (Genesis 4:25–26); see also Friedman's similar treatment of 5:29 in *Hidden*, 74. In other words, J's Noah is a descendant of Cain, not Seth.

[32]   It is worth noting that Dante identified Nimrod as a giant (*Inferno*, canto 31).

epithet, "mighty hunter before Yahweh" (Genesis 10:9). Moreover, he founds his empire at Babel (i.e., Babylon) – indicating the common cultural heritage underlying both the Tower and the Nephilim – from where it subsequently spreads across Mesopotamia.[33] The patriarchal figure of Abraham represents a type of counterculture in this period, one defined by its covenant with Yahweh. Like the rest of the age he was born into, Abraham also aspires to leave behind a great "name," but his will be achieved not in the present through heroic feats and imposing monuments but rather in a divinely promised future through the begetting of numerous offspring (Genesis 12:1–3). Thus, if his appearance in the middle of this epoch does not constitute an actual rupture in history, it does portend a time in the future when his descendants will conquer the land of Canaan and usher in the age of Israel.

If J's history, not unlike P's, is punctuated by revolutionary breaks, it is not a story of divinely imposed dispensations. According to J, humans actively shape the world in which they live. The Cainites invent civilization and thus lay the foundation for the rest of human history. The Hamites establish the great empires, with all their influence on later developments. Finally, one glimpses the historical contribution Israel is destined to make in Abraham's God-given duty to "charge his sons and his household after him to observe the way of Yahweh by doing righteousness and justice" (Genesis 18:19). It will ultimately involve playing a part in bringing the Hamite age to an end, as announced already by Noah in his prophetic curse on Canaan, son of Ham (9:25–27). For this reason, J repeatedly refers to the native populations already inhabiting Canaan: these are the remnants of the old order that Israel must eventually destroy (Genesis 12:6, 13:7, 15:18–21; Exodus 3:8, 34:11). It will specifically entail dispossessing the "Anakites of the Nephilim" (Numbers 13:33). If Friedman is correct in tracing J into the Deuteronomistic History,[34] it is none other than David who completes Israel's divinely appointed task by slaying Goliath (1 Samuel 17).

The historical mechanism behind J's succession of ages is the dialectic between human evil and divine judgment. The Cainites, although they were ingenious inventors, stumbled into a downward spiral of violence – from Cain's fratricide (Genesis 4:8) to Lamech's boundless vengeance (Genesis 4:23–24). It is this trajectory that led to the point in Noah's generation where "every inclination of the thoughts of their heart was only evil all the day"

---

[33] Nimrod's exploits call to mind the famous monumental reliefs of the royal hunt scenes – discovered at Nineveh and housed in the British Museum – and the epic hero Gilgamesh, king of Uruk, who is immortalized in epic for slaying Humbaba and the Bull of Heaven and for constructing the monumental walls of Uruk.

[34] *The Hidden Book in the Bible* (San Francisco, CA: HarperCollins, 1998).

(Genesis 6:5) and thence to the death of the first age by drowning. Behind the fall of the second age lies a more subtle notion of decadence. According to J, the Jordan plain – before being scorched and salted by divine wrath – used to be "well-watered . . . like the Garden of Yahweh, like the land of Egypt" (Genesis 13:10). This carefully chosen comparison implies that to live in a state of paradisiacal ease, where one can simply "irrigate by foot" (Deuteronomy 11:10–12), inevitably leads human societies into moral decline. For since the time of Adam, Yahweh has decreed that mortals should live in a state of anxiety, as befits their creatural status – like a farmer nervously scanning the horizon for signs of rain as he wrests sustenance from the earth "by the sweat of [his] brow" (Genesis 3:19).[35] Eden is thus long lost to humankind. The destruction of Sodom and the other cities of the plain – due to "pride, surfeit of bread, and quiet ease," according to another witness (Ezekiel 16:49) – is a morality tale about the fate of overly prosperous empires and the beginning of the second age's fated end. Egypt, the reader already knows, is next.

If P's so-called plot traces God's gradual descent into the world, step by ineluctable step, J's three ages proceed instead according to an almost Hegelian logic. In that strictly prehistoric phase known as Eden, Yahweh and humanity originally live next to one another within the divine estate in the naïve bliss of a natural or primitive unity (Genesis 2–3). Even after Adam and Eve come of age by becoming "like God, knowing good and evil" and are sent off – now alienated from the divine parent – to lead their own lives as autonomous adults, Yahweh, it is understood, continues to live within his earthly abode, next to which the garden remains undisturbed – thus, the need for guardians who will prevent humans from reentering the palace grounds (Genesis 3:24). The flood brings this state of affairs to a close. Henceforth, the mortal and immortal planes are irrevocably separated as Yahweh forsakes the earth: sacrifices must now rise up to heaven in the form of smoke (Genesis 8:20)[36]; those still dwelling below shall die an early death (Genesis 6:3); and nature itself is left to run its course undisturbed (Genesis 8:22). This does not, however, make the age of Ham a godless one. That Nimrod's prowess is celebrated "before [*lipne*] Yahweh" (Genesis 10:9) suggests that at least during this early stage of history, the heroic–monumental empires are still near to the

---

[35] On "sweat" as a metonymy for worry rather than work, see Daniel E. Fleming, "By the Sweat of Your Brow: Adam, Anat, Athirat and Ashurbanipal," in *Ugarit and the Bible*, eds. G. J. Brooke, A. H. W. Curtis, and J. F. Healey (Münster: Ugarit-Verlag, 1994), 93–100.

[36] Cain and Abel merely "brought" their "offering" to Yahweh's home (Genesis 4:3–5), much like an Israelite was to "bring" his "offering" to the temple priest (e.g., Leviticus 2:1–3), who would, in turn, perform the sacrifice proper (Kawashima, "*Homo Faber*," 497).

divine – in sharp contrast, one might add, to Cain and his descendants, who have been "hidden from the face of [*mippane*] Yahweh" (Genesis 4:14). Nonetheless, one senses in their glorious achievements the height, if not yet *hubris*, of human independence. Therefore, as their civilization finally and inevitably begins to collapse under the weight of its own prosperity, Yahweh inaugurates a new phase in divine–human relations: namely, that sublation or synthesis effected in his call to Abraham (Genesis 12:1–3). This turning point in history sets the stage for the joint venture that will eventually take shape between Yahweh and the future nation of Israel – mortals now reconciled with the immortal in a cultural rather than natural unity, viz., a covenant.

REDACTION

Having isolated and interpreted the Pentateuch's sources, criticism must still confront the interpretive problem posed by the Pentateuch in its final redacted form. Here, we find ourselves on unfamiliar terrain. True, there has existed for some time a criticism devoted to redaction, but it has been unevenly realized in relation to different biblical books and underdeveloped in the case of the Pentateuch.[37] Friedman's vision of a future synthesis in source criticism thus includes "a larger treatment" that would "deal with the place of the corpus" (viz., source) "in relation to the other corpora."[38] Furthermore, if it is indeed the case that the individual sources have not received adequate treatment as coherent literary works, the proposed goal, at least, is abundantly clear: having reconstructed the sources to a reasonable degree of precision, biblicists must now analyze and interpret them as would literary critics any other single-author piece of literature. But what of the Pentateuch as such? What does it mean to read this (or any other) composite text critically – that is, in a way that is consistent with the research program of philology and its modern concept of meaning?

One might be tempted to turn again for guidance to the discipline of literary studies. In fact, it is worth recalling that literary scholars were among the first to defend the "final text" of the Pentateuch (not to mention other portions of the Bible) as an aesthetic object in its own right. Apart from Robert Alter and David Damrosch, however – both of whom offered suggestive if brief remarks on the Bible's "composite artistry"[39] – literary critics of the Bible have

---

[37] See John Barton, "Redaction Criticism (Old Testament)," in *The Anchor Bible Dictionary*, ed. D. N. Freedman (New York: Doubleday, 1992), Vol. 5, 644–7.

[38] "Recession," 99.

[39] See Alter, *Art of Biblical Narrative*, 131–54; and Damrosch, *The Narrative Covenant* (San Francisco, CA: Harper & Row, 1987).

generally failed to approach the redacted text in a consistently modern way, resorting to facile notions of the "final text" based on theoretical constructs (viz., the "implied author" and "intertextuality"), which, however useful to literary theory, are of dubious value to biblical criticism. The implied author was originally conceived of as a type of idealized textual projection of the actual author.[40] Although this entity is arguably compatible with philology, it cannot be said to exist in the case of a composite text such as the Pentateuch. By extension, one might posit an implied author who is the anthropomorphic projection of the text in and of itself. This absolute text, however, is no longer a modern text – one constituted in relation to the author – and its implied author is thus incompatible with criticism. The same holds true for intertextuality, according to which principle (so the argument goes) any combination of texts, even accidental, creates meaning. Indeed, by extension, one might as well interpret accidental permutations of letters and words. After all, that infamous pseudoscientific study, *The Bible Code*, demonstrated that the letters of the biblical text – when recombined according to an arbitrary mathematical function – will produce, purely by chance, short readable strings that a nonmodern reader might choose to interpret. Philology, however, crucially rejects these random strings as unintentional and therefore meaningless. In precisely the same way, "intertextuality" is by design an irretrievably post-philological concept, which as such can contribute nothing to modern interpretation.

It was partly in response to such nonmodern approaches to the composite text that Friedman called on scholars to attend to the figure of the editor, on whom, he recognized, a modern interpretation of the redacted text must be grounded. "One must have some conception," he proposes, "of the world that produced the *combination* of those works"[41] – namely, the world of the editor. "The focus now," he maintains, "is upon the literary figure who assembled the received texts into a single work. The combinatory design which this redactor conceived did more than house the received texts. It gave birth to new narrative syntheses."[42] His recourse to "narrative syntheses," however, is incompatible with philological criticism: "Whatever one learns about the mind of the author in literary analysis of other works, one learns about the

---

[40] Wayne C. Booth, e.g., who is generally credited with inventing the "implied author," defines it wholly in relation to the real author: "As he writes, he creates not simply an ideal, impersonal 'man in general' but an implied version of 'himself' that is different from the implied authors we meet in other men's works" (*The Rhetoric of Fiction* [2d ed.; Chicago: University of Chicago Press, 1983], 70).

[41] "Recession," 99.

[42] "Sacred History and Theology: The Redaction of Torah," in *The Creation of Sacred Literature*, ed. Richard Elliott Friedman (Berkeley: University of California Press, 1981), 25.

complex *meeting* of minds (intended or not) that were brought together to fashion this work."[43] To conceptualize the redacted text as a "meeting of minds (intended or not)" is, in effect, to reject the redactor in favor of an "implied author" who merely personifies a false textual unity or to resort to that strictly post-philological concept of intertextuality.[44] Ironically, it is structurally identical to the attempt to ward off source criticism by appealing to literary patterns in the received text as evidence of its unity – a misguided project that Friedman himself dismantled elsewhere.[45]

To interpret the redacted text in a modern fashion, one must extend criticism's basic concept of meaning so as to account for the contribution of the redactor.[46] By a strict and simple analogy, one arrives at the concept of "editorial intention." Intention, however, presupposes choice. In precisely this respect, the activity of the redactor is qualitatively different from that of the author, being far more constrained. The author, even when obliged to remain faithful to an inherited plot (e.g., the preliterary traditions of the Pentateuch), exercises a broad freedom of expression.[47] The redactor, in stark contrast, inherits one or more texts, which he merely manipulates – by combining, reordering, embellishing, censoring, and so forth. The meaning of redaction is to be found entirely in this manipulation by reconstructing the original text or texts and then analyzing which specific editorial changes were made and why. Conversely, to the extent that a text's redaction was determined by the mechanical necessities of constructing a logically coherent narrative, the editor cannot be said to have contributed to its final meaning, any more than

---

[43] "Recession," 99.

[44] N.B., Friedman also espouses looking for "evidence of the presence of a theological consciousness on the part of the Priestly tradent" but only in those cases where the sources "do not stand in tension but are bound together to form a richer narrative" ("Redaction," 31) (e.g., the plague narrative in Exodus). My point, however, is that one must always look for this "theological consciousness" (i.e., editorial intention).

[45] Friedman ("Some Recent Non-arguments Concerning the Documentary Hypothesis," in *Texts, Temples, and Traditions: A Tribute to Menahem Haran*, eds. Michael V. Fox et al. [Winona Lake, IN: Eisenbrauns, 1996], 87–101) specifically attacks Isaac M. Kikawada and Arthur Quinn, *Before Abraham Was: The Unity of Genesis 1–11* (Nashville, TN: Abingdon Press, 1985); his criticisms also apply to Gary Rendsburg, *The Redaction of Genesis* (Winona Lake, IN: Eisenbrauns, 1986).

[46] The significance of the Parry–Lord hypothesis largely consists in the fact that it enabled Homer scholarship to interpret the collective and cumulative intention of the oral tradition.

[47] Van der Toorn, by insisting on the merely "traditional" and "conventional" style of the biblical writers (whom he refers to as "craftsmen"), fails to recognize the creativity these literary artists could and did exercise, even within the limits imposed on them by a predominantly oral culture (*Scribal Culture*, 14–16, 47, 51, 110–18). See my arguments to the contrary in "Verbal Medium and Narrative Art in Homer and the Bible," *Philosophy and Literature* 28 (2004), 103–17.

someone who correctly assembles the pieces of a jigsaw puzzle can be credited with its final design.[48] In other words, the modern critic must interpret redaction strictly in relation to the range of options available to the redactor, as the expression of editorial freedom as opposed to literary necessity.

Some of what is at stake in the redacted text becomes visible in a case of textual corruption found in Immanuel Kant's *Prolegomena to Any Future Metaphysics*. Hans Vaihinger convincingly argued (in philological fashion) that a galley of Kant's "Preamble" was misplaced during the printing process.[49] Faced with this difficult (because corrupted) text, readers are obliged, to be sure, to make sense of it as best they can. Once criticism has revealed, however, that it contains an unintended collocation of two discontinuous passages, most readers will reject readings based on the defective text in favor of those based on the emended one – as is the case with the variant readings of Genesis 4:8 discussed previously. Yet, one might ask, now that literary theory has provided us with tools such as the implied author and intertextuality, are we not able – perhaps ethically obligated – to rescue the *Prolegomena*'s "final text as it is"? Philological criticism's answer is an unqualified "no." The goal of modern interpretation is to recover Kant's thought, for which the implied author (here, the personification of a textual defect) and intertextuality (here, the reification of a misplaced galley) are poor substitutes indeed. One can certainly cling to the "text as it is" under the banner of a post-philological research program, but one should then have the honesty to admit that Kant's thought is no longer at issue. Now, in terms of the resultant tension and even confusion, a bit of misplaced text in Kant is not unlike a juncture in the Pentateuch where two originally independent passages have been secondarily juxtaposed. By the same logic, then, the modern critic, when confronted with the latter, must decide whether it results from an error in transmission or an editorial decision and then emend or interpret the composite text accordingly. Again, one can insist on reading the text "as it is," but one should then be prepared to admit that the thought of a speaking being is no longer at issue.

Let us return to the two Creation stories and consider their side-by-side placement. It will not do to pronounce Genesis 1–3 a "narrative synthesis with [new] exegetical possibilities" and proclaim that it is now "quite literally more than the sum of its components."[50] The juxtaposition of the two stories indeed may produce suggestive echoes that encourage the reader to draw interesting

---

[48] See Friedman, "Redaction"; and Baruch Halpern, "What They Don't Know Won't Hurt Them: Genesis 6–9," in *Fortunate the Eyes that See*, 16–34.

[49] Vaihinger, "Eine Blattversetzung in Kants *Prolegomena*," *Philosophische Monatshefte* 15 (1879), 321–32, 513–32.

[50] Friedman, "Redaction," 25–6.

(or imaginative) connections between them, but if these literary effects were unintended by the redactor, they cannot be credited with any "meaning" in the modern critical sense of the word.[51] To attribute meaning to redaction, one must find evidence in the text for viewing the effect under consideration as no mere accident but rather as the result of an editorial choice the redactor was in a position to make. In so gross a procedure as placing two entire texts side by side, the editorial options are severely restricted. One can certainly profit from comparing the two stories in all their details in order to bring their respective meanings into proper relief, but R's limited intervention here will not sustain attempts such as Friedman's to interpret J and P together as part of a textual unity: "In the final product we call Torah" – note his invocation of the traditional text – "one cannot separate the creation in *imago Dei* [in P] from the natures of the humans who disobey the divine instruction [in J]." By the same token, Friedman should adduce evidence of positive editorial activity before maintaining that R has created a "metamorphosis in the portrayal of Yhwh," a "synthetic theological formulation"[52] – namely, that God is at once both personal (JE) and impersonal (P), both graciously merciful (JE) and unrelentingly just (P). The fact that R has preserved (but not necessarily endorsed) both theological positions merely may reflect his belief that "Both these and these are the words of the living God" (Babylonian Talmud *Eruvin* 13b).

Rather, a fully critical interpretation of Genesis 1–3 must begin with the options that lay before R. If we grant that splicing the two Creation stories together into a single continuous narrative would be an awkward and clumsy procedure given the nature of the material, we are left with two basic possibilities: P followed by J or vice versa. A useful thought experiment, then, is to consider the effect of placing J before P. In this hypothetical arrangement, the progression from "in the day" (Genesis 2:4b) to "in the beginning" (Genesis 1:1) seems illogical and the move from the intimate space of the garden to the vast expanse of heaven and earth is disorienting. R's decision, then, may have simply consisted in choosing the most (or only) elegant permutation of

---

[51] There are postmodern works of art that are meant to incorporate extrinsic, accidental phenomena as part of the meaning effect they produce within the viewer, listener, and so forth, who now constitute both a site of and a participant in this effect. John Cage's famous musical composition 4'33", for example, consists of nothing but silence on the part of the musician(s), and thus contains no intrinsic "meaning" in the modern sense: "I have nothing to say, and I am saying it," he has maintained. Rather, its intended meaning effect is to produce within the audience an awareness of whatever ambient noise happens to be perceptible within the performance space. It should be obvious that this is a far cry from the intentions of the biblical writers and redactors, but one must be prepared to admit that the Bible is not postmodern.

[52] "Redaction," 26–7.

Creation accounts. Even in light of this limited choice, however, it still seems fair to say that R's intended effect was precisely what many readers intuitively infer on reading the combined text: P provides a broad perspective into which J is subsequently fitted in as a type of "close-up." One can go further: the fact that R chooses to set the stage for his grand narrative synthesis with P and its sublime opening words – which have become one of the most famous phrases in all of world literature – demonstrates R's Priestly loyalties. This agrees with the compelling case Cross has made that R used P (or material pertaining to P) to create the framework of the entire Pentateuch, essentially making it a Priestly composition, within which the other sources merely have been allowed to find their place.[53] In the end, however, little can be said of R's actual contribution to the meaning of Genesis 1–3 because there was little that could actually be done.

A more interesting case is the redaction of the flood story, around which the remainder of this study revolves. Here, J and P have been so ingeniously woven together that Hermann Gunkel declared the analysis of Genesis 6–9 into its constituent sources a "masterpiece of modern criticism."[54] In constructing this seamlessly combined, more-or-less continuous story, R had greater opportunity to shape the final narrative. There is evidence, furthermore, that R added to the redacted flood story, thereby imposing on it certain ideas. In cases such as this, an interpretation that takes the Pentateuchal sources and redaction fully into account must begin with the individual components – here, J and P – and then carefully interpret the redactor's (or redactors') editorial intentions insofar as these can be inferred from the text.

To discern the complex meaning of the flood, then, let us begin with the two underlying sources, J and P. One can bring out their distinctive ideas most fully by comparing them on three key points: the motive for the flood, the function of the flood, and the conclusion to the flood. If P was actually written as a direct response to J, these comparisons also reveal how P revised J.

(1) According to J, the motive for the flood is "evil" and the culprit is humankind (Genesis 6:5).[55] It continues and develops the theme of humanity's

---

[53] Specifically, Cross posits a "Book of Generations" (see Genesis 5:1) – whence the recurring phrase "these are the generations" – and points to the list of "stations" now found in Numbers 33 (*Canaanite Myth and Hebrew Epic*, 293–325). He does not distinguish between P and R, but these details need not concern us here.

[54] Gunkel, *Genesis*, trans. Mark E. Biddle (Macon, GA: Mercer University Press, 1997), 138–9.

[55] Since antiquity (see, e.g., Jubilees 5), it has often been thought (and for good reason) that the giants are at least partly to blame for the flood. As I argue elsewhere, however, J's brief account of the Nephilim (Genesis 6:1–4) originally followed the flood. It was R who moved it to its present location, precisely in order to impute guilt to these "men of name" – an ingenious

"knowledge of good and evil," which is both creative and destructive. For P, in contrast, the reason for the flood is the "corruption" of the "earth" itself, due to the "corruption" and "violence" of "all flesh" – that is, both humans and animals (Genesis 6:11–13). Thus, the problem in P is not related specifically to that moral agency peculiar to humans. As Knohl observed, P uses passive constructions to describe this corruption in order to downplay the question of agency altogether.[56] Furthermore, the allusion Hendel identifies in Genesis 6:12 – "And God saw the earth, and look, it had been corrupted" – to Genesis 1:31 – "And God saw all that he had made, and look, it was very good"[57] – demonstrates that for P, the operative distinction is clean versus unclean, not good versus evil.

(2) It follows, then, that J's flood functions as a nearly universal punishment for the crimes of humanity. Yahweh, who experiences "pain" and "regret" at having created them (Genesis 6:6), decides to "wipe out humans" along with all living things (Genesis 6:7), the animals being mere innocent bystanders. Is it coincidence that the next time Yahweh contemplates inflicting collective punishment, when "fire" is about to "rain" down from the sky (Genesis 19:24), Abraham distinguishes himself by boldly questioning "the judge of all the earth" (Genesis 18:25) whether it is just to "sweep away the righteous with the wicked" (Genesis 18:23)? In contrast, P's flood cleanses the earth from pollution, apparently caused by bloodguilt.[58] The "end of all flesh . . . come[s] before" God (Genesis 6:13) like a mere side effect. "Destruction" (Hiphil, *šḥt*) is first and foremost a means to undo "corruption" (Niphal, *šḥt*). For this reason, the flood is described as a partial reversal of Creation: opening "the springs of the great deep" and "the windows of heaven" is the mirror image of the separation God achieved in the second day of Creation (Genesis 1:6–8); stopping the flood by shutting up the skies and sending forth a "wind"

and remarkably effective editorial maneuver ("The Flood, the Day of Atonement, and the Priestly Redaction of Genesis 1–11," paper read at the Annual Conference of the Association for Jewish Studies, December 2008). N.B., with both 5:29 (see n. 31) and 6:1–4, R employs the same minimalist procedure (movement), in order to create the same effect: setting up a dualism between good seed (Seth, Noah the Sethite) and bad (Cain, the Nephilim). In both cases, the bad seeds are eliminated by the flood.

[56] Knohl, "The Priestly Conception of Evil," paper read at the Twelfth World Congress of Jewish Studies, Jerusalem, 1997; see also *The Divine Symphony* (Philadelphia, PA: Jewish Publication Society, 2003), 11–16.

[57] Ronald S. Hendel, "The Poetics of Myth in Genesis," in *The Seductiveness of Jewish Myth: Challenge or Response?*, ed. S. Daniel Breslauer (Albany, NY: SUNY Press, 1997), 163.

[58] See Tikva Frymer-Kensky, "The Atrahasis Epic and its Significance for our Understanding of Genesis 1–9," BA 40 (1977): 147–55; idem, "Pollution, Purification, and Purgation in Biblical Israel," in *The Word of the Lord Shall Go Forth: Essays in Honor of David Noel Freedman in Celebration of His Sixtieth Birthday*, eds. Carol L. Meyers and M. O'Connor (Winona Lake, IN: Eisenbrauns, 1983), 399–414.

(Genesis 8:1–3) is nothing less than a recapitulation of P's Creation account (Genesis 1:2).

(3) J's flood concludes with Noah's sacrifice of one of every clean animal and bird as a burnt offering to Yahweh; hence, his earlier directive to bring seven pairs of clean animals and one pair of unclean animals onto the ark (Genesis 7:2–3). Without being asked, Noah sends up their "pleasing odor" to Yahweh, who remarkably is appeased by it and reconciled with human evil – which has not, in his eyes, changed as a result of the flood (Genesis 8:20–22). In fact, as the first ritual sacrifice in J, Noah's burnt offering may well constitute J's etiology of sacrifice: sacrifices are gifts freely given to Yahweh that appease his wrath and win his favor.[59] E, in contrast – to judge from "the Binding of Isaac" (Genesis 22) – appears to view sacrifice as an act of unquestioning obedience to God's absolute word (viz., God's demand, beyond good and evil, that Abraham sacrifice his son) and/or as an efficacious substitution of an animal for a human, who would have otherwise been forfeited to divine negation.[60] For P, as is well known, sacrifice purifies, but only the sons of Aaron can sacrifice to Yahweh, and they do so only in strict conformity to the instructions revealed at Mount Sinai. It is thus unthinkable for P that Noah did so. For this reason, P insists that Noah brought only one pair of all the animals onto the ark (Genesis 6:19–20), failing even to mention the distinction between clean and unclean, which has not yet been revealed. P's flood thus concludes instead with the giving of ad hoc universal laws designed to avoid the pollution caused by the shedding and eating of blood (Genesis 9:1–7).

How have these two stories been combined? To be sure, much of R's redaction was determined by the mechanical necessities of constructing a logically coherent narrative.[61] As Bernard Levinson argued, however, R intervened in the question of the number of animals brought on board the ark.[62] Specifically, R sides with P: "From the clean animals and from the animals which are not clean … two, two they came to Noah, to the ark, male and female, just as God had commanded Noah" (Genesis 7:8–9). This mixture of ideas

---

[59] Cain and Abel's offerings were not fully executed sacrifices (see n. 36). Nonetheless, both cases operate according to the principle of gift exchange.

[60] As Friedman points out, it appears that Abraham actually sacrificed Isaac in an earlier version of the story (*Who Wrote the Bible*, 256–7; *The Bible with Sources Revealed* [San Francisco, CA: HarperSanFrancisco, 2003], 65).

[61] See Halpern, "What They Don't Know."

[62] See Levinson, "'The Right Chorale': From the Poetics of Biblical Narrative to the Hermeneutics of the Hebrew Bible," in *"Not in Heaven": Coherence and Complexity in Biblical Narrative*, eds. Jason P. Rosenblatt and Joseph C. Sitterson (Bloomington: Indiana University Press, 1991), 137–41. Israel Knohl has made similar observations (personal communication).

taken from J and P betrays the later hand of R. R alludes to J's distinction between clean and unclean animals but confirms P's report that only one pair of all the animals were saved. I add that R's wording, "two, two ... male and female," is an amalgam of J – "seven, seven, man and his woman" (Genesis 7:2) – and P, "two from all ... male and female" (Genesis 6:19). R similarly altered Genesis 7:15 ("two, two from all flesh") to conform with Genesis 7:9 by adding a second "two." Remove it and Genesis 7:15 ("two from all flesh") is now nearly identical with P's earlier statement in Genesis 6:19 ("from all flesh, two from all").[63] The number is the number of P, but the syntax is the syntax of J. As such, assigning Genesis 7:8–9 and Genesis 7:15 to either J or P would result in nonsense because interpreting them in conformity with the language of either J (Genesis 7:2) or P (Genesis 6:19) would lead to the conclusion that Noah finally decided to bring two pairs of all the animals onto the ark. They only make sense as secondary, composite references to J and P. Considering that all three of the factors discussed herein – motive, function, and conclusion – revolve around the presence or absence of sacrifice, R's small decision entirely shifts the final narrative in P's favor, making the flood a divine act of purification.

CONCLUSION

The complex interpretive procedure I employ in this chapter, to be sure, is fraught with difficulties. The flood story, having rather clear source divisions, provides a relatively simple test case – like an experiment performed under controlled conditions. The more complicated and therefore conjectural the composition of a passage is, however, the more complicated and therefore conjectural must its interpretation be. In such cases, conventional wisdom will likely complain that this procedure is too "speculative." True, the critic who dares to imaginatively extrapolate from the available evidence runs the risk of erring boldly, but only a critic who risks being wrong can hope to be right, because only he has allowed for the fact that we have at our disposal only a part of the relevant evidence. The timid scholar, whose lack of imagination is often mistaken for "rigor," is all but guaranteed to err because he offers "cautious" interpolations, which foolishly treat the available evidence – or, to use empiricist terminology, the directly perceived evidence – as if it were all the evidence, an error akin to believing that an iceberg consists only of that which appears above the water's surface. Ultimately, from the standpoint of

---

[63] A less elegant solution, unsupported by variant readings, would be to emend 7:9 and 15 as cases of dittography.

philology, there simply is no other choice because the inherent difficulty of this project neither constitutes an argument against its validity nor justifies inventing a more attractive (because simpler) alternative. Modern criticism must refuse such false comforts.

Finally, I reemphasize that there is nothing "anti-literary" in the analysis of sources and redaction. On the contrary, there is – as I have already observed – a direct historical relationship between philology and the modern academic study of literature. As Barthes perceived so clearly, the class of those who are "obsessed by" the text includes both authors and linguists, philologists and critics.[64] It seems to be only in biblical studies – for reasons having to do with the history of scholarship – that philology and literary interpretation are seen to be at odds with one another. One does well to recall, then, that source criticism used to be called "literary criticism" because only the most lovingly precise attentions paid to the Pentateuch could have gained access to its complicated textual past. What I demonstrate here is that awareness of the sources and redaction of biblical texts is not only helpful but also necessary to their interpretation. Far from obscuring or neglecting or denying literary art, it makes possible the retrieval of the intentions of the biblical writers and redactors, which have been lost with the passing of the centuries and obscured by modern notions of the single-author book.

[64] Barthes, *Pleasure of the Text*, 21, 63.

4

‍

Gender and Sexuality

Ronald Hendel, Chana Kronfeld, and Ilana Pardes

In her groundbreaking study of gender, *The Second Sex* (1949), Simone de Beauvoir evokes the story of the creation of woman in Genesis 2 as a primary text whose impact on Western perceptions of gender relations cannot be overlooked. Beauvoir writes:

> Eve was not fashioned at the same time as the man; she was not fabricated from a different substance, nor of the same clay as was used to model Adam: she was taken from the flank of the first male. Not even her birth was independent; God did not spontaneously choose to create her as an end in herself.... She was destined by Him for man; it was to rescue Adam from loneliness that He gave her to him, in her mate was her origin and her purpose; she was his complement on the order of the inessential.[1]

Beauvoir's renowned claim that "one is not born, but rather becomes, a woman"[2] – the formulation that became the very base for the definition of "gender" as a social construct – turns out to be particularly relevant to the "birth" of the first woman. Eve's birth is by no means a natural event, innocent of cultural presuppositions regarding the role of woman. She is subjected to God and to Adam, shaped as the perfect Other whose very purpose is to serve as "dream incarnate," to enable the first man to define himself as Subject within the realm of the essential.

Beauvoir did not devote much attention to the Bible, but her reading of Genesis had great impact on the first biblical scholars to engage in feminist criticism of the Bible. Phyllis Trible, the founding figure of this trend, positions her feminist rhetorical criticism against Beauvoir's treatment of the biblical text. To be more precise, she offers a critique of both sexist and feminist approaches to Scripture. What previous readers have neglected to take into

---

[1] Simone de Beauvoir, *The Second Sex* (New York: Vintage Books, 1953), 141.
[2] Ibid., 267.

account, she claims in "Depatriarchalizing in Biblical Interpretation" (1973), is that patriarchy does not have "God on its side." "The women's movement," she suggests, "errs when it dismisses the Bible as inconsequential or condemns it as enslaving. In rejecting Scripture women ironically accept male chauvinistic interpretations and thereby capitulate to the very view they are protesting."[3] "Depatriarchalizing" then, is a "hermeneutic operating within Scripture itself," evident to those willing to strip away the layers of patriarchal commentaries and read anew.[4]

Genesis 1:27, from the Priestly version of Creation, serves as the primary exegetical "clue" in Trible's more elaborate work, *God and the Rhetoric of Sexuality* (1978). She construes the parallelism between the phrases "in the image of God" and "male and female" (Genesis 1:27) as "a semantic correspondence between a lesser known element and a better known element."[5] By turning this parallelism into a guiding metaphor – God being the tenor and human sexuality the vehicle – Trible highlights the pluralism and equality that "God's image" embodies. She uses this egalitarian "clue" as a springboard to explore the hitherto neglected female metaphors (mother, above all) of the deity.

Trible's most pronounced departure from Beauvoir is evident in her reading of the Yahwistic tale of Creation in Genesis 2. She ventures to refute the notion that God created man first and shows that even if this were the case, it does not necessarily imply his superiority vis-à-vis woman. Relying on the fact that *ha'adam* is a generic Hebrew term meaning "humankind," she suggests that it is not man who is created in 2:7 but rather a sexually undifferentiated "earth creature" (from *'adamah*, earth). Human sexuality is created only in Genesis 2:22–23, when God "operates on this earth creature, to produce a companion."[6] When dealing with the material from which woman was created, Trible, unlike Beauvoir, sees God's building of woman from the rib as a sign of her uniqueness (Adam and all the other living creatures were made of dust). Depicting the complex work that the creation of woman involved, she concludes that "woman is no weak, dainty, ephemeral creature. No opposite sex, no second sex, no derived sex – in short, no 'Adam's rib.' Instead, woman is the culmination of creation, fulfilling humanity in sexuality."[7]

---

[3] Phyllis Trible, "Depatriarchalizing in Biblical Interpretation," *Journal of the American Academy of Religion* 41 (1973), 31.

[4] Ibid., 48.

[5] Phyllis Trible, *God and the Rhetoric of Sexuality* (Philadelphia, PA: Fortress Press, 1978), 17.

[6] Ibid., 98.

[7] Ibid., 102. But cf. Beauvoir's response to this kind of interpretation (*Second Sex*, xxxix): "Some say that, having been created after Adam, she is evidently a secondary being; others say on the contrary that Adam was only a rough draft and that God succeeded in producing the human being in perfection when He created Eve.... Each argument at once suggests its opposite... If we are to gain understanding, we must get out of these ruts; we must discard

In its bold revisionism, Trible's work is an admirable scholarly continuation of the pioneering exegesis of suffragists such as Sarah Grimké, who wrote in 1838: "Men and women were CREATED EQUAL: they are both moral and accountable beings, and whatever is *right* for man to do, is *right* for woman."[8] However, it has also been criticized for some of its conservative presuppositions. Elizabeth Schüssler Fiorenza in her influential *In Memory of Her* (1983) offers a critique of Trible's lack of attention to the patriarchal stamp of the biblical text. A feminist reading of the Bible that does not take into account the ways in which this text legitimizes the oppression of women, she writes, is in danger of rehabilitating patriarchal norms.[9] Later, as the first woman president of the Society for Biblical Literature, she advocated a new ethics of historical reading that raised "the question of power" both within the biblical world and in the interpretive project, taking into account "the ideological distortions of great works of religion."[10]

An entirely different perception of gender emerged within the newly con- solidated field of biblical literary studies. In Mieke Bal's *Lethal Love: Feminist Literary Readings of Biblical Love Stories* (1987), a groundbreaking postmodern study of the biblical text, the Bible is regarded as neither "a feminist resource" nor a "sexist manifesto." Such an assumption, Bal claims, "can be an issue only for those who attribute moral, religious, or political authority to these texts, which is precisely the opposite of what I'm interested in."[11] Accordingly, she does not set out, as Trible does, to "restore" an "original" or privileged meaning of the Bible but rather attempts to provide a "different" reading that would highlight "the relative arbitrariness of all readings, including the sexist readings we have become so used to."[12]

Bal's alternative readings are meant to serve as a critique of the misogynist monolithic stance that most interpretations of the Bible share, despite their diversity. To illustrate this point, she discusses different types of reception – from literary scholarship to children's Bibles – in her analysis of five biblical

the vague notions of superiority, inferiority, equality which have hitherto corrupted every discussion of the subject and start afresh."

8 Sarah M. Grimké, *Letters on the Equality of the Sexes and the Condition of Woman* (New York: Burt Franklin, 1838; reprint, New Haven, CT: Yale University Press, 1988), 3–4.

9 Elizabeth Schüssler Fiorenza, *In Memory of Her: A Feminist Theological Reconstruction of Christian Origins* (New York: Crossroad, 1983), 21. For a more recent critique of Trible, see John J. Collins, *The Bible after Babel: Historical Criticism in a Postmodern Age* (Grand Rapids, MI: Eerdmans, 2005), 86–96.

10 Elizabeth Schüssler Fiorenza, "The Ethics of Biblical Interpretation: Decentering Biblical Scholarship," *Journal of Biblical Literature* 107 (1988), 14–15; revised in idem, *Rhetoric and Ethic: The Politics of Biblical Studies* (Minneapolis, MN: Augsburg Fortress, 1999), 27–8.

11 Mieke Bal, *Lethal Love: Feminist Literary Interpretations of Biblical Love Stories* (Bloomington: Indiana University Press, 1987), 1.

12 Ibid., 2.

love stories. What Bal attempts to show in each case is how the heteroge-
neous ideology of the text is turned into a monolithic one in the respective
patriarchal interpretations she criticizes. How different is this from Trible's
depatriarchalizing of biblical interpretation? First, unlike Trible, Bal engages
in an extensive semiotic analysis of the interpretations to which she refers,
laying bare the reading strategies at work. Second, her perception of gender
and misogyny are informed by deconstruction and postmodernism. What
bothers Bal "is not the sexist interpretation of the Bible as such. . . . It is the
possibility of dominance itself, the attractiveness of coherence and authority
in culture."[13] In keeping with the writings of Derrida and Lacan, Bal defines the
feminine as that which exceeds the comprehension of the Cartesian subject,
that which is non-decidability and non-knowledge.[14]

At the same time as feminist biblical scholarship was being consolidated in
its literary, philosophical, and political multiplicity, the appearance of Michel
Foucault's three-volume *History of Sexuality* (1976–1984) initiated a new turn
in the study of gender and sexuality. Rather than contesting misogyny or
other oppressive practices as such, Foucault contested the stability of our
concepts of gender and sexuality – which misogyny, homophobia, and the like
presume – through a rigorous exploration of their historical formations from
ancient Greece to the Victorian era. In some respects, Foucault's genealogy of
sexuality represents a return to Beauvoir's argument that gender is made, not
found: "Woman is determined . . . by the manner in which her body and her
relation to the world are modified through the action of others than herself."[15]
Foucault extended this insight to both sexes and to sexuality as such.

Foucault explored the domains of sexuality in each era by examining their
conceptual, legal, and personal dimensions. He unpacks these three levels of
inquiry as follows:

> [sexuality as] a complex experience is constituted from and around certain
> forms of behavior: an experience which conjoins a field of knowledge (with
> its own concepts, theories, diverse disciplines), a collection of rules (which
> differentiate the permissible from the forbidden, natural from monstrous,
> normal from pathological, which is decent from what is not, etc.), a mode of
> relation between the individual and himself (which enables him to recognize
> himself as a sexual subject amid others).[16]

---

[13] Ibid., 3.
[14] For an extensive consideration of Bal's approach, see Ilana Pardes, *Countertraditions in the
     Bible: A Feminist Approach* (Cambridge, MA: Harvard University Press, 1992), 5–6 and passim.
[15] Beauvoir, *Second Sex*, 725.
[16] Michel Foucault, "Preface" to *The History of Sexuality, Vol. 2*, in *The Foucault Reader*, ed. P.
     Rabinow (New York: Pantheon Books, 1984), 333.

The study of sexuality, therefore, is an inquiry into historically specific configurations of knowledge, power, and agency. One important consequence of this method is an awareness that our modern categories and rules regarding sexuality – codified in labels such as "heterosexual" and "homosexual," and in the laws that enforce their difference – are relatively recent cultural phenomena. As Beauvoir observed (and as Judith Butler further explored in Foucauldian fashion), "woman" is also a contingent and socially constructed category, which conjoins specific historical formations of knowledge, power, and agency.[17]

Foucault's contribution to the study of gender and sexuality has inspired important recent work in biblical studies. In light of the absence of biblical and rabbinic material in Foucault's work, Daniel Boyarin pertinently asked, "Are There Any Jews in 'The History of Sexuality'?" (1995) and concluded that "biblical and Talmudic texts confirm rather than refute Foucault's general hypothesis of the 'history of sexuality,'" focusing on the biblical laws of sexual intercourse, bestiality, and cross-dressing.[18] Biblical rules, categories, and narratives concerning sexual and gendered behaviors are richly illuminated by a Foucauldian style of inquiry, as recent studies by Saul Olyan, Ken Stone, and Susan Ackerman have shown.[19]

More recently, the study of gender and sexuality has focused (among other topics) on the critique of binary oppositions such as sex/gender, gay/straight, and even male/female.[20] If such distinctions, as Butler argues, are culturally produced through discourse and performance, then it may be misleading to ask how these mark, in any meaningful sense, different kinds or essences. In this spirit, Butler contends (invoking Beauvoir), "one is not born, but rather one is *called* a woman, and it is discourse that does the metaphorical 'calling.'"[21]

[17] Judith Butler, *Gender Trouble: Feminism and the Subversion of Identity* (New York: Routledge, 1990), 3–9 and passim.

[18] Daniel Boyarin, "Are There Any Jews in 'The History of Sexuality'?" *Journal of the History of Sexuality* 5 (1994–1995), 333–55, quote from 353.

[19] See Saul Olyan, "'And with a Male You Shall Not Lie the Lying Down of a Woman': On the Meaning and Significance of Leviticus 18:22 and 20:13," *Journal of the History of Sexuality* 5 (1994–1995), 179–206; Ken Stone, "Gender and Homosexuality in Judges 19: Subject-Honor, Object-Shame?," *Journal for the Study of the Old Testament* 67 (1995), 87–107; idem, *Practicing Safer Texts: Food, Sex and the Bible in Queer Perspective* (London: T. & T. Clark, 2005); Susan Ackerman, *When Heroes Love: The Ambiguity of Eros in the Stories of Gilgamesh and David* (New York: Columbia University Press, 2005).

[20] See Nikki Sullivan, *A Critical Introduction to Queer Theory* (New York: New York University Press, 2003); and on Genesis, see Ken Stone, "The Garden of Eden and the Heterosexual Contract," in *Bodily Citations: Religion and Judith Butler*, eds. Ellen Armour and Susan St. Ville (New York: Columbia University Press, 2006), 48–70.

[21] Introduction to "The Lesbian Phallus and the Morphological Imaginary," in *The Judith Butler Reader*, eds. Sara Salih with Judith Butler (Oxford, UK: Blackwell, 2004), 139.

Without pressing the point, we note that the original articulation of "male and female" (*zakar unᵉqebah*) in Genesis already complicates this gender binary, while nesting it in the metaphysical binary of God and human:

> God created the human (*ha'adam*) in his image (*ṣalmo*);
> in God's image he created him (*'oto*);
> male and female he created them (*'otam*). (Genesis 1:27)

The parallelistic effects of this poetic triplet simultaneously call into being and partially erase the sharp distinctions of God/human and male/female. Humans are not gods but are created in (or as) God's image (a phrase whose meaning is anything but clear).[22] "The human" is grammatically masculine singular but is specified as "male and female" and plural. The grammatical and ontological singularity and plurality of "the human" is mirrored in God, who is morphologically plural but grammatically masculine singular, and who in the previous verse addresses a divine plurality: "Let us make a human (*'adam*) in our image, after our likeness" (Genesis 1:26). In this first poem in the Bible, "our image" becomes "his image," reducing the plurality to a singularity, as the verses move from God's subjective intentions to the narrator's objective report.

The expressive use of rhyme – *'adam/'otam, ṣalmo/'oto* – and the shifting chiasms and word order in each line, which are the biblical poem's stock in trade, help rearticulate "the human" (and, by implication, God's image) *as both* "male and female." That is, the poem complicates, intensifies, and reorients the duality of male/female in its very moment of linguistic origin. As Butler writes, "the self is from the start radically implicated in the 'Other'"[23] – according to Genesis 1:27, the self, inasmuch as it is "human," is implicated in both terms of "male and female," just as it is simultaneously singular and plural, human and divine replica. The first human(s) is thus called into being as a composite equality in which male, female, and God are related to one another.

A reading of the first Creation story inspired by contemporary gender theory would thus argue that gender and sexuality are inaugurated as physical and metaphysical qualities in a continuum rather than as purely dichotomous essences or types. This poem unpacks the seemingly natural binaries – human/God and male/female – into a highly nuanced and reflective theory of gender and self.[24]

---

[22] W. Randall Garr, *In His Own Image and Likeness: Humanity, Divinity, and Monotheism* (Leiden, the Netherlands: Brill, 2003).

[23] Butler, "Imitation and Gender Subordination," 132.

[24] It should be stressed that the biblical concepts of the self are deeply embedded in the extended "self" of the family, in contrast to the modern unembedded self; see Robert A. Di Vito,

THE STORY OF SODOM (GENESIS 19)

Recent developments in the study of gender and sexuality are particularly pertinent to the story of Sodom and Gomorrah.[25] This narrative turns on the sexual violence that the men of Sodom seek to perpetrate on Lot's mysterious guests, and it concludes with incest between Lot and his daughters. Like the stories of sexual conflict elsewhere in Genesis, the implicit rules of gender, sexuality, and morality are of central importance to the story. We pay particular attention to the triad of knowledge, power, and agency that Foucault identifies as the force fields of sexuality and to the pliable frameworks of male, female, and divine.

The Sodom narrative opens with a scene of hospitality, setting up the righteous Lot as a foil for the wicked men of Sodom. As many commentators have observed, the Sodomites' "crime consists in the violation of hospitality."[26] Hospitality is both gendered and social: it is an obligation for the male head of a family, a public expression of his honor and his power to protect. These two intertwined values – hospitality and honor – bear crucially on the conflicts of gender and sexuality in the story. The story begins as follows:

> Two divine messengers came to Sodom in the evening, while Lot was sitting at the gate of Sodom. Lot saw them and rose to face them and bowed his face to the ground. He said, "Please, my lords, please turn aside to your servant's house and spend the night, and wash your feet, and rise in the morning and go on your way." They said, "No, we will spend the night in the street." He pressed them greatly and they relented and they came into his house. He made them a feast with baked flatbread, and they ate. (Genesis 19:1–3)

"Old Testament Anthropology and the Construction of Personal Identity," *Catholic Biblical Quarterly* 61 (1999), 217–38; and Jon D. Levenson, "Individual Mortality and Familial Resurrection," in idem, *Resurrection and the Restoration of Israel* (New Haven, CT: Yale University Press, 2006), 108–22.

[25] See the discussions in Boyarin, "History of Sexuality," 348–51; Stone, *Safer Texts*, 77–80; and Martti Nissinen, *Homoeroticism in the Biblical World: A Historical Perspective* (Minneapolis, MN: Fortress Press, 1998), 45–9. On the related dynamics in Judges 19, see Stone, "Gender and Homosexuality."

[26] Claus Westermann, *Genesis 12–36: A Commentary* (Minneapolis, MN: Augsburg, 1985), 298; see further Victor Matthews, "Hospitality and Hostility in Genesis 19 and Judges 19," *Biblical Theology Bulletin* 22 (1992), 3–11; Weston W. Fields, *Sodom and Gomorrah: History and Motif in Biblical Narrative* (Sheffield, UK: Sheffield Academic Press, 1997), 54–85; Lyn Bechtel, "A Feminist Reading of Genesis 19:1–11," in *Genesis: A Feminist Companion to the Bible (Second Series)*, ed. A. Brenner (Sheffield, UK: Sheffield Academic Press, 1998), 108–28; and Phyllis A. Bird, "The Bible in Christian Ethical Deliberation Concerning Homosexuality: Old Testament Contributions," in *Homosexuality, Science, and the "Plain Sense" of Scripture*, ed. D. L. Balch (Grand Rapids, MI: Eerdmans, 1999), 147–9.

There are two movements in this first scene – the strangers' entry into Sodom and their entry into Lot's house. This sets up a parallel between city and house and between their respective thresholds: gate and door. As an adult male "sitting at the gate" (an image typical of a city elder, a privileged male) and as the head of his own household, Lot is the guardian of both thresholds. As the keeper of these boundaries, he offers the vulnerable strangers hospitality and protection. The verb for entering – they "came (*wayyavo'u*) to Sodom" and "they came (*wayyavo'u*) into his house" – emphasizes the crossing of thresholds and implicitly signals vulnerability and danger. As Lyn Bechtel observes – following Mary Douglas – "boundaries are powerful because they protect the group, but dangerous because they can be violated, threatening the existence of the group."[27]

The ambiguous status of boundaries is thematized in the movement of the strangers, setting up a threefold analogy: entering the city gates, crossing the threshold of the house, and (in the next scene) the threat of sexually penetrating the male or female body. Lot acts as the guardian of each threshold, with different problems and bodies to confront at each.

The divine strangers enter city and house under Lot's protection, but the description of his invitation – "he pressed (*wayyifṣar*) them greatly (*me'od*) and they relented and they came into his house" – anticipates the dangerous scene later at his house – "they pressed (*wayyifṣeru*) the man Lot greatly (*me'od*), and they pushed to break the door" (v. 9). This repetition of "pressed . . . greatly" sets up a resonance between the two scenes, which mingles foreshadowing and dramatic irony. Lot's "pressing" the strangers to stay at his house is a gesture of hospitality, portraying Lot as a righteous man – just as Abraham was in his effusive hospitality to the traveling strangers in the previous chapter (Genesis 18:1–8). However, Lot's hospitality also stands in proleptic contrast to the wickedness of the men of Sodom, who "press" Lot and nearly break the door in order to sexually penetrate the strangers. The intention to violently rape is the antithesis of hospitality – it turns guests into victims and strips them of honor and humanity. It graphically depicts the social and moral disintegration of Sodom.

A Foucauldian analysis would focus on the opposing relations of agency, power, and knowledge in the competing systems of hospitality and sexuality in Sodom. In the hospitality system, agency resides with the host as the receptive party; this is an active receptivity, a "bringing-in of guests" into one's home (*haknasat 'orḥim* in rabbinic Hebrew). In hospitality, the receiver is open

---

[27] Bechtel, "Feminist Reading," 113.

to that which is not himself.[28] The active receptivity to the other and to the unknown lends the host ethical, epistemological, and social power. This power, in turn, explains why hospitality is the domain of male agency, even though the home is symbolically and socially a female space. Conversely, in sexuality systems – whether Mesopotamian, Greek, or Israelite – power and agency are associated with penetration, and sexual receptivity (as discussed below) is a feminizing position. Rape, as the most extreme – and socially abhorrent – violent appropriation of power is thus the symmetrical opposite of the willing receptivity of hospitality.

Hospitality is therefore implicitly linked to sexual danger, which is its opposite and which it attempts to prevent. Lot's behavior in this opening scene displays the honor and generosity of the male head of household, but it is also a strategy for containing violence and seduction that could issue from the strangers or the natives. As Carol Delaney explains with regard to traditional village and nomadic societies:

> Any outsider who enters the village is usually taken at once into someone's house, not only as an act of hospitality but also as a way of disarming the visitor. For once you have passed through the gate you are a guest, under the protection of the host.... By nomadic traditions of hospitality, travelers granted refuge in an encampment must abide by their host's rules of hospitality. In particular, they may not steal, harm, or make sexual advances to the women; otherwise they relinquish protection and their lives are in danger.[29]

Lot does not know who the strangers are but, by insisting on hospitality, he exercises his power not only to protect them from harm but also to bind them to an implicit social contract not to harm his household. There is potential sexual danger in having strange men inside his house at night, in close quarters with his wife and unmarried daughters. The rule of hospitality guards against seduction or rape. Lot will extend his protection to the strangers only as long as they do not violate the rules of the household, including violating the female bodies in the house – a crucial concern for the male head of household. As Lot says, "they have come under the shadow of my roof-beam" (ṣel qorati,

---

[28] As Elaine Kaufman argued (*The Delirium of Praise: Bataille, Blanchot, Deleuze, Foucault, Klossowski* [Baltimore, MD: Johns Hopkins University Press, 2001], 137), Foucault treats the laws of hospitality in terms of radical openness, to the point of merging with the other: "the relationship of hospitality is ... predicated on the *in*distinguishability between guest and host and the possibility of encountering an unknown entity"; see Michel Foucault, "The Prose of Acteon," in *Aesthetics, Method and Epistemology: Essential Works of Foucault 1954–1984*, ed. J. D. Faubion (Harmondsworth, UK: Penguin, 2000), 123–35.

[29] Carol Delaney, *The Seed and Soil: Gender and Cosmology in Turkish Village Society* (Berkeley: University of California Press, 1991), 233.

v. 8), an idiom that conveys an image of protection (literally, *shade*; a refuge from the merciless sun of the Plains) but that also marks the home as a place of protected sexuality.

As Bal points out, in biblical narrative, the house of the father is a structure with strongly gendered meanings. It is the liminal threshold of private and public, female space and male space, mingled with sexual dangers. Her observations refer to the horrifying scene of rape in Judges 19, which shares keywords and themes with the Sodom story:

> The images of the threatening men surrounding the house, the enforced opening, the expulsion of the victim become . . . the very image of rape. The door of the house represents, then, the female body itself; the impossibility of keeping the door closed, the female body's vulnerability to rape.[30]

This description holds for Sodom as well. The attempted violation of the house by the threatening men of Sodom is the very image of rape – at first, it is male bodies that are at risk of penetration, then the daughters of the house, and finally even Lot himself. In all narratives of sexual violence in the Bible, doors and entryways are central concepts in establishing narrative space – marking a clear boundary between inside and outside – and the site of violation is always on the rapists' own territory.[31] This is very much the case in the next scene of Genesis 19, in which the men of Sodom demand that the guests be brought out to them:

> Before they lay down, the men of the city – the men of Sodom – surrounded the house, from youths to old men, all the people from the entire city. They called out to Lot, saying to him, "Where are the men who came to you tonight? Bring them out to us so that we may know them." (Genesis 19:4–5)

The time marker – "before they lay down (*yišk^{e}vu*)" – provides a clue to the impending dangers. The verb "to lie down" may be used to denote sexual intercourse, as it does later in the chapter (seven times in vv. 32–35) when Lot's daughters lie with their father on successive nights. It does not have an explicit sexual sense here but rather serves as a foil and foreshadowing of the sexual violence that the men of Sodom intend to bring to the house. This is the customary time and place – at night and at home – when people "lie down" in sexual intimacy. The norms of biblical society mandate that the intimate sexual partners be a married couple; the men of Sodom have other ideas.

---

[30] Mieke Bal, *Death and Dissymmetry: The Politics of Coherence in the Book of Judges* (Chicago: University of Chicago Press, 1988), 183.

[31] Yael Shemesh, "Biblical Stories of Rape Narratives: Common Traits and Unique Features" [in Hebrew], in *Studies in Bible and Exegesis, Vol. 6*, eds. R. Kasher and M. Zipor (Ramat Gan, Israel: Bar-Ilan Press, 2002), 315–44.

Their demand is a literal reversal of hospitality: they require a bringing-out rather than a bringing-in of guests. Rape is indeed "topsy-turvy" hospitality.[32]

The men of Sodom act as a collective mob – "from youths to old men, all the people from the entire city" – in their desire to violate the strangers. The diction emphasizes the complicity of every male in the city, from adolescents to elders. The men "surrounded the house" so that there is no exit for those inside, indicating a strategic and deliberate act. Is violent rape the normal treatment of guests in Sodom? As Robert Alter observes, the behavior of the Sodomites is presented as an emblematic violation of civilized norms:

> The story of the doomed city is crucial not only to Genesis but to the moral thematics of the Bible as a whole (compare the use of Sodom in Isaiah 1 and Judges 19) because it is the biblical version of anti-civilization, rather like Homer's islands of the Cyclops monsters where the inhabitants eat strangers instead of welcoming them.[33]

The men of Sodom are sufficiently civilized not to eat the strangers, but they instead seek to humiliate them by gang rape: "bring them out to us so that we may know (*weneda*) them" (v. 5). The desire to "know" can have several meanings, but Lot's reply – "I have two daughters who have not known (*yade'u*) a man. Let me bring them out to you, and do to them as you please" (v. 7) – and the men's angry response make it clear that sexual knowledge is their intention. They intend to rape the male guests, penetrating their bodies by force to deprive them of power, honor, and humanity.

Ironically, the "men (*'anse*) of Sodom" do not know what kind of "men (*'anašim*) who came to you" they are intending to violate. Their desire to *know* (sexually) will be confounded because they do *not know* who these men are. Their gendered plan of male rape fails because they do not understand the true nature of their victims. The strangers are divine messengers – angels – who seem to have male bodies but possess supernatural powers. The confident gender perceptions of the men of Sodom, in this case, are utterly flawed.

The sentiments expressed by the Sodomites' demand for male-to-male rape rely on the implicit meanings of this act, which involve the interrelated fields of knowledge, law, and agency in the Bible. Many readers anachronistically project modern concepts of homosexuality onto this text; indeed, as Bechtel points out, the exegetical tradition has often "become preoccupied with the morality of homosexuality."[34]

---

[32] Stuart Lasine, "Guest and Host in Judges 19: Lot's Hospitality in an Inverted World," *Journal for the Study of the Old Testament* 9 (1984), 38–41.

[33] Robert Alter, "Sodom as Nexus," in *The Book and the Text: The Bible and Literary Theory*, ed. R. M. Schwartz (Oxford, UK: Blackwell, 1990), 151.

[34] Bechtel, "Feminist Reading," 119, n. 20.

In fact, as recent scholarship has shown, biblical concepts of gender and sexuality are structured somewhat differently than modern concepts and – importantly – do not include *homosexual* as a term of identity or orientation in the modern sense.[35] The Bible knows of sexual acts and behaviors – some licit and some illicit – and two genders, male and female, but does not categorize them according to innate sexual orientation. Foucault and others demonstrated that sexual categories and contrasts such as "homosexual" versus "heterosexual" are modern constructs, products of the post-Enlightenment taxonomic drive and of the "sexual science" that by the nineteenth century replaced the "erotic arts" typical in many traditional societies.[36]

Biblical norms promote sexual intercourse between a male and a female within marriage and prohibit adultery, incest, bestiality, and male seduction or rape of an unmarried woman. They also prohibit male–male anal intercourse for reasons that illuminate the motives of the men of Sodom. These rules regulating sexual acts are based on two principal social values. The first is the patrilineal principle, which mandates that the lineage – and the material and symbolic wealth of inheritance – are passed along the male line. This means that the chastity of women is of crucial concern so that paternity is unquestioned. As Delaney observes, a man's honor "depends on his ability to guarantee that a child is from his own seed."[37] The patrilineal principle guarantees the normative legal status of male–female intercourse within marriage.

The second principle, which complements the first, is the prohibition against mixing incommensurate categories. As Douglas emphasized, biblical law insists that "different classes of things shall not be confused" in order to "keep ... distinct the categories of creation."[38] Therefore, the normative sexual behaviors of males and females should not be confused, just as one must not cross-breed farm animals, sow different seeds in the same field, or mix different fabrics in the same garment. The key terms are *kil'ayim* and *ša'aṭnez*, forbidden mixtures of two different kinds, as in the following law: "You shall not let your cattle mate with different kinds; you shall not sow your field with different kinds; you shall not wear clothing made of different kinds"

[35] See Boyarin, "History of Sexuality," 333–55; Olyan, "And with a Male," 179–206; and Nissinen, *Homoeroticism*, 37–56.
[36] Michel Foucault, *The History of Sexuality. Vol. I: An Introduction* (New York: Vintage Books, 1978); the discussion of *scientia sexualis* is on pp. 53–73. For a cogent exegesis and refinement of Foucault's position, see David M. Halperin, "Forgetting Foucault," in idem, *How to Do the History of Homosexuality* (Chicago: University of Chicago Press, 2002), 24–47.
[37] Delaney, *Seed and Soil*, 39.
[38] Mary Douglas, *Purity and Danger: An Analysis of the Concepts of Pollution and Taboo* (London: Routledge & Kegan Paul, 1966), 53.

(Leviticus 19:19). Normative male and female behaviors – which follow from the patrilineal principle – must not be subverted or confused.[39]

In short, the interplay of power, knowledge, and agency – the norms of patrilineal society, the conceptual categories of Creation, and the contrast of active and receptive agency (see the following discussion) – are responsible in varying measures for determining the categories of forbidden sexual relations. The law prohibiting male–male penetrative sex follows from these principles.

Leviticus 18:22 commands: "With a male you shall not lie down the lying-down of a woman – it is an abhorrence." As Saul Olyan demonstrates in his careful elucidation of this verse, the command is addressed to the insertive partner, who is condemned for causing the "feminization" of his male partner: "The laws . . . viewed the receptive partner as the legal equivalent of a woman: he is not addressed directly; he is very likely seen as a patient rather than an agent; he is viewed as 'feminized.'"[40]

In other words, the male receptive partner is viewed as a victim whom the insertive partner has feminized by penetrating him sexually, in the manner of "the lying-down of a woman." This is a crime of violating the gender of the penetrated man, treating "him" as a "her." Such a violation of gender categories and the hierarchy of power implicit in them illustrate (in Butlerian terms) the social constructedness of the binary discursive opposition of masculine/feminine.

Turning a male into the receptive, feminized partner is construed by biblical law as an act of sexual shaming and dehumanization. This analysis is supported by the language of an Assyrian treaty curse addressed to a disloyal vassal, dating to the eighth century B.C.E. (roughly contemporary with the composition of Genesis 19):

> If Mati'ilu sins against this treaty with Ashurnirari, king of Assyria, may Mati'ilu become a (female) prostitute, his soldiers women, may they receive [a gift] in the square of their cities like any prostitute.[41]

As Martti Nissinen explains, "The curses of the treaty do not mention rape but threaten to make a man a prostitute, which amounts to the same effect. . . . [T]o become subjected to (anal) intercourse by another man involves shame and suppression."[42] Both the biblical law and the Assyrian treaty curse define male–male penetrative sex as an act of aggression, in

---

[39] See Boyarin, "History of Sexuality," 342–4.
[40] Olyan, "And with a Male," 205.
[41] Quoted in Nissinen, *Homoeroticism*, 26–7.
[42] Ibid., 27.

which the penetrated man is feminized and shamed. It is a reversal of social norms, conceptual categories, and gendered agency.

In this nexus of bodily movements, cognitive categories, and social norms, we may be able to glimpse how such webs of meaning are constructed. Pierre Bourdieu argued that the sexual motions of male and female bodies are a "preconstructed" field for the cultural construction of the categories and norms of gender and sexuality:

> [T]he elementary acts of bodily gymnastics ... and, most importantly, the specifically sexual, and therefore biologically preconstructed, aspect of this gymnastics (penetrating or being penetrated, being on top or below, etc.) are highly charged with social meanings and values.[43]

Hence, the "elementary acts" of inserting and receiving are projected outward into behavioral, social, and legal norms. Everyday practices become symbolic "signifiers" in the culturally constructed fields of gender and sexuality.

Back to the story: the men of Sodom aim to humiliate the strangers and Lot, their host, by feminizing and publicly shaming the strangers through violent gang rape.[44] They are collectively enacting the curse of the Assyrian treaty but unlawfully because they seek to punish men who have done them no wrong. In so doing, the men of Sodom show themselves to be outside of civilization – they are barbarians who know no shame. In a culture in which honor is the highest value, the Sodomites are the antitype of human moral worth.

Lot's reply to the men of Sodom brings another dimension to the gender trouble that they have raised. As he shuts the door behind him – closing the threshold to his household and to the vulnerable bodies within – Lot offers instead his two daughters "who have not known a man." The demand to shame two male bodies has its riposte in an offer to shame his two daughters. The vortex of power, gender, and sexuality takes a new turn:

> Lot came out of the opening to them, and he shut the door behind him. He said, "Please, my brothers, do not do this evil. Behold, here I have two daughters who have not known a man. Let me bring them out to you, and do to them as you please. But to these men, do not do anything, for surely they have come under the shadow of my roof-beam." They said, "Move aside," and then said, "This one came to sojourn among us, and now he dispenses

---

[43] Pierre Bourdieu, *The Logic of Practice* (Stanford, CA: Stanford University Press, 1990), 71.

[44] On the similar dynamics in the rape episode in Judges 19, see the comments of Bal quoted previously; and Stone, "Gender and Homosexuality," 87–107.

justice? We will do more evil to you than to them." And they pressed the man Lot greatly, and they pushed to break the door. (Genesis 19:6–9)

The architecture of the house – the opening and the door, inside and outside, the protecting roof-beam – is, as noted previously, the actual and symbolic space of this confrontation. At this symbolic threshold, Lot displays – and surrenders – his patriarchal authority. When Lot "shut the door behind him" and the men of Sodom "pushed to break the door," we detect both physical and sexual meanings. First the guests, then the daughters, and finally Lot are each threatened with sexual violence. As Fewell and Gunn noted, "a glance at the imagery of locking, latches, and doors in the Song of Songs (e.g., 4:9–5:8) is enough to suggest a perverse double entendre here. Rapidly Lot himself has become the rape object."[45]

But the narrative's most disturbing turn is Lot's offer to "bring out" (*'oṣi'ah*) his daughters "who have not known (*yadᵉʿu*) a man" as a surrogate rape object – which precisely echoes the men's demand, "bring them out (*hoṣi'im*) to us so that we may know (*wᵉnedᵉʿah*) them" (v. 5). As Bal observes (speaking of Jephthah and his daughter), "the open door signifies the openness, the vulnerability of Jephthah's position as [warrior] and father."[46] The open door also signifies the vulnerability of Lot's position as host and father. At the same time, as Bal remarked previously, "[t]he door of the house represents . . . the female body itself, the impossibility of keeping the door closed, the female body's vulnerability to rape."[47] How can Lot, as father, open the door, handing over his virginal daughters to these violent men? How can he speak the words, "Let me bring them out to you, and do to them as you please"?

One of the hallmarks of the system of honor is the obligation of males of the household to protect the virginity of daughters and sisters. This is the explicit issue in the story of Dinah in Genesis 34, in which the brothers massacre every male of the city of Shechem to avenge the rape of their sister. When Jacob rebukes them – in fear that the Canaanites will massacre Jacob's family – his sons Simeon and Levi reply, "Shall our sister be treated like a whore?" (Genesis 34:31). This is the language of honor and shame, as in the Assyrian case of a male who is "treated like a whore."

In ancient Israel, as in other village-based traditional societies, the daughter's shame stains the entire household. As J. G. Peristiany observed, "For an unmarried woman, shame reflects directly on parents and brothers, especially

---

45 *Gender, Power, and Promise: The Subject of the Bible's First Story* (Nashville, TN: Abingdon Press, 1993), 59.

46 Bal, *Death and Dissymmetry*, 181.

47 Ibid., 183.

unmarried ones, who did not protect or avenge her honor."[48] This is the obligation of honor, and this is why Jacob remains silent after Simeon and Levi rebuke him.

Lot's choice to offer his daughters to the men of Sodom involves a dangerous exchange. He chooses to value the rule of hospitality higher than his duty to protect his virgin daughters. In so doing, he preserves his honor as host but is stained with shame as father. It would seem that – to Lot's eyes – his duty to other males is a higher value than his duty to his daughters. The hierarchy of power is such that daughters can be sacrificed in deference to male obligations. His speech makes the gender hierarchy clear: "... but to these men, do not do anything." This is a heightened example of the inner contradictions of the patriarchal value system, which are exposed in a moment of crisis.

In keeping with the poetics of reticence typical of biblical narrative, especially at moments of great moral and emotional upheaval,[49] there is no explicit comment about the morality of Lot's choice. The text is gapped and terse. In retrospect, however, an implicit judgment is suggested in the final scene (see the following discussion) with an analogy that strikes a note of punishment and poetic justice. The father who had offered his daughters to be raped by the mob is unknowingly seduced by them. The father is "objectified" by the daughters as a sexual body – his mind dulled by wine – and they "rape" him on successive nights. In some respects, this feminizes Lot and he, like Mati'ilu, is treated like a whore. This poetic justice, such as it is, is supplied retrospectively.

Ironically, the male strangers who are guests in Lot's house are the ones who actively protect the daughters' virginity – and the household's honor. They afflict the mob with blindness to undo the threat of sexual violence.

> The men stretched out their hands and brought Lot to them inside the house, and they shut the door. And they struck the men at the opening of the house with blindness, from small to great, and they could not find the opening. (Genesis 19:10–11)

The evil outsiders can neither penetrate the door nor the bodies within it. Human blindness and divine power seal the barrier between outside and inside. The mob that was morally blind – exemplars of anti-civilization – now

[48] J. G. Peristiany, "Honour and Shame in a Cypriot Highland Village," in *Honour and Shame: The Values of Mediterranean Society*, ed. J. G. Peristiany (Chicago: University of Chicago Press, 1966), 182.

[49] See Robert Alter, *The Art of Biblical Narrative* (New York: Basic Books, 1981), 114–30.

become physically blind at the door to the house. The failure of the attempted rape, with its assertion of power and knowledge ("Bring them out to us so that we may know them"), becomes a failure of bodily power and knowledge ("And they could not find the opening"). In view of the sexual symbolism of house and opening, the men of Sodom are now symbolically impotent. (Compare Oedipus's self-blinding when he discovers his own sexual crime.) They can no longer find the door, much less penetrate it. This is an ironic – and richly deserved – reward for the violent mob. As Freud might say, they are now unmanned, symbolically castrated.

As Alter observes, the theme of vision and blindness occurs elsewhere in the story as well.[50] Lot's wife leaves the house – the gendered domestic space, her body's double – but tragically violates the angels' command, "Do not look behind you" (v. 17). Her longing for home makes her look back, despite the danger. She becomes an object, a memorial of salt, forever looking back at the destroyed city. This image is followed by Abraham's long view of the destruction: "He looked and, behold, the smoke of the land rose up like the smoke from a kiln" (v. 28). Seeing, insight, ignorance, and blindness – a mingling of moral and sensory perception – are thematically intertwined in the story, from Lot's first sight of the mysterious strangers to his unknowing seduction by his daughters.

After the destruction of the city and the demise of Lot's wife, Lot and his daughters come to dwell in a cave. The cave serves as a metonymy of anti-culture, far from the comforts of home and civilization. A cave is a home for wild animals and Cyclops, where cultural norms do not apply. It is, at the same time, a body double, a house without a door, a symbolic female body vulnerable to penetration. With no barrier to this threshold, the sexual honor of Lot and his daughters is once again at risk. The absence of the normative sexual partner – Lot's wife – intensifies the risk. But now – in an extended example of the fragility and constructedness of gender and sexuality – the daughters take the position of active agents, choosing to preserve the family despite the onus of sexual shame and the fracture of the patrilineal principle:

> They dwelled in a cave, he and his two daughters. The first-born said to the younger one, "Our father is old, and there is no man on the earth to come to us in the manner of all the earth. Come, let us serve our father wine, and let us lie down with him, so that we may bring to life seed from our father." They served their father wine that night, and the first-born came and lay

50 Alter, "Sodom as Nexus," 152.

down with her father, but he did not know of her lying down and her rising up. The next day the first-born said to the younger one, "Behold, I lay down last night with my father. Let us serve wine again tonight, and come, lie down with him, so that we may bring to life seed from our father." They served wine again that night to their father, and the younger one arose and lay down with him, but he did not know of her lying down and her rising up. And the two daughters of Lot conceived from their father. The first-born bore a son and she named him Moab [literally, "from the father"] – he is the father of Moab until the present day. The younger one also bore a son, and she named him Ben-Ammi [literally, "son of my kin"] – he is the father of the sons of Ammon until the present day. (Genesis 19:30–37)

Lot's daughters – like their mother – are not named. They are known by their kinship relationship with Lot – they are "his daughters," the "first-born" and the "younger one." Their identities are embedded in the kinship hierarchy of their father's household. Now that they are removed from the house itself – which is smoking rubble – they act to save the household itself from destruction. The first-born's first words are decisive: "Our father is old, and there is no man on the earth to come to us in the manner of all the earth." The patrilineal principle is on the verge of extinction because there is "no man on earth" – with the exception of "our old father" – to impregnate them. As we know, the elder daughter is mistaken because the destruction only involved the cities of the plain. But given her knowledge, she makes a moral choice, opting for the family's survival over its honor. Lot's daughters – like Lot previously – choose to protect a cherished value but, in doing so, they violate another one. Their choice involves a clash of sexual norms and knowledge.

The children – the eponymous ancestors of Moab and Ammon – bear the shame of incestuous origins. Incest is the ultimate mixing of incommensurate categories: sex and father–daughter relations. Like male–male penetrative sex, it violates the rule of *kil'ayim* and *ša'aṭnez*, the forbidden blurring of norma-tive categories. In these cases, the violation involves two parties who are *too* close. Sexual penetration between two kinds that are too closely related, by kinship (father–daughter) or gender (male–male), threatens the coherence of the system. So, the daughters' seduction of their father is an inverted echo of the sexual trouble in Sodom: it is a forbidden combination of incest, rape, and premarital and extramarital sex. The daughters' motivation is noble – preserving the family from extinction – but their actions produce perma-nent shame for the family line, the nations of Moab and Ammon, who are permanently marked as bastards (in Israelite eyes) by their shameful origins.

The scene is unsparing in its shaming of Lot, father of these foreign nations. The repetitions of "she lay down with her father" (five times with variations) within the span of four verses heightens the shame of the incestuous seductions:

"Let us lie down with him." (v. 32)
"She lay down with her father, but he did not know of her lying down and her rising up." (v. 33)
"I lay down last night with my father." (v. 34)
"Come, lie down with him." (v. 34)
"She lay down with him, but he did not know of her lying down and her rising up." (v. 35)

Like the penetrated partner in male–male intercourse, Lot is feminized in these seductions as the passive recipient, even though he is the biological penetrator. He now reverses his former role as protective host, in which he was the active agent, welcoming and sheltering his guests. The gendered roles of agency are also reversed for the daughters as they become sexual aggressors, with Lot their submissive sexual object. The cave narrative is a reversed – and sexually perverse – response to a scene of total destruction. The gendered norms of the civilized world are inverted as the daughters seduce their unconscious father in a cave at the end of the world.

The scrambling of honor and family relationships in this scene is highlighted by the play of knowledge in the shifting semantics of the verb "to know" (*yada*ʿ). Twice we are told that "he did not know of her lying down and her rising up" (vv. 33, 35). Lot does not know that his daughters – who had previously "not known a man" (v. 8) – are now knowing him sexually. Their intention is honorable – "so that we may bring to life seed from our father" (vv. 32, 34) – but what they think they know is faulty. There is a slippage between faulty cognitive knowledge and forbidden sexual knowledge. The daughters' limited knowledge is mitigated by their limited power – they do not know the wider world outside their house and their cave. They lack the panoramic perspective that the reader, narrator, God, and Abraham share. The "slippery slope" of false and forbidden knowledge yields the preservation of the patrilineal principle but it is tainted by the stain of forbidden mixtures.

The story ends with the birth of the eponymous ancestors of Moab and Ammon. According to biblical law, the people of these two nations are prohibited from entering "the assembly of Yahweh" (the Israelite community) forever (Deuteronomy 23:4). This law immediately follows the same prohibition for a "bastard" (*mamzer*) – that is, the child of a prohibited mixed union.

The names of Moab and Ammon – "from the father" (*mo-'ab*) and "son of my kin" (*ben-'ammi*) – are memorials "until the present day" of this scene of incestuous seduction (vv. 36–37). The two nations, the devastation of the Dead Sea region, and the lone pillar of salt are reminders of the dangerous history of sexuality in Sodom, the antitype of civilization.

BEYOND SODOM AND GOMORRAH

Lot and his family seem at first as a swerve in the course of Genesis. But even when the focus returns to the history of the founding figures of the house of Israel, we discover that sexual scandal – although not as crude – does not quite disappear. In the following chapter (Genesis 20), Abraham presents Sarah as his sister to Abimelech. This is a ruse that does not entail literal incest, but the scene is not innocent of incestuous innuendo. More importantly, other women in Genesis depart from sexual norms in their insistence on preserving lineage. Consider the story of the mandrakes in Genesis 30, in which Rachel and Leah strike a dubious deal. Each gives up her particular prerogative in order to gain the prize she lacks. Rachel trades Jacob for a night and Leah gives her sister the mandrakes – the fruit that promises fertility, the object that metonymically represents the son: *duda'e b^eni* ("the mandrakes of my son," 30:15). Here, Jacob descends to the humiliating position of being a token of exchange between two women who, for a brief moment, manage to attain sexual agency and power. He is neither drunk as Lot nor does he lie with his daughters, but he is feminized in a curious way as he becomes a powerless Other in an unconventional sexual act that leads to the expansion of his household.

The story of Tamar and Judah in Genesis 38 is another case in point. The childless widow Tamar sleeps with her father-in-law, unbeknownst to him, in the guise of a prostitute. The role reversal is complete: the socially powerless widow plays the role of an objectified female but, in her performance, she gains agency, knowledge, and power over the family's patriarch. When Judah accuses her of whoring on discovering her pregnancy, Tamar presents the tokens he had given her. Judah cannot but admit that in her audacious struggle to preserve the familial line, she has been "more in the right" than him.

Beyond Genesis, the story of Ruth the Moabite, the descendant of Lot and his daughters, is particularly pertinent. Ruth's encounter with Boaz at the threshing floor clearly evokes the scene at the cave – Boaz, in fact, calls her "my daughter" (Ruth 3:11) – but, in this case, the "daughter" is only figuratively speaking an offspring. This too, however, is a scene of sexual seduction, in which the older and younger women (Naomi and Ruth) use sexual knowledge to secure themselves a modicum of power within their extended Israelite family. Within the biblical worldview, Ruth's seduction of Boaz is deemed appropriate not because it grants two otherwise unmoored women some security but rather because it leads to the preservation of the patriline, levirate law (as is the case in Genesis 38), and the land within the framework of a blessed marriage.

Sodom never ceases to cast a shadow on issues of gender, sexuality, and procreation in the Bible. It is a primal scene that lurks in the background, endangering the primary codes of biblical civilization. As Isaiah, Jeremiah, and Ezekiel make clear, the sins of Jerusalem are often grave enough to merit the dire punishment of Sodom.[51] What makes it all the more difficult to avoid Sodom's end is the fact that deviation from normative sexual conduct seems to be part and parcel of the history of the House of Israel. The story of Sodom opens these issues in bold strokes and allows them to resonate throughout the Bible.

[51] Isaiah 1:9, Jeremiah 23:14, and Ezekiel 16:48–49.

Inner-Biblical Interpretation

Yair Zakovitch

INTRODUCTION

Inner-biblical interpretation is the light that one biblical text casts onto another – whether to solve a problem within the interpreted text or to adapt the interpreted text to the beliefs and ideas of the interpreter. The interpreting text may stand far from the interpreted text, or be next to it, or may even be incorporated within it. Not always does a text function solely as the interpreting or as the interpreted one: sometimes the two will mutually interpret one another. In this chapter, we look at the phenomenon of inner-biblical interpretation through the example of one story, Genesis 27, the tale of Jacob deceiving his father, Isaac, in order to receive the blessing that Isaac had intended for Esau, Jacob's brother and Isaac's firstborn – and the many interpretations of that story that we find inside the Hebrew Bible.

Before turning our attention to the story and its interpretations, let us consider more fully the phenomenon of inner-biblical interpretation. There are both *overt* and *covert* types of inner-biblical interpretation. Examples of overt interpretation, in which a text openly refers to another well-known text, are found – to name a few examples – in Chronicles' paraphrase of the historiographic literature; in the way in which the writer of the historical psalm, Psalm 78, treats its Pentateuchal sources; and even in the way the law of the Hebrew slave in the Book of the Covenant (Exodus 21:2–11) is interpreted in Deuteronomy 15:12–18.[1] The covert type of inner-biblical interpretation is more difficult to discern. To detect this type of interpretation, the reader must be alert and sensitive to allusions planted by writers, editors, compilers, and annotators who embedded a literary unit in a certain place or who placed it within or juxtaposed it to another unit in order to cast the latter in new light.

---

[1] See Y. Zakovitch, *Introduction to Inner-Biblical Interpretation* [in Hebrew] (Even-Yehuda: Reches Publishing, 1992).

That the Bible is embedded with interpretation was not unrecognized by previous generations of scholars (even when they did not use the term *inner-biblical interpretation*). Usually, however, these researchers limited themselves to observations about particular aspects, their focus denying them the scope necessary to present the entire picture.[2] Biblical scholarship waited for the insightful architect who might raise the edifice of inner-biblical interpretation in all its manifestations, who would determine its various divisions and categories. Such a scholar was Michael Fishbane, in his book, *Biblical Interpretation in Ancient Israel*.[3] The book is divided into four parts: "Scribal Comments and Corrections," "Legal Exegesis," "Aggadic Exegesis," and "Mantological Exegesis." Each part describes one realm of overt and covert interpretation and points to sociohistorical forces that characterized the types of interpretation in the different periods. Fishbane's book is important for the threads that run through all four of the parts.[4]

The book equips readers with tools for identifying typical forms of inner-biblical exegesis, a welcome outcome because objectivity must always be striven for in this matter. When we are able to isolate exegetical elements – whether they are opening formulae or terms that are typical of interpretation, techniques of citation, or insertions or allusions to interpreted texts within the interpreting texts – we are better able to understand the interpretative process. Fishbane does not view the exegetical work as a purely literary phenomenon but rather as reflecting and expressing history and ideology. Interpretation is always relevant and current – an expression of the needs and problems of a generation. Fishbane tries to determine the *Sitz im Leben* of each interpretative type, identifying who created it and in what sociohistorical circumstances it was created.

Fishbane's book is significant for its exploration of the relationship between inner-biblical interpretation and postbiblical interpretation that appears at

[2] See, e.g., H. W. Hertzberg, "Die Nachgeschichte alttestamentlicher Texte in nerhalb des Alten Testament," in *Werden und Wesen des Alten Testaments*, eds. P. Volz, F. Stummer, and J. Hempel (Berlin: Töpelman, 1936), 110–21; I. L. Seeligmann, "Voraussetzungen der Midraschexegese" and "Anfänge der Midraschexegese in der Chronik," in *Gesammelte Studien zur Hebräischen Bibel*, ed. E. Blum (Tübingen: Mohr Siebeck, 2004), 1–54; H. L. Ginzberg, "Daniel" (addition to entry) [in Hebrew], *Encyclopedia Miqra'it*, 2.949–52; M. Z. Segal, *The Interpretation of the Bible* [in Hebrew] (2nd ed.; Jerusalem: Kiryat Sefer, 1971), 5–7; N. Sarna, "Psalm 89: A Study in Inner Biblical Exegesis," in *Biblical and Other Studies*, ed. A. Altmann (Cambridge, MA: Harvard University Press, 1966), 29–46, 37–52; F. F. Bruce, "The Earliest Old Testament Interpretation," in *The Witness of Tradition*, ed. M. A. Beek (Oudtestamentische Studiën 17; Leiden, the Netherlands: Brill, 1972), 37–52; and J. Weingreen, *From Bible to Mishna: The Continuity of Tradition* (Manchester, UK: Manchester University Press, 1976).
[3] Oxford: Clarendon Press, 1985.
[4] On the strengths and weaknesses of Fishbane's book, see Y. Zakovitch, "The Variegated Faces of Inner-Biblical Interpretation" [in Hebrew], *Tarbiz* 56 (1987), 136–43.

Qumran (in the *pesharim* literature) and in the various formulations of rabbinic literature, both in *halakha* and *aggadah*. Recognition of this relationship
leads to a better understanding of biblical literature: the clear and visible path
of interpretation in rabbinic literature helps uncover the covert beginnings of
the interpretative process in the Bible. An awareness of this relationship helps
us to better understand postbiblical literature and its history as well: exegetical
techniques that formerly were perhaps viewed as having been borrowed from
the philological schools of Alexandria indeed can be found in the basement
of our own home, in the Bible. The biblical corpus contains parallels both to
forms of *halakhic* Midrash (e.g., in instances of harmonizations within biblical
law codes) and to the ways in which the writers of the Mishnah worked (e.g.,
the pledge in Nehemiah 10). In writings composed in the period between the
Bible and rabbinic literature, one finds correspondences with these two types
of *halakhic* interpretation, as can be seen in a comparison of the methods
employed in the Temple Scroll on the one hand and the Damascus Document
on the other.

Likewise, the Bible was not fashioned *ex nihilo*, and Fishbane emphasizes
the relationships between biblical literature and the surrounding cultures
of the ancient Near East. This relationship is apparent in both the smallest
details (e.g., glosses of scribes) as well as larger matters (e.g., updatings of
prophecies).

In my book, *Introduction to Inner-Biblical Interpretation*,[5] I further widened
the scope, addressing the following topics: the beginnings of inner-biblical
interpretation; interpretative comments and interpolations; juxtaposition as a
tool for interpretation; double stories interpreting one another; interpretation
within the redactional work; stories in circles of interpretation; biblical poetry
interpreting biblical narrative; biblical speeches interpreting biblical narrative;
the interpretation of biblical law within the law itself; the interpretation
of a law within other biblical law codes; the interpretation of biblical law
in nonlegalistic material; the interpretation of biblical sayings in biblical
narratives and prophecies; the interpretation of biblical sayings within the
book of Proverbs; the book of Chronicles as a commentary; and motives for
interpretation. The book's final chapter provides readers with an "appetizer"
for the volume that I recently published, *Inner-Biblical and Extra-Biblical
Midrash and the Relationship between Them*.[6]

[5] See n. 1.
[6] Y. Zakovitch, *Inner-Biblical and Extra-Biblical Midrash and the Relationship between Them* [in
    Hebrew] (Tel Aviv: Am Oved, 2009). Important contributions that broaden the discussion
    on the world of inner-biblical interpretation have been made in recent decades, including
    G. Vermes, "Bible and Midrash: Early Old Testament Exegesis," in idem, *Post-Biblical Jewish
    Studies*, 59–91 (Leiden, the Netherlands: Brill, 1975); J. L. Kugel and R. A. Grier, *Early Biblical*

Interpretation is a creative act in the fullest sense, which makes the distinction among writers, editors, compilers, and interpreters difficult and artificial. The editor is an interpreter; so also is the writer who interprets one story by writing another and placing it next to the one it interprets. A writer who adds to an already existent work is a writer–interpreter. These titles do not preclude the writer–interpreter from also being an editor (or one of a series of editors) of a story cycle or a biblical book.

The Bible's profusion of interpretative strategies testifies to its being a branching network of relationships that connect distant texts, binding them to one another. Writings from different historical periods and a variety of literary genres call out and interpret one another, with the interpreted texts being reflected back – somewhat altered – from a multitude of mirrors. Poets interpret stories, storytellers interpret poetry, and prophets interpret the Pentateuch. Indeed, it is not an exaggeration when I propose that no literary unit in the Bible stands alone, isolated and independent, with no other text drawing from its reservoir and casting it in a new light. When we turn our attention to the interpretative relationships among different literary units, we actually address issues of intertextuality, a topic much dealt with in modern literary criticism.[7] In a similar way, it is worthwhile to view our approach also as an expression of canonical interpretation.[8] The relationships that are revealed push the reader to understand the meaning and strength of the conversations that exist among different literary units, conversations that cross the boundaries between books included in the biblical canon, which – despite its comprising elements of various genres and types – is perceived as a unified whole.

CANON, CONTEXT, AND MIDRASHIC INTERPRETATION

It is worth reflecting on the meaning of *canon*, a term used already by the *rhetors* of Alexandria to refer to a list of classical, authoritative writings.[9]

Interpretation (Philadelphia, PA: Westminster Press, 1986); B. Sommer, *A Prophet Reads Scripture, Allusion in Isaiah 40–66* (Stanford, CA: Stanford University Press, 1986).

[7] For expressions of this phenomenon in the Bible, see, e.g., the following collections: *Intertextuality in Biblical Writings: Essays in Honour of Bas van Iersel*, ed. S. Draisma (Kampen, the Netherlands: Kok, 1989); *Reading between Texts: Intertextuality and the Hebrew Bible*, ed. D. N. Fewell (Louisville, KY: Westminster John Knox Press, 1992); and *Intertextuality and the Bible*, eds. G. Aichele and G. A. Phillips (*Semeia* 69/70; Atlanta, GA: Scholars Press, 1995).

[8] The champion of canonical interpretation is B. S. Childs, *Introduction to Old Testament as Scripture* (Philadelphia, PA: Fortress Press, 1979), esp. pp. 46–106. Childs gave expression to this approach in his commentary on Isaiah: B. S. Childs, *Isaiah* (Old Testament Library; Louisville, KY: Westminster John Knox Press, 2001).

[9] See M. Haran, *The Biblical Collection. Its Consolidation to the End of the Second Temple Times and Changes of Form to the End of the Middle Ages*, Part 1 [in Hebrew] (Jerusalem: Bialik, 1996), 25.

First and foremost, *canon* signifies a community's set of classical books, a collection that crystallized over time and became fixed.[10] *Canon* signifies a body of literature toward which its readers are not ambivalent; literature that people will be ashamed to admit that they have not read or studied; literature that has left its imprint on other writings that were written within the same community; literature that its readers read also through the eyes of others who interpreted it, directly or indirectly, in their own writings. It is a literature that attained its status slowly, in an extended process that, for the most part, was hidden and that functions as a shared cultural platform for the members of the community and as the foundation of its historical–cultural memory. In Descartes' well-known dictum, "I think, therefore I am," we make a slight change: "I remember, therefore I am." A society's literary canon is what secures it from oblivion; it is what protects it against erosion and loss.

When a canon consists of the sacred writings of a group of believers, it becomes fortified with recognized boundaries: the identities of the texts' authors are obscured or the texts are attributed to ideal figures from the distant past, whereas the text derives its particular validation from its comprising a divine truth. Hence, its authority in the eyes of the believers is absolute.[11] It was in this way that the term functioned in the early Church; it is a term that binds together the authoritative collection that is Scripture.[12]

Readers who have knowledge of the canon, who are well versed in its writings and sensitive enough to recognize the network of connections that crisscrosses within it, will be aware of the exegetical role of the connections between a unit and the allusions to it, whether they are in the same book or in other biblical books. This brings up the important issue of identifying the micro-environments within the canon.

Whenever we want to interpret a biblical narrative, we find ourselves facing the challenge of determining its borders and context: is the narrative an independent literary unit that should be understood without connection to its literary context, or was it written, from the start, as part of a larger cycle of stories onto which it casts its light and from which it receives light? This question must be asked in the course of analyzing each and every biblical narrative. No single answer exists for all.

In addition to these possibilities – of an independent narrative and one dependent on others – there is a third that lies somewhere between the two: a story that was originally independent but that at some point in its transmission, whether still in an oral stage or already in the written stage,

---

[10]   Seeligmann, "Voraussetzungen der Midrashexegese," 151.
[11]   Haran, *Biblical Collection*, 23.
[12]   Ibid., 25.

became embedded into a broader literary complex that promotes a different idea than the isolated story. In this way, the story comes to hold two meanings. Its effect as an isolated stone is not its effect as part of the multijeweled necklace. In such a case, the meaning of the story that is imparted by the redactor may seem to depart from what we call *peshat* and enter more into the realm of *midrash*. Let us examine these terms.

Peshat, as Sarah Kamin explained, is "the elucidation of a verse by way of its language, syntax, context, literary genre and structure, while taking into account the reciprocal relations between the various elements. In other words, an interpretation following the *peshat* is one that takes into consideration the mix of linguistic elements and grants to each one a meaning according to the whole."[13] An important component was added to the definition by Yonah Fraenkel, who determined that the interpreter of the *peshat* "does not wish to be novel, but to reveal the original, that which was in the past."[14]

What is the meaning of *midrash*? The noun appears twice in the Bible, both in Chronicles: "The other events of Abijah's reign, his conduct and his acts, are recorded in the story [*midrash*] of the prophet Iddo" (2 Chronicles 13:22); and "As to his sons, and the many pronouncements against him, and his rebuilding of the House of God, they are recorded in the story [*midrash*] in the book of the kings..." (2 Chronicles 24:27). The Septuagint to Chronicles translated the term *midrash* in the first case with *biblion* (book) and in the second with *graphei* (writing). Several manuscripts of the Hexapla, however, translate the word in 2 Chronicles 13:22 with *enzeiteisis* (inquiry, study), exactly as *lidroš* (the verb from the same root as *midrash*) was translated in the Septuagint to Ezra 7:10: "For Ezra had dedicated himself to study the Teaching of the LORD and to observe it, and to teach laws and rules to Israel."[15]

The root *d-r-š*, Avi Hurvitz has shown, was increasingly used in the Second Temple period for the study and investigation of the Torah, such as in the late Psalm 119 where one finds the expressions: "for I have *studied* your precepts" (vv. 45, 94), "for they have not *studied* your laws" (v. 155).[16] This contrasts with the earlier use of the root, which conveyed the sense "to seek," as we find in prophetic literature: "They have not *sought* the LORD" (Isaiah 31:1; Jeremiah

---

[13] S. Kamin, *Rashi's Exegetical Categorization in Respect to the Distinction between* Peshat *and* Derash [in Hebrew] (Jerusalem: Magnes Press, 1986), 14.

[14] Y. Fraenkel, *The Ways of the Aggadah and the Midrash* [in Hebrew] (Givatayim, Israel: Yad la-Talmud, 1991).

[15] S. Liebermann, *Hellenism in Jewish Palestine* (New York: Jewish Theological Seminary, 1950), 15.

[16] A. Hurvitz, *The Transition Period in Biblical Hebrew* [in Hebrew] (Jerusalem: Bialik, 1972), 131–4.

10:21). The noun *midrash* appears also in Ben Sira ("in my house of *study*"; 51:23).[17]

In its paraphrase of the verse in Deuteronomy 6:17 ("Be sure to observe [*šamor tišmᵉrun*] the commandments... of the LORD your God"), 1 Chronicles 28:8 states: "Observe and study [*šimru wᵉdiršu*] all the commandments of the LORD your God." In contrast to Joshua 1:8, "Let not this Book of the Law cease from your lips but recite it day and night," Qumran's Community Rule 6:6 reads: "Let not cease... a man from studying [*doreš*] the Law day and night" – that is, a man who is studying, inquiring, and interpreting the Torah. Also the noun *midrash*, in the sense of "the study of the law," appears in the Dead Sea Scrolls. This meaning of d-r-š seems also to appear in Isaiah 34:16: "*Study* the Book of the LORD and read."

How should *midrash* be defined? Shinan and I wrote:[18]

> Midrash is a mode of approaching a text – derived from a religious world view and motivated by various needs (historical, moral, literary, etc.) – which enables and encourages multiple and even contradictory meanings to be discovered in the text, while the intention of its author(s) is perceived as elusive....

> Midrash became of particular significance when all channels of direct communication with God were considered blocked. In the rabbinic period, it was believed that prophecy had ceased,[19] the Urim and Thummim were hidden and even a heavenly voice [*bat-qol*] was not to be relied upon.[20] The text, then, becomes the only avenue to knowledge about God's will and demands upon man. Reading and rereading this text in many different ways, and revealing its innumerable twists and turns, became a religious task of central importance to one's life. The well-known saying regarding the Torah (*m. 'Abot* 5:22), "turn it and turn it again," expresses this task in its essence. "For everything is in it," the second half of this maxim, emphasizes that Scripture always has relevance for the present; hence, to give but a few examples, midrashic interpretations even claim that Christianity and the fall of Byzantium are mentioned in the Bible....

> [In midrash] it is believed that everything one reveals in the text is true and has been valid from the text's inception. This is why midrash does not involve any drive toward finding the one original meaning of the text. The interpreter never invents new truths, he only finds existing ones. Moses at

---

[17] M. Z. Segal, *The Book of Ben Sira* [in Hebrew] (2nd ed.; Jerusalem: Bialik, 1958), 362.

[18] A. Shinan and Y. Zakovitch, "Midrash on Scripture and Midrash within Scripture," in *Studies in Bible*, ed. S. Japhet (*Scripta Hierosolymitana* 31; Jerusalem: Magnes Press, 1986), 258–61. On rabbinic midrash, see Chapter 6 by Dina Stein in this volume.

[19] See E. E. Urbach, "When Did Prophecy Cease?" [in Hebrew], *Tarbiz* 17 (1945), 1–11.

[20] See Liebermann, *Hellenism in Jewish Palestine*, 194–9.

Sinai was told all that students of Scripture will ever learn: "And even what a faithful disciple would in the future say in the presence of his master, was communicated to Moses in Sinai" (*Leviticus Rabbah* 22:1). . . .

Midrash has boundaries of tolerance which change with shifts in religious or philosophical values. The kabbalist midrashist, for instance, finds his conception of the upper *sefirot* in the word *bereshit* in Genesis 1:1 (by dividing it into two: *bara'* and *šit* = "created the six [*sefirot*]"),[21] while the Christian midrashist finds in the very same sentence, "the Son" (*bara'*).[22]

Let me be clear: the midrashic dimensions of inner-biblical interpretation do not make it irrelevant to modern practitioners of biblical criticism. On the contrary, it is critical that modern scholars of the Bible are familiar with the modes of inner-biblical interpretation – modes that we detect in the very formation and compilation of biblical literature. Indeed, the skills of biblical criticism, a field based on the rules of philology, are a prerequisite for determining the boundaries of literary units and for detecting additions and sorting out duplications, contradictions, and all the other difficulties that arise.

When applied to ancient interpretation, either biblical or extrabiblical, the distinction between *peshat* and *midrash* is anachronistic. Even when one finds in the vast "ocean" of ancient exegesis interpretations that agree with the concept of *peshat*, they are but one "drop," and their authors did not intend to confer on these interpretations exclusive or primary status.

A word about source criticism and its relationship to inner-biblical interpretation is in order.[23] Philological–historical research discerned the different sources from which the Torah was constructed. In the book of Genesis in general and in the Jacob cycle in particular, one may trace three sources, J, E, and P, which sometimes duplicate and sometimes contradict one another. Some source critics wrongly ignore the interrelationships among the sources. These sources are not autistic writings, existing in splendid isolation one from the other, but rather relate to, polemicize against, and interpret one another. In this chapter, we see how – more than once – E interprets J and how P interprets both J and E.

Separating the combined whole into the basic elements makes it possible to view and evaluate the character and sense of each part, yet we have an interest in the mixture as it is because that is the finished product, the real

---

[21] See M. M. Kasher, *Torah Shelemah* (Jerusalem: Bet Torah Shelemah, 1927), 1.14 nos. 57, 59, 60, 61, and 62 (all quoted from the *Zohar*).

[22] For an interesting example, see A. Diez Macho, *Neophyti 1* (Madrid: Consejo Superior de Investigaciones Científicas, 1968), 3.

[23] On source criticism, see Chapter 3 by Robert Kawashima in this volume.

and the certain. This wondrous, artistic mosaic was not created accidentally, like cards randomly dealt. Biblical criticism, therefore, may not excuse itself from examining the creative–exegetical process by which texts became fused together or from following the process by which the whole complex came into being.

To conclude this introduction, I add that it is hardly surprising to find that a story from Genesis, in particular, has multiple echoes and interpretations in biblical literature, because the book of Genesis is a sort of "table of contents" or "genetic code" for the Bible. Many of the Bible's writers were drawn almost magnetically to the Genesis stories, as though to a prototype from which they could mold their stories and thereby make possible and encourage comparisons between their newly created text and this already well-known work.

CIRCLES OF INTERPRETATION: JACOB'S DECEPTION OF ISAAC (GENESIS 27)

Genesis 27:1–45 provoked a surfeit of interpretations due to its discomfiting storyline. One cannot help but acknowledge Jacob's deceitfulness in the blatant lie with which he answers his father's request to identify himself: "'Which of my sons are you?' ... 'I am Esau, your firstborn'" (vv. 18–19). Isaac later confesses to Esau, his firstborn, that "your brother came with guile and took away your blessing" (v. 35).

Already in the chapter, we detect two distinct and conflicting forces at work: on the one hand, Jacob's transgression is openly recognized (as in the verses just quoted); on the other hand, we find attempts to justify Jacob, to find extenuating circumstances that will ease our judgment of him. These tendencies can also be traced in the circles of interpretation that radiate out from the story.

We can point to two reasons that the Bible admits Jacob's sin. First, oral tales of Jacob's trickery and fraud were already well known. As mentioned previously, biblical stories were not created *ex nihilo* from the imaginations of writers. Most biblical stories represent adaptations of oral traditions, traditions that were modified to suit the interests of the writers. Yet, motifs appropriate for tales told in secular contexts do not necessarily fit a religious context that seeks to engage readers with a writer's beliefs and ideas. Indeed, the beginnings of interpretation lie in this process of coping with prior oral traditions. That said, writers tended to adapt popular traditions by making only minimal changes and interpretations. On the one hand, they wanted to elevate the traditions to their own religious worldview. On the other hand, they tried to preserve the maximal resemblance to the source story to gain the trust of the reader, who was familiar with the original story. The balance struck by these writers as they carefully tread between preservation and innovation is an interpretative process that imparted new meaning to the old traditions.

The method followed by these writers was one of covert polemics. Avoiding any overt opposition to the popular traditions, they wrote the stories in a way that both expressed their disagreement with them and offered an alternative that would be accepted by readers.[24] In our case, Jacob of the oral traditions represented the archetypal trickster – cunning and wise – whose exploits produced endless laughter among listeners. Any attempt to completely alter that image by denying Jacob's trickery would have been pointless. Readers aware of the oral tradition about Jacob the trickster would not have accepted a story that erased that dimension of the patriarch's character.

The second reason for admitting Jacob's misdeeds has to do with the character of biblical literature from the First Temple period. That literature, we find, avoids providing readers with perfect heroes: what can we mortals learn from heroes who possess no speck of wrongdoing? On the contrary: only characters that have sinned, atoned for their mistakes, and changed their behavior can provide models for us. Only from the experiences of such imperfect, human heroes can we comprehend the moral fallibility of humans and the mysterious workings of God in human affairs. Moreover, characters who transgress, make amends, and learn from their sins provide more depth and interest than those who tread only the virtuous path. We are able to identify and empathize with flawed, complex figures.

Some of the classical rabbis emphasized that the Bible neither suppresses unpleasant stories about its heroes nor tries to beautify their image:

> Two good leaders stood for Israel: Moses and David, King of Israel. Moses said before the Holy One, blessed be He: "Master of the world, Let the transgression that I committed be recorded [in the Torah], so that people will not say it seems that Moses wrote falsely in the Torah or that he said something that he was not commanded. . . . " David spoke before [God], "A transgression that I have committed should not be written." God said to him: "It is not worthy of you that people will say, 'because He loved him He forgave him.'" (*Sifre* Deuteronomy *Va-'ethanan* 26)[25]

With this text, the rabbis wanted to make clear that the Bible always revealed a hero's transgressions – even when describing the greatest of heroes, David,

---

[24] For examples of covert polemics and ways for reconstructing the ancient traditions against which the biblical stories polemicized, see A. Shinan and Y. Zakovitch, *When Women Seduced the Gods and Other Stories the Bible Doesn't Want Us to Know* (Philadelphia, PA: Jewish Publication Society, in press).

[25] Cf. *b. Sanhedrin* 97a.

who himself wished to hide them. The origin of this idea, I think, must be explained against the backdrop of skeptics, who assumed that the Bible sometimes stifled unflattering traditions.

Evidence for the existence of these skeptics is found in the argument between Rabbi Yossi ben Ḥalafta and a Roman matron:[26]

> One matron asked Rabbi Yossi and she said to him: "Joseph was seventeen years old and was in full heat [i.e., was filled with youthful desires] and he would have done this thing [i.e., run from the house of the Potiphar's wife]?" He brought before her the book of Genesis and began reading to her the story of Reuben and Bilhah, the story of Judah and Tamar; he said to her, "Regarding those who were already adults and under the authority of their father, the Bible doesn't cover what they have done, all the more so one who is young and on his own." (*Genesis Rabbah* 87:8).[27]

The significance of this dispute is clear: coverups meant untruths on the part of the Pentateuch.

An opposite tendency in the Bible's narration and interpretation of Genesis 27 was to cleanse Jacob's image of wrongdoing. This tendency stemmed from the need to relate the well-known tale while discouraging readers from identifying with the hero's deceitful acts, to tell an entertaining story but not imply that cheating is tolerated or that disingenuous behavior would be rewarded. Let us turn to this second tendency.

JUSTIFYING JACOB

Chapter 27:1–45 (attributed to J) presents a Jacob who has been partially vindicated. The reason for Isaac's desire to bless the firstborn Esau is his craving for meat: "Then prepare a dish for me such as I like, and bring it to me to eat, so that I may give you my innermost blessing" (v. 4). Isaac is ready to seal the fate of his sons and descendants for generations (as becomes apparent from the blessing, vv. 28–29), all for the satisfaction of his most basic physical needs: taste and smell (v. 27).

A further way in which the writer absolves Jacob from responsibility is to focus on Rebekah, Jacob's mother. The storyteller emphasizes that it was Rebekah – and not Jacob – who initiates the deception. It is Rebekah who loves Jacob (v. 6ff) and who commands him to listen to her and obey her words (v. 8). Just as Esau must carry out the bidding of their father, who loves him, so must Jacob carry out the requests of their mother. When Jacob hesitates

---

[26] See J. Licht, *Storytelling in the Bible* (Jerusalem: Magnes Press, 1978), 18.

[27] Cf. *Midrash ha-Gadol*, Genesis, p. 665.

(vv. 11–12), Rebekah urges him on, expressing her readiness to take her husband's curse onto herself if he discovers the duplicity. She presses Jacob, "Just do as I say and go fetch them for me" – "for me," she says, not "for you" (v. 13)! Rebekah plans the stratagem and plays an active role in carrying it out:

> ... and his mother prepared a dish. ... Rebekah then took the best clothes of her older son Esau, which were there in the house, and had her younger son Jacob put them on; and she covered his hands and the hairless part of his neck with the skins of the kids. Then she put in the hands of her son Jacob the dish and the bread that she had prepared. (vv. 13–17)

Rebekah leaves no room for Jacob to falter. She dresses him (!) in his disguise and places into his hands the food that he will take to his father as part of the impersonation. The reader is left with the impression that if only she could, Rebekah would have gone to Isaac instead of her son. The writer refers to Jacob as "her younger son," reminding us of Jacob's powerlessness and dependence on his mother, who made all the decisions and who performed all the necessary preparations.[28]

At the story's end, Rebekah tries to disassociate herself from the scheme when she instructs Jacob to stay away until Esau "forgets what you have done to him" (v. 45) – "you" and not "I"! However, the reader is already aware of the degree to which Rebekah is responsible, and Rebekah will be punished for her scheming: when Jacob later returns from Haran, he will not meet his mother. She who thought that the separation from her son would last "a few days" (v. 44) will never see him again, and it is certainly ironic that Isaac, the father who is certain that he will soon die (v. 4), will still be alive to meet Jacob when he returns (35:27).

The words "a few days" return in chapter 29: "So Jacob served seven years for Rachel and they seemed to him *like a few days* because of his love for her" (v. 20). But Jacob's servitude in Laban's house will extend even beyond those seven years, to twenty. The repetition of Rebekah's words, "a few days," again inserts irony: her "few days" have now become seven years and will indeed turn out to be many more.

Another way that Jacob is made acceptable to the reader is by discrediting Esau, thereby presenting Esau as undeserving of the blessing. This method can be found at the end of chapter 26 in verses 34–35, which derive from a different literary document (P) and were added as a prelude to our story specifically to appraise readers of Esau's having taken two Canaanite wives who "were a source of bitterness to Isaac and Rebekah." In marrying these women, the

---

[28] See M. Buber, *The Way of the Bible* [in Hebrew] (Jerusalem: Bialik, 1964), 291.

author of these verses asserts, Esau proved himself to be an unworthy successor of his forefathers. These two verses, together with ten others (also from P) that were added at the end of our story (Genesis 27:46–28:9), effectively create a frame around the story of the stealing of the blessing. In the verses added at the end of the story, Rebekah expresses her fear that Jacob will follow in Esau's footsteps and take Canaanite wives as well: "I am disgusted with my life because of the Hittite women. If Jacob marries a Hittite woman like these, from among the native women, what good will life be to me?" (Genesis 27:46). Isaac now sends his younger son to Paddan-aram to find a wife from among the daughters of Laban (Genesis 28:1–2). Jacob's departure from the land of Canaan, according to these verses, no longer results from a need to escape his brother's wrath but rather from the praiseworthy desire to find a wife from among his family – the same family from which his father and grandfather had found their wives.

In fact, the additional ten verses do even more to change our reading of Jacob's behavior. Whereas in the main narrative, it is through trickery that Jacob receives the blessing that was meant for his brother, in these verses, Isaac intentionally blesses his younger son:

> Isaac sent for Jacob and blessed him.... May El Shaddai bless you, make you fertile and numerous, so that you become an assembly of peoples. May He grant the blessing of Abraham to you and your offspring, that you may possess the land where you are sojourning, which God assigned to Abraham. (Genesis 28:1–4)

This time, Isaac blesses Jacob with the most supreme blessing, "the blessing of Abraham" – undoubtedly superior to the blessing that had been meant for Esau (and which Isaac only accidentally gave to Jacob). These verses firmly assert that in any case, Isaac intended the more important blessing for Jacob, that which contains the blessing of the inheritance of the land of Israel.

For other ways in which Jacob is vindicated, we must leave the story and move outward to the broader circle, back to the preceding story about Jacob's buying the birthright from Esau (Genesis 25:27–34; J). Here, we find Isaac paying the price of Jacob's vindication. At the story's beginning, we find an asymmetry in the characterization of the brothers:

> Isaac loved Esau because he had a taste for game,
> but Rebekah loved Jacob. (25:28)

The verse foreshadows our story because it explains the parents' subsequent behavior toward their sons. It gives no reason for Rebekah's love for Jacob, which is unrestricted and unqualified, whereas Isaac's love for Esau is conditional, depending on the substantial food supplies that Esau brings him. In this way, the narrator succeeds in heightening our esteem for Jacob (and Rebekah); lowering our estimation of Esau (and Isaac); and putting the subsequent scene, Genesis 27, in a broader context.

The story of the selling of the birthright also relates to the etymology of Jacob's name that is voiced by Esau in our story, when he complains about the stealing of both the birthright and the blessing: "Was he, then, named Jacob that he might cheat me these two times? First he took away my birthright and now he has taken away my blessing!" (Genesis 27:36). The reader, of course, recalls how in the story of the birthright, Esau expressed no interest whatsoever in his future, or even in what would follow the immediate moment, when he said, "I am at the point of death, so of what use is my birthright to me?" (Genesis 25:32). The biblical narrator closes the birthright story with an unambiguous declaration of Esau's contempt for his birthright: "Thus did Esau spurn the birthright" (Genesis 25:34). The reader cannot help but appreciate the significance of these two expressions of Esau's scorn: we do not so easily disregard Esau's derision of his birthright, now that he has satisfied his hunger and thirst and is no longer reacting only to his bodily needs. As a result of this small story, Esau's complaint in Genesis 27:36 sounds more like that of a whiny boy: because he already completely renounced his birthright in chapter 25, we are not particularly sympathetic to his complaint about Jacob after the stealing of the blessing.

Moreover, in the story of the birthright, Esau is depicted like his father, as a materialistic man whose sole interest lies in the immediate satisfaction of his most earthly needs and physical desires: "Stuff me with that red stuff, for I am famished" (v. 30). The imperative "stuff me [hal'iteni]" is a *hapax legomenon*. In rabbinic literature, the word is used in reference to feeding animals (*m. Shabbat* 24:3); Esau's use of it in reference to himself betrays his animal nature. Even after Jacob satisfies his brother's physical needs by feeding him, Esau's crude behavior is still emphasized by the quick succession of verbs that describe his impulsivity and proclivity to act without forethought: "he ate and drank and rose and went away. Thus did Esau spurn the birthright."[29]

TAMING THE NAME

Esau's etymology of the name Jacob (Genesis 27:36), which is interpreted as deriving from *'aqob* ("deceitful, treacherous"), differs from the official

---

[29] See R. Alter, *The Art of Biblical Narrative* (New York: Basic Books, 1981), 42–5.

name derivation that is given in the birth story, which relates the name to
'aqeb, "heel": "his brother emerged, holding on to the heel of Esau" (Genesis
25:26). In fact, Esau's explanation of Jacob's name may reflect its original
interpretation. Other echoes of this same derivation can be found in the
Bible's peripheral books, which often preserve traditions that were rejected
from the center. Such is the birth tradition in Hosea: "In the womb he cheated
('aqab) his brother" (Hosea 12:5).[30]

Another prophecy in the periphery, this one in Jeremiah 9:3–5, also preserves
this ancient interpretation of Jacob's name:

> Beware, every man of his friend!
> Trust not even a brother!
> For every brother cheats ('aqob ya'aqob)
> Every friend is base in his dealings
> One man deceives the other,
> They will not speak truth;
> They have taught themselves to lie
> They wear themselves out working iniquity
> You dwell in the midst of deceit
> In their deceit, they refuse to heed Me, declares the LORD.

Wanting to show the extent to which iniquity has become widespread among
the people, Jeremiah calls forth the memory of the story of Jacob and Esau. It
is not enough to protect yourself from friends, he warns: even brothers cannot
be trusted. In these verses, which have a chiastic structure, it is the brother
and not the friend who cheats the other, just like the nation's forefather did
when he cheated his brother.[31]

Another verse in Jeremiah proves that the tradition about Jacob cheating his
brother was known to both the prophet and his audience (because he would
not allude to a story that did not awaken associations among his listeners):
"Most devious ['aqob] is the heart; it is perverse – who can fathom it? I the
LORD probe the heart, search the mind – to repay every man for his conduct
according to his deeds" (Jeremiah 17:9–10). Although Jeremiah does not speak
about Jacob, the use of the root '-q-b is no coincidence. It is clear that he wrote

---

[30] Hosea also may preserve the more ancient tradition of the birth, according to which Jacob
      cheats Esau already inside their mother's womb, and he emerges first (similar to the story
      about Perez and Zerah in Genesis 38:27–30). See Shinan and Zakovitch, *When Women Seduced
      the Gods*. Hosea 12 preserves a number of ancient traditions about the patriarch Jacob.
[31] N. Leibowitz, *Studies in the Book of Genesis* [in Hebrew] (Jerusalem: World Zionist Organi-
      zation, 1967), 186, insisted that in these verses the prophet recalls the story of Jacob and Esau
      and reveals a disapproving attitude toward Jacob. See also Buber, *Way of the Bible*, and J. P.
      Fokkelman, *Narrative Art in Genesis* (Assen, the Netherlands: Van Gorcum, 1975), 291.

with the archetype deceiver, Jacob, in mind because of the last words, "to repay every man for his *conduct according to his deeds*," which are taken from Hosea: "and punished Jacob for his *conduct*, requited him *for his deeds*" (Hosea 12:3), where they follow immediately after the prophet's name derivation of Jacob's name, which we mentioned previously, "In the womb he cheated [*ʿaqab*] his brother" (v. 5).[32]

A different strategy for fighting the unflattering association of the name Jacob was changing the name in a way that would express an antonym of "deceit" and "cheating." This is how the name Yeshurun, which means "honest, upright," was created.[33] The success of the name Yeshurun was quite limited, however, and it appears only in Deuteronomy (32:15; 33:5, 26) and Deutero-Isaiah (44:2). In Deutero-Isaiah's consoling prophecy, we find evidence also of the polemic against the notion that Jacob cheated already in his mother's womb:

> Thus said the LORD, your Maker,
> Your Creator who has helped you from the womb:
> "Fear not, My servant Jacob,
> Yeshurun, whom I have chosen."

The prophet emphasizes that God's choosing Jacob and His giving him the name Yeshurun are complementary acts, occurring already in his mother's womb prior to (or simultaneous with) Jacob's rivalry with Esau.

Although the name "Yeshurun" did not find broad acceptance in the Bible, we find a similar attempt to ascribe the meaning of the root *y-š-r*, the antonym of *ʿ-q-b*, to the name Israel, in which also appear the consonants of *y-š-r*; see Numbers 23:10: "Who can count the dust of Jacob, Number the dust-cloud of Israel? May I die the death of the upright [*yᵉšarim*], May my fate be like theirs!"[34] The prophet Micah knew well that this meaning was related to the name Israel, and he uses it in his argument with his people: "The one who *is said to be the House of Jacob* [*heʾamur bet yaʿaqob*], Is the LORD's patience short? Is such His practice? To be sure, My words are friendly to those who walk in rectitude [*hayyašar holek*]" (Micah 2:7). In his addressing "the one who is said to be the House of Jacob," the prophet alludes to the story of the changing of Jacob's name to Israel in Genesis 32:29: "Said he, "Your name shall no longer *be said Jacob*, but Israel." Micah disagrees with what is written

---

[32] For the influence of Hosea on Jeremiah, see K. Gross, *Die literarische Verwandtschaft Jeremias mit Hosea* (Leipzig, Germany: Noske, 1930).

[33] See W. Bacher, "ישרון," *ZAW* 5 (1885), 161–3.

[34] Also Buber (*Way of the Bible*, 292) argued that the change of the name Jacob to Israel was meant to cancel the shame inherent in the former.

in Genesis: the people' name remains Jacob because they are still cheaters and they do not deserve the name Israel, which befits only "those who walk in rectitude (*yašar*)."

The prophet Micah plays one further time with these two names that are so loaded with antithetical meanings:

> Hear this, you rulers of the House of Jacob,
> You chiefs of the House of Israel,
> Who detest justice.
> And make crooked what is straight (*hayšarah y^e'aqešu*). (Micah 3:9)

The nation's principal name, which reflects its essence, is "House of Jacob," and the prophet initially gives that name in the first hemistich. Then he immediately explains why they are undeserving of the second name, Israel: because all that is straight they make crooked. The verb "make crooked" plays on the sound and sense of the name "Jacob": the root '-q-š is similar in meaning to '-q-b and shares two of its consonants.[35]

AN INNOCENT MAN

At the beginning of the birthright story, the narrator reports Jacob's innocence, when Jacob's disposition is presented as antithetical to that of Esau: "And the boys grew up, Esau became a skillful hunter, a man of the outdoors; but Jacob was an innocent man, who dwelled in tents" (Genesis 25:27).[36] The description of the two brothers is stylistically symmetrical. Each characterization contains three elements in which the first is the name of the brother and the third identifies his work-sphere: Esau the hunter is "a man of the outdoors," whereas Jacob "dwelled in tents." Conversely, there is no symmetry between the contents of the descriptions. About Esau we learn of his profession as "a skillful hunter," whereas about Jacob we learn that he was "innocent" (*tam*): a direct assertion that his nature is not that of a liar.

Jacob's birth story in Genesis 25:19–26 also affects our reading of Genesis 27. The divine oracle in Genesis 25:23 represents an effort to extricate Jacob from any blame in the story of the blessing. This may be a secondary insertion because the exclamation, "And behold! There were twins in her womb" (v. 24) seems to indicate surprise, even though there is no reason for surprise

---

[35] This is not the place to discuss the other interpretations of the name Israel from "king" (*š-r-r* associated with its synonym *m-l-k*; Genesis 35:11); "dominion" (*š-r-r* and *m-š-l*; Psalm 114:2); "one who has striven" with God (*š-r-h*; Genesis 32:29; Hosea 12:4); "strove against" (*yaśar 'el*; Hosea 12:5).

[36] For a discussion of this antithesis, see L. Frankel, *Studies in the Bible* [in Hebrew] (Jerusalem: World Zionist Organization, 1981), 136–9.

because, in the previous verse, God had already revealed to Rebekah that "two separate peoples shall issue from your body . . . and the older shall serve the younger." The secondary nature of Rebekah's request for an oracle also may be indicated by its uniqueness in Genesis. An "inquiry" of God (i.e., a request for knowledge of the future or of guidance direct from God) is found in descriptions of Israelite religion in the era of the monarchy (e.g., 1 Samuel 9:9; 1 Kings 22:8; 2 Kings 3:1, 8:8, 22:13, 18) but is not found elsewhere in Genesis. It is anachronistic in the patriarchal narratives, in which God speaks to the characters without cultic intervention.

The divine oracle in Genesis 25:23 was meant to defend Jacob by depicting his ascent to power not as the result of any treachery on his part, but rather as part of God's initial plan. According to this interpretative clue, the determining factor in Jacob's future was not Isaac's blessing, because that future had already been determined before birth, by God.[37] There is even a defense of Rebekah in these verses: each of her actions, it seems, only pushes Jacob closer to his promised role, thereby bringing God's plan to fulfillment. Rebekah, of course, commits a transgression when she tries to hurry the fulfillment of God's promise (God is not interested in human help),[38] but Jacob does not achieve anything that would not have fallen into his hands anyway.

We now move from efforts to justify Jacob's character in the stories that precede the story of the blessing to those in the stories that follow it. When the time comes for Jacob to return to Canaan, we read of Rachel's stealing Laban's household idols in a story attributed to J: "Rachel stole her father's household idols. Jacob stole the heart of Laban the Aramean, by not telling him that he was fleeing, and he fled" (Genesis 31:19–20). The storyteller makes a partial admission in order to rescue Jacob from the guilt of stealing: he did not take anything from Laban. Rachel was the thief; if Jacob became stuck with the reputation of one, it is because he stole Laban's heart when he "stole

---

[37] Fokkelman, *Narrative Art*, 86–94, sees the function of verses 22–23 as part of the divine plan, although he does not sense their secondary nature.

[38] On the phenomenon of characters who provide assistance to God and are then punished for it – a prominent theme in Genesis – see, e.g., Sarah and her treatment of her Egyptian servant, Hagar, whom she offers to Abraham (Genesis 16:1–2). Hagar becomes pregnant and scorns her mistress (v. 4) who, in turn, maltreats her, providing one of the contributing factors in the Israelites' future enslavement in Egypt. See Zakovitch, "*And You Shall Tell Your Son . . .*": The Concept of the Exodus in the Bible (Jerusalem, Magnes Press, 1991), 27–30. Another example: when Rachel presses Jacob, "Give me children, or I shall die" (Genesis 30:1), she precipitates her own death: in her having "children," plural (i.e., in giving birth to her second son), she will die (Genesis 35:16–20). And again Rachel: when Rachel seeks to purchase her sister's mandrakes – out of the belief that through them she will conceive – Leah sells them to her in exchange for one night with Jacob. It is Leah who then conceives two sons – Issachar and Zebulun – before God remembers Rachel and causes her to conceive (30:14–18).

away" without first notifying him. Laban, we find, blames Jacob, first, for stealing his heart: "What did you mean by stealing my heart and carrying off my daughters like captives of the sword? Why did you flee in secrecy and steal (mislead?) me?" (Genesis 31:26–27). The expression "and steal me" is vague. Laban is accusing Jacob of theft, although he is clearly not referring to the idols because he specifically speaks of them a few lines later, at the end of verse 30.

The phrases "stealing my heart" and "and steal me" were intended to remove any impression that Jacob stole something material from Laban. Jacob's alleged crime – the writer is telling his readers – was nothing but a verbal expression, a turn of phrase; all he is blamed for is "stealing" away. Concerning that crime, Jacob is not even guilty because he had no other choice, as he explains to Laban. Laban presented himself as one who, first and foremost, worried about his daughters (Genesis 31:26–29), and to this Jacob defends himself: "I was afraid because I thought you would take your daughters from me by force" (Genesis 31:31).

Laban's second accusation against Jacob, "but why did you steal my gods?" (Genesis 31:30), is also baseless because it was Rachel who stole and hid them. Jacob knew nothing of Rachel's act, as is clear from his declaration about the man with whom the idols would be found: "but anyone with whom you find your gods shall not remain alive." Had he known it was Rachel, his beloved wife, who took the idols, he would never have made such a perilous promise.[39] Moreover, the accusation of theft makes it possible for Jacob to address the issue directly and to come to his own defense, making clear that not only did he not steal but also when Laban's property had been stolen, Jacob paid for the lost property from his own money: "that which was torn by beasts I never brought to you; I myself made good the loss; you exacted it of me, whether stolen by day or stolen by night" (v. 39).

Clear evidence that the story about the stealing of the household idols and Rachel's deception of her father is brought in order to balance the story of Jacob's deceiving his father, Isaac, is found in the repeated use of the verbs *mašaš/muš*, "to feel, touch," in both. In chapter 27, Isaac "feels" Jacob: "So Jacob drew close to his father Isaac, who *felt* him" (v. 22; see also vv. 12 and 21); in chapter 31, Laban rummages through Rachel's tent in an attempt to find the stolen idols: "and Laban rummaged [literally, "felt"] through the tent without finding them" (v. 34; see also v. 37). These verbs appear in both stories at the most dramatically heightened moment, when the deception might

---

[39] According to the Midrash, Rachel's death was caused by Jacob's curse when he inadvertently and unknowingly prophesied the thief's death: "In the opinion of Rabbi Yosi she died because of the curse of an old man, like an error committed by a ruler (Ecclesiastes 10:5), 'and Rachel stole,' 'and Rachel died'" (*Genesis Rabbah* 4:3); see also Rashi's commentary.

be – but is not – discovered. In both stories, this act of touching fails to help the father discover the truth.[40]

The story of Rachel's stealing the idols is brought, I believe, in order to clear Jacob's name of any accusation of stealing. Because a partial admission is necessary, the storyteller grants that Jacob did steal Laban's heart – a consequence of Laban's character and behavior – and also that an actual act of thievery did occur during the escape from Haran – but of that Rachel was guilty, not Jacob.[41] The depiction of Jacob as an "innocent man" is achieved, therefore, at the expense of Rachel, the thief.

After returning from Haran, Jacob no longer engages in deception. True, he still desires blessings and is even ready to fight for them – this time with no less than a divine being – but he will no longer deceive. In the story of the name change from Jacob to Israel that follows his wrestling with a divine being at the Jabbok crossing, he is ready to consent to the request, "let me go, for dawn is breaking" (Genesis 32:27), only if the divine being blesses him: "He answered, 'I will not let you go, unless you bless me,'" and the divine being does so: "and he blessed him there" (v. 30).

In a different telling of the changing of Jacob's name to Israel, this time in Bethel (in P), there is no longer any wrestling. On the contrary, it is repeated three times that God only spoke with Jacob at that place (see Genesis 35:13–15). This time, it is God who blesses Jacob, willingly and on his own initiative:

---

[40] On Rachel's being a bigger "deceiver" than Jacob, with her behavior in the story of the household idols, see Fokkelman, *Narrative Art*, 163.

[41] R. S. Hendel, *The Epic of the Patriarch: The Jacob Cycle and the Narrative Traditions of Canaan and Israel* (Harvard Semitic Monographs 42; Atlanta, GA, 1987), 95–7. For stealing the household idols, Rachel is punished with a measure-for-measure punishment. Following the principle of "Parents have eaten sour grapes and children's teeth are blunted" (Jeremiah 31:28): the story of the pursuit after Jacob and his household is similar to the story of the pursuit of Jacob's sons, which leads to the discovery of Joseph's goblet in Benjamin's bag (Genesis 44):
   a. The departure of Jacob's family from a foreign land for Canaan.
   b. A holy object is stolen (or appears to have been stolen) – Laban's household idols and the goblet with which Joseph divines the future (what is more, the household idols have an oracular function, as becomes clear, e.g., from Ezekiel 21:26 and Zechariah 10:2).
   c. The pursuit ends with the pursuers catching up to the others (31:23; 44:4).
   d. The accusation of theft (31:30; 44:4–6).
   e. The innocent are vindicated: Jacob (31:32); Joseph's brothers (44:7–9).
   f. The vindicated are willing to hand over the guilty one – if such a one is found – to die (31:32; 44:9).
The two stories are also antithetical and deliberately so: Rachel steals and is not caught, whereas her son Benjamin does not steal but is caught. The rabbinic sages were aware of the relationship between the stories; Benjamin, who is suspected of stealing from Joseph, is blamed by his brothers who call him "a thief, son of a thief [*ganevet*]" (*Midrash Tanḥuma, Miqqeṣ* 13).

"God appeared again to Jacob on his arrival from Paddan-aram, and He blessed him" (Genesis 35:9).[42]

One more effort that is made to soften our judgment of Jacob can be detected in the reconciliation scene between Jacob and his brother, when Jacob expresses his desire to atone for his actions. On his return from Haran, Jacob meets Esau and offers him a gift. The term Jacob uses is *birkati* (literally, "my blessing"): "Please accept my gift/blessing which has been brought to you, for God has favored me and I have plenty" (Genesis 33:11). Once Jacob has given Esau a "blessing" in place of the blessing that he stole from him, the brothers are even, and the account between them is clear.[43]

A justification of the younger son taking the blessing that was intended for his firstborn brother can be found in the Joseph story, when Jacob is already an old man and he knowingly grants the better blessing to Ephraim, Joseph's younger son, instead of to the firstborn Manasseh (Genesis 48; E). Jacob is blind, just as his father had been: about Isaac, it was said, "When Isaac was *old* and his *eyes were too dim to see*" (Genesis 27:1); and about Jacob: "Israel's eyes were *dimmed* because of his *old* age; he could not *see*" (Genesis 48:10). When Joseph sees his father placing his right hand onto the younger son's head, he tries to correct the error and remove it (v. 17), but Jacob reassures him that he is well aware of his action: "I know, my son, I know. He too shall become a people, and he too shall be great. Yet his younger brother shall be greater than he, and his offspring shall be plentiful enough for nations" (v. 19). In his subsequent blessing, Jacob indeed blesses Ephraim before Manasseh: "So he blessed them that day, saying, 'By you shall Israel invoke blessings, saying: God make you like Ephraim and Manasseh.' Thus he put Ephraim before Manasseh" (v. 20). Ephraim's blessing and his being granted precedence over his elder brother is meant to show how the divine plan does not always correspond with the rights of the firstborn son. Just as Ephraim was chosen, so also was Jacob, and so also was he preferred over his firstborn brother by God.

CONDEMNING JACOB

Now that we have found the justifications of Jacob's behavior in the different sources that form the Jacob story cycle and beyond, let us look for the work of the other force: the disapproving voice that acknowledges and condemns Jacob for stealing the birthright and shows how he was punished for it. First

---

[42] Regarding Jacob's name change at Bethel, see also Hosea 12:4b-5.
[43] See Hendel, *Epic of the Patriarch*, 130.

and foremost, Jacob was punished by having to flee from Canaan and by being enslaved to his uncle, Laban, for twenty years – a heavy penalty indeed. The narration of Jacob's flight, enslavement, and release from Laban's control (chapters 30–31) echoes the paradigm of the Israelites' enslavement and flight from Egypt, both of which occurred under God's guidance.[44] The molding of the story according to that model demonstrates its plain intention to punish and purge Jacob prior to his return to Israel.

Jacob is further punished with the switching of the daughters of Laban on his wedding night (Genesis 29:21–27; J). Despite Laban's promise to give his daughter Rachel to Jacob as wife, he switches Rachel with her sister, the firstborn Leah, and so manages to marry off the less attractive daughter and keep the hardworking and faithful Jacob indebted to him for seven more years. The switch is performed under the cover of darkness: "When morning came, behold, there was Leah" (v. 25). Jacob blames Laban for treachery: "Why did you deceive me?" In his defense, Laban does not deny the act but rather declares, "It is not the practice in our place to marry off the younger before the older" (v. 26).[45] Laban's words, "it is not the practice in our place," contain a thinly veiled taunt that recall Jacob's own behavior toward his brother, Esau. In the words of the commentator R. Eleazar Ashkenazi, "in our place the rights of a first born will not be passed on to the younger one, as was done in your place, that the younger took the firstborn [rights] from his brother – measure for measure."[46]

The story of switching the daughters plainly corresponds with Jacob's own behavior in the story of the stolen blessing: hidden by his father's blindness, the younger brother (Jacob), directed by his mother, impersonates his elder brother; likewise – but conversely – the elder sister (Leah), hidden by darkness and directed by her father (who is the brother of Jacob's mother), impersonates her younger sister. This purposeful – and perfect – symmetry is noted in the Midrash, which claims that the substitution of Leah represents Jacob's "measure-for-measure" punishment.[47]

Moreover, if the penalties of enslavement and the switching of the daughters (which leads to further enslavement) are not sufficient, one more measure-for-measure punishment is found outside the boundaries of the Jacob story cycle in the Joseph story, where another deception is played on Jacob – this

[44] See D. Daube, *The Exodus Pattern in the Bible* (London: Faber and Faber, 1983), 62–72; Zakovitch, *And You Shall Tell Your Son*, 46–8.

[45] Among the scholars who have noted how the sisters' behavior reflects Jacob's just rewards, see Fokkelman, *Narrative Art*, 291, and Hendel, *Epic of the Patriarch*, 95.

[46] According to Leibowitz, *Studies*, 187.

[47] *Genesis Rabbah* 70:17.

time by his sons who bring him the tunic that belonged to his beloved son Joseph:

> Then they took Joseph's tunic, slaughtered a kid, and dipped the tunic in the blood. They had the ornamented tunic taken to their father, and they said, "We found this. Please examine it; is it your son's tunic or not?" He recognized it and said, "My son's tunic! A savage beast devoured him! Joseph was torn by a beast!" (Genesis 37:31–33; J).

Just as Jacob deceived his father by using the clothes of the father's favorite son, so his own sons now deceive him with the clothes of his favorite son.[48]

EDOM AS ENEMY

We have seen how the prophets did not hesitate from offering reproving interpretations of Jacob's name when they wished to criticize the Israelites – the patriarch's descendants who continue in his crooked ways. At the same time, Jacob was fully rehabilitated in other prophecies that dealt with the relations between Israel and Edom and looked on Edom as Israel's enemy. In the Jacob cycle, a notable balance is struck between the characterizations of Jacob and Esau, with Esau's portrayal – despite his initial depiction as a dumb creature with poor table manners – as increasingly sympathetic. In

---

[48] After Jacob is punished with Joseph's bloodstained clothes, the chain of disguises and punishments continues with Judah in Genesis 38: Judah is punished for the pivotal role he played in the sale of Joseph and for lying to their father. He lied to his father with a piece of clothing, and his daughter-in-law now deceives him with clothing when she disguises herself as a prostitute (Genesis 38:14–15). The story of Judah and Tamar has a number of elements that identify it as Judah's measure-for-measure punishment. Just as Jacob's sons tell their father about the tunic, "Examine it: is it your son's tunic or not?" (37:32), so will Tamar shame Judah when she presents him with the objects he had left with her: "Examine these: whose seal and cord and staff are these?" (38:25). The expression "examine these/it" appears nowhere else in the Bible. The rabbis noted the purposeful connection between the sin and the punishment (e.g., *Genesis Rabbah* 85:1).

The chain of transgressions and penalties continues with the punishment of all the brothers for their part in the disguising of Joseph's tunic. This time, Joseph appears before his brothers dressed splendidly as the vizier of the King of Egypt and they do not recognize him. The father identified his son's tunic, just as the brothers had planned (37:33), but the brothers do not recognize Joseph in his new clothes. Joseph's punishment of his brothers, to a certain extent, is also Jacob's punishment for his sins – his sin of disguising himself as his brother and his more recent sin of favoring Joseph with the ornamented tunic. Joseph's disguise now inspires great fear in Jacob about the fate of his sons Simeon, who is imprisoned by Joseph, and particularly Benjamin, Joseph's younger brother.

At the story's end, when Joseph's brothers will withstand the test and not abandon their brother to imprisonment or death, it becomes apparent that the chain of disguises portends life for Jacob's house, as revealed by Joseph to his brothers (45:5–7). On the chain of knowledge, deception, and revelation, see also Alter, *Art of Biblical Narrative*, 159–77.

the prophecies that we look at now, Jacob is depicted as entirely virtuous, whereas Edom is portrayed as being utterly bad, the brutal enemy of Israel who deserves vengeance: a result of the blood-filled history of wars between Israel and Edom throughout the generations.

Amos's prophecy about Edom (Amos 1:11–12) – one of Amos's prophecies about foreign nations (Amos 1:2–2:16) – blames Esau "because he pursued his brother with the sword and repressed all pity" (v. 11). Although it is true that in the blessing Esau receives from his father it is said that "by your sword you shall live" (Genesis 27:40), it adds "you shall serve your brother." Esau was forbidden to turn his sword against his brother. Yet, over the course of history, Esau did threaten Israel with the sword. During Israel's journey to the land of Canaan, when Israel turned to Edom for mercy and requested that they be allowed to pass through Edom's borders – "thus says *your brother* Israel, You know all the hardships that have befallen us" (Numbers 20:14) – Edom answered: "You shall not pass through us, else we will go out against you with *the sword*" (v. 18). Edom, we see, did "repress all pity."[49]

Amos's portrayal of Edom's hatred for Jacob, "because his *anger* raged unceasing and his *fury* stormed unchecked," returns us to Rebekah's command to Jacob to flee to Laban's house "until your brother's *fury* subsides – until your brother's *anger* against you subsides and he forgets what you have done to him" (Genesis 27:44–45). Although the book of Genesis tells of the conciliatory reunion between the brothers, Amos makes the claim that Esau's hatred for his brother continued unabated and that Rebekah's hope that Esau's anger would diminish was disappointed.

Hatred toward Edom increased with the destruction of Jerusalem and its Temple, in which the Edomites participated (see, e.g., Psalm 137:7 and Lamentations 4:21–22). Ezekiel 35 speaks of Edom's "eternal hatred" for Israel and how Esau sought to inherit Israel, even saying, "the two nations and the two lands shall be mine" (v. 10). Of course, "the two nations" return to the oracle in Genesis 25:23: "two nations are in your womb, two separate peoples shall issue from your body." Esau denies the divine plan voiced in the oracle and dreams of prevailing over his brother, and for this God will have vengeance. Esau hates Israel and God will take retribution: "I will act with the same anger and passion that you acted with in your hatred of them" (Ezekiel 35:11), one more reminder of Esau's anger toward Jacob (Genesis 27:44–45). God's retribution for Edom's anger against Israel is expressed also in Ezekiel 25: "I will wreak My vengeance on Edom through My people Israel, and they

---

[49] Rashi and Abarbanel understood Amos's words as referring to Numbers 20:18. N. H. Tur-Sinai (*The Language and the Book. Vol. 1: Language* [in Hebrew; Jerusalem: Bialik, 1954], 84) observed that the blame of Edom returns to Genesis 27.

shall take action against Edom in accordance with My blazing anger and fury and they shall know My vengeance" (v. 14).

The first prophecy in the book of Malachi also emphasizes that God "loved Jacob and hated Esau":

> I have shown you love, said the LORD. But you ask, "How have You shown us love?" After all, declares the LORD, Esau is Jacob's brother; yet I have loved Jacob and hated Esau. I have made his hills a desolation, his territory a home for beasts of the desert. If Edom says, "Though crushed, we can build the ruins again," thus says the LORD of Hosts: "They may build, but I will tear down. And so they shall be known as the region of wickedness, the people damned forever of the LORD. Your eyes shall behold it, and you shall declare, 'Great is the LORD beyond the borders of Israel!'" (Malachi 1:2–5)

In Genesis, it is Rebekah, Jacob's mother, who loves him, while Isaac, the father, loves Esau (25:28). Yet, in the prophecy, it is not the parents' love that is spoken of but rather divine love and hate, and God's unambiguous choice of Jacob. In Genesis, Esau hates Jacob for stealing his blessing: "Now Esau loathed Jacob because of the blessing which his father had given him" (Genesis 27:41) whereas in Malachi, God takes revenge and hates Esau. In Genesis, Isaac yielded to Esau's insistent pleas to grant him a blessing of plenty (although it would be poorer than that granted Jacob): "See, your abode shall enjoy the fat of the earth and the dew of heaven above" (Genesis 27:39). However, in Malachi, God curses him with a desolation that will not desist: "and so they shall be known as the region of wickedness, the people damned forever of the LORD" (vv. 3–4).[50]

The story in Genesis served as raw material for the prophets, who pushed and prodded, separating it from its most simple and obvious sense. The prophets' hatred for Edom reilluminates and reinterprets the story in Genesis. In this new prophetic light, Esau is no longer the blameless, duped brother but rather has become a villain who deserves vengeance and who must be punished, measure for measure.

JUSTIFYING JACOB IN POSTBIBLICAL LITERATURE

Before we conclude, it is worth noting that justifying Jacob became the rule in postbiblical literature. The writer of *Jubilees*, for example, deleted Jacob's lie to Isaac. Jacob does not say, "I am Esau your firstborn" (Genesis 27:19) but rather "I am your son. I have done according to your words" (*Jubilees*

---

[50] See also God's bloody "day of vengeance" against Edom in Isaiah 63:1–6; and Y. Zakovitch, *Through the Looking Glass: Reflection Stories in the Bible* [in Hebrew] (Tel Aviv: Hakibbutz Hameuchad, 1995), 96–7.

26:13). Some rabbinic sages tried to hide Jacob's lie in another way by dividing his answer – "I am Esau your firstborn" – in half. According to a tradition attributed to Rabbi Levi, Jacob's response actually comprised two distinct parts: "*I am* destined to receive the Ten Commandments, but Esau is *your firstborn*" (*Genesis Rabbah* 65:18). A different tactic was taken in the Aramaic translation of *Targum Onqelos*. There, the sting of Isaac's accusation that "your brother came with guile and took away your blessing" (v. 36) is weakened by replacing "with guile [*b^emirmah*]" with "with wisdom [*b^eḥokmah*]" (so also in *Targum Pseudo-Jonathan*, and cf. *Genesis Rabbah* 66:4: "in the wisdom of His Torah").

Yet another way to justify Jacob's actions in postbiblical literature was to trace the younger son's rightful claim to the blessing to a superior authority: Abraham. In *Jubilees*, Abraham identifies Jacob as deserving the blessing: "And Abraham saw the deeds of Esau, and he knew that in Jacob should his name and seed be called" (*Jubilees* 19:16). Furthermore, Rebekah's preferential treatment of Jacob receives Abraham's full approval:

> And he said unto her: My daughter, watch over my son Jacob, for he shall be in my stead on the earth, and for a blessing in the midst of the children of men, and for the glory of the whole seed of Shem. For I know that the LORD will choose him to be a people for possession unto Himself. . . . And behold, Isaac my son loves Esau more than Jacob, but I see that you truly love Jacob. (*Jubilees* 19:17–19)

Abraham even blesses Jacob in Rebekah's presence:

> And he called Jacob before the eyes of Rebekah his mother, and kissed him, and blessed him, and said: "Jacob, my beloved son, whom my soul loves, may God bless you from above the firmament, and may He give you all the blessings." (*Jubilees* 19:26–27; see also 22:10–30)

In *Jubilees*, even Isaac (who, in our story, blames Jacob for deceiving him) distinguishes Jacob for his uprightness. After the latter is sent to Paddan-aram, Isaac reassures Rebekah:

> For I know that his ways will be prosperous in all things, wherever he goes, until he returns in peace to us, and we see him in peace. Fear not on his account, my sister, for he is on the upright path and he is a perfect man. (*Jubilees* 27:16–17)

God's blessing to Jacob, given on His own initiative (Genesis 28:13–15), provided later sources with the justification to view Isaac's blessing as part of a divine plan and not the result of a fraudulent act.

In the Midrash, emphasis is placed on the divine plan that stands behind Jacob's lies and on the fact that God sent His angels to help Jacob in his deception:

> When Esau was hunting and tying [his catch], the angel was untying and setting it free . . . and why? In order to prolong the hours until Jacob will go and do [what he needs] and goes in to his father and his father will eat and Jacob will take the blessing. (*Tanḥuma Buber, Tolᵉdot* 10)

Other examples of acts of divine intervention clear Jacob's name of accusations of deceit. *Genesis Rabbah* 65:19 contains the following:

> When Israel told Jacob, "Come closer that I may feel you, my son" (Genesis 27:21), Jacob urinated onto his calves, and his heart became as soft as wax, and God assigned to him two angels, one on his right and one on his left, in order to hold him up by his elbows.

Here, the climactic moment of Jacob's deception is interpreted differently: the upright Jacob was overcome with fear, and it was God's angels who held him steady so that he could fulfill God's plan. The book of *Jubilees* describes a similar act of intervention: "and [Isaac] discerned him not, because it was a dispensation from heaven to remove his power of perception" (*Jubilees* 26:18).

CONCLUSION

We have seen how different forces were at work in the formation and interpretation of the story of Isaac's blessing: on the one hand, Jacob's transgression is admitted and his subsequent punishment (measure for measure) is described; on the other hand, Jacob is vindicated, if only partially. We saw how both forces left their mark on the Jacob cycle in its various sources and in the Joseph story. J is not reluctant to admit Jacob's deceit – even as it also indicates positive traits – whereas E and P interpret Jacob's behavior favorably. Prophecies about the two brother-nations, Israel and Edom, were generally guided by the inclination to vindicate Jacob, with some variation among the pre-exilic prophets. Different genres of postbiblical interpretation – biblical translations, rewritten Bibles, and Midrash – continued the trend that began with the later biblical writers: clearing the names of biblical heroes of any wrongdoings, thereby presenting them as morally perfect exemplars, worthy of our imitation.

6

Rabbinic Interpretation

Dina Stein

MIDRASH AND ITS PRECURSORS

Rabbinic interpretations of Scripture – unlike the creation of the world (at least according to some ancient exegetes) – were not a creation *ex nihilo*. They were preceded by a long and varied chain of tradition that, in turn, was adapted by the rabbis to suit their own cultural needs. To fully appreciate the rabbinic exegetical enterprise, we must pay attention to the legacy (at times hidden) that informed their practice and, at the same time, recognize the astonishing novelty of their project. The novelty lies not only in the thematic plan but also, as I argue, predominantly in the formal–rhetorical aspect of their writings. That is, what we see in rabbinic interpretation of Scripture is a new epistemology, one that situates the text itself as an *explicit* locus of knowledge. This epistemological shift is implicated in the self-reflexive character of rabbinic texts themselves, which in turn render the characters they embody – whether they are the projected biblical protagonists or the implied rabbinic subjects – self-reflective. Before addressing this epistemological shift, we must first turn to the beginning.

The book of Genesis begins with a seemingly simple, although grammatically awkward, statement: "In the beginning God created heaven and earth." Yet, already in Scripture itself we find that imagining the very moment of creation did not end (nor did it begin) in Genesis 1. When Wisdom, the speaker in Proverbs 8, announces, "The LORD made me *the beginning* of his course, the first of his acts of old" (8:22), it inscribes itself as a transformative force in the primordial moment. Here and elsewhere, the first traces of the retelling of the Genesis story are to be found within the Bible. Whether imagined in the conceptual framework of *Sophia-Ḥokmah* (as in Proverbs), or as God's battle with mythological beasts (as in Psalms or Job), or in the creation language of the building of the tabernacle (as in Exodus), these texts tell a different story

than the one told in the opening chapter of the canon. Not only do mythological beasts – conspicuously absent from the Genesis Creation narrative (albeit
etymologically alluded to in the name *Tehom/Tiamat*) – resurface in other
texts, but also the universalistic paradigm that the Genesis story outlines is
later linked to a particularistic trajectory concerning Israel and its redemption
from Egypt.[1] Competing or reworked traditions, and even exegesis of Genesis narratives, are contained within Scripture itself, attesting to the different
schools and the long process that informed its formation until it reached the
final stage of canonization sometime in the first century C.E.

If the Bible already contains its own reworking of tradition, this is all the
more so in the literature of the Second Temple period – particularly in the
last two centuries B.C.E and the first century C.E. – which offers a glimpse of
narratives and traditions that did not make the final cut. The books of Enoch
tell of the celestial voyages of this enigmatic biblical figure; the *Testaments
of the Patriarchs* is a first-person *Rashomon* of sorts in which each of Jacob's
sons gives his own account of the family history; and the *Book of Jubilees*
retells the biblical history from Creation to the Giving of the Torah on Mount
Sinai. These are just a few texts that retell parts of Genesis and, whether
contingent on the biblical text or independent narratives, they are powerful
manifestations of the creative literary turmoil of that period.

What was the impetus for this textual–cultural activity? James Kugel has
drawn a compelling picture of the rise of a text-oriented discourse in the
Second Temple period, following the Babylonian Exile, as necessitated by the
need to bridge unavoidable gaps between the old texts and the perceptions
and needs of their later consumers. Not only did the interpreters of that period
share the basic assumption of the Scripture as a sacred text, they also shared
several exegetical principles. The Bible is fundamentally a cryptic text and, as
such, it requires elucidation of its obscure or hidden meanings; it constitutes
one great Book of Instructions and, as such, it is a fundamentally *relevant* text;
Scripture is perfect and perfectly harmonious; and all Scripture is somehow
divinely sanctioned, of divine provenance, or divinely inspired.[2]

According to this historical picture, the Second Temple period formed
the exegetical kernel for subsequent generations of Bible readers, and the
Second Temple literary creativity was largely a scholarly enterprise. Clearly,
ancient and Late Antique reworkings of biblical traditions are products of
an intellectual elite. However, one must remember that the sources of those
traditions may have originally resided in wider circles, which were articulated – for whatever cultural or ideological reasons – by members of a scribal

---

[1] Similarly, other texts in Genesis (e.g., allusions to a less complimentary etymology of Jacob
    as a trickster can be found in the Prophets), see Chapter 5 by Yair Zakovitch in this volume.
[2] James L. Kugel, *The Bible As It Was* (Cambridge, MA: Harvard University Press, 1997), 17–23.

elite. That is, it should be kept in mind that the impetus for retelling Scriptural narratives may have been, phenomenologically, closer to folk-retelling of widespread tales than to an academic-like zeal for verse-by-verse exegesis. Yet, the ability to ascribe specific materials to different social groups or settings where they may have originated is problematic, if not entirely impossible, when addressing Late Antique texts that are fashioned by the elite.[3] This textual barrier continues into the rabbinic period: although scholars (particularly Galit Hasan-Rokem) have pointed out folk-elements in the rabbinic corpus, it remains unclear whether folk-motifs, genres, or practices relate to or stem from the "folk" as opposed to any "rabbinic" group.[4]

THE NOVELTY OF MIDRASH

By the time we reach the rabbinic era, whose earliest texts are from the third century C.E., the Bible is not only a canonized text but also one that is handed down with a legacy of interpretations, some of which are in Scripture itself. In this sense, the rabbis are one more link in the chain of tradition whose origins can be traced as far back as the sixth century B.C.E. Yet, the rabbis introduce Midrash as their cultural hallmark. *Midrash*, derived from the root *d-r-š* means in rabbinic literature "to interpret, explicate, or investigate" first and foremost a biblical text in order to produce new exegetical insights. It is crucial for understanding the rabbinic enterprise to recognize that never before has interpretation been, in its *explicit* form of Midrash, a defining cornerstone of other groups sharing the sacred text. Not that traces of it cannot be found in the Second Temple period; however, even if we acknowledge that the rabbis were not innovators of the explicit exegetical form per se, they did turn one rhetorical option that existed alongside other forms (exegetical or not) into their main hermeneutical and literary marker. Intratextual relationships no doubt exist within the Bible, and the author of *Jubilees* consciously rewrote and commented on the Creation story as he knew it from a Genesis version. However, neither the author of *Jubilees*, the author of the *Testaments*, nor the various authors of the Enoch literature explicitly anchor their tales in Scriptural citations.

---

[3] The category of "folklore" has served scholars such as Eli Yassif in reading Second Temple materials. Although his reading exposes interesting aspects of the texts, they do not point necessarily at distinguishing markers that set them apart from any central-hegemonic social group or world of ideas; see idem, *The Hebrew Folktale: History, Genre, Meaning*, trans. J. S. Teitelbaum, introduction by D. Ben-Amos (Bloomington: Indiana University Press, 1999), 38–69.

[4] See: Galit Hasan-Rokem, *Web of Life: Folklore and Midrash in Rabbinic Literature*, trans. B. Stein (Stanford, CA: Stanford University Press, 2000). See also Dina Stein, "Let the 'People' Go: On the 'Folk' and Their 'Lore' in Reconstructing Rabbinic History" (forthcoming).

There are two exceptions to this hermeneutical–narratological character of Second Temple literature. One is the *pesharim* of the Qumran community, in which Scriptural verses are quoted and, in turn, interpreted as referring to the historical context of interpreter. The other is Philo – the Jewish Hellenistic Scholar of Alexandria (ca. 20 B.C.E.–50 C.E.) – who often quoted Scripture. However, if the *pesharim* are in the formal sense predecessors of rabbinic Midrash, they are nonetheless not the exclusive or major narratological option of the (imagined) Qumran community. Similar citations appear in Philo's writings, but they function as the springboard from which the author takes his lead or the end to which he drives his argument.[5] Unlike Midrash, his writings are far from a mosaic of citations.

For Philo, the design of the Creation narrative is meant to enhance philosophical investigation, resulting in the philosopher's (i.e., Torah reader's) experience of "sober intoxication" in the face of the divine.[6] In turn, the Torah itself is rendered the *Logos*. For the rabbis, too, the Torah serves as an underlying cosmic principle of wisdom, shared by both God and humans. Here, the rabbis are clearly carrying a torch that was handed down to them from earlier times. As they write in the opening of *Genesis Rabbah*, a fifth-century C.E. Palestinian compilation that provides *aggadic* (i.e., nonlegal) commentary on the book of Genesis (and often provides more than one Midrash for a word or a verse):

> The Torah said: I was the tool which the Holy One, blessed be He used. As it is the way of the world: a king of flesh and blood builds a palace, he does not build it basing it on his own knowledge but on the artisan's. And the artisan does not build it on his own accord but rather he has parchment and writing tablets to instruct him how to build rooms, how to build little gates. Likewise the Holy One, blessed be He, looks at the Torah and creates the world. And the Torah said: "In the beginning God created" (Genesis 1:1). And "the beginning" is Torah, as it is written "God made me the beginning of his course" (Proverbs 8:22). (Genesis Rabbah 1:1)

---

5 See Steven D. Fraade, "Rewritten Bible and Rabbinic Midrash as Commentary," in *Current Trends in the Study of Midrash*, ed. Carol Bakhos (Leiden, the Netherlands: Brill, 2006), 59–77. Fraade seeks to present a more nuanced comparison between Second Temple retellings of the Bible and rabbinic Midrash, one that takes into account not only thematic but also formal similarities. Although his reading is convincing, it should not – as I suggest here – blur the broader (and, to be sure, unavoidably reductionist) picture of the epistemological innovation encapsulated in Midrash as a central discursive rabbinic paradigm (as Fraade himself acknowledged in his *From Tradition to Commentary: Torah and its Interpretation in the Midrash Sifre to Deuteronomy* [Albany, NY: SUNY Press, 1991]).

6 *On the Creation*, Loeb Classical Library, § 70–1.

This short narrative seems to echo Middle Platonic notions of Ideal Forms with which Philo is identified, although it has often been argued that rabbinic Judaism – counter to its evolving sibling, Christianity – did not incorporate Platonic concepts.[7] Leaving aside this complex question (and issues of Philonic–Platonic allegorical style), the narrative presents rhetorical markers that are distinctly rabbinic: it speaks by referring to Scripture itself as its locus of authority, rendering Midrash, in Daniel Boyarin's apt characterization, explicitly "intertextual."[8]

Philo is the recognized author of his works, and his authority is granted by the philosophical principles that underlie his reading of Scripture. For him and for his designated, albeit varied, audience, the two paradigms – the philosophical–allegorical and Scripture – are to be harmonized. Narratologically, his authority does not depend on Scriptural citations (even where he clearly addresses Scriptural verses). Similarly, the authority of *Jubilees* in retelling the story of Creation is not Scripturally based: it is a ministering angel who recounts the events that preceded the giving of the Torah to Moses, while the latter waits on Mount Sinai for forty days. *The Testaments of the Patriarchs* is granted authority by its first-person narrative, in which each of Jacob's sons delivers his own account – Testament – of the trials and tribulations of the extended Israelite family. Revelation and testimony construct an authorial position that is based on direct, unmediated knowledge. It is exactly these authorial positions that, by and large, the rabbis relinquish. In their conscious recognition of the loss of prophetic knowledge (after the destruction of the Second Temple, or even earlier), it is textual interpretation – Midrash – that is the rhetorical marker of their authority.

Because the Torah is the means by which God created the world – as in the example cited – and the Torah is the means by which the rabbis live and understand the world and interpret God's creation, the rabbis are granted a share in divine creativity and authority. By staging the Torah as the instructive tool with which God created the world, the Torah, in turn, is rendered the key for deciphering the structure of the world with its rooms and little gates. The Torah is thus not only the facilitator of the world but also – as a specifically *rabbinic* etiological myth of interpretation – of Midrash. Finally, divine epistemology – how God Himself gained the required knowledge for creating the world – is seen as residing in the text and in His ability to read it.

---

[7] On the association of "beginning," Wisdom," and "Logos," and the underlying platonic notions of Ideal Forms, see James L. Kugel, *Traditions of the Bible: A Guide to the Bible as It Was at the Start of the Common Era* (Cambridge MA: Harvard University Press, 1998), 63–6.

[8] Daniel Boyarin, *Intertextuality and the Reading of Midrash* (Bloomington: Indiana University Press, 1990).

THE RECEPTION OF MIDRASH AS (VALID) INTERPRETATION

Returning to the book of Genesis, it would seem that nothing in the plain sense of the Creation narrative alludes specifically to the Torah's role in the process. Moreover, is comparing God to a king of flesh and blood (albeit in parabolic form) who is not self-sufficient enough to perform an independent act of creation not a diminishment of the Almighty? Indeed, Midrash was not only a source of inspiration but also posed difficulties for later generations, starting with the Geonim (i.e., the leaders of the Jewish academies in Babylonia and Palestine of the eighth – eleventh centuries) and ending with modern scholars of our day. It is also the explicit exegetical rhetoric that characterizes rabbinic writings that has been found to be objectionable. For the Geonim and many of the traditional commentators of the medieval and early modern periods, rabbinic Midrash and *aggadic* (i.e., nonlegal) narratives often created a dissonance between the basic authority – especially in legal matters – with which the rabbis were accorded, and their own sensibilities. The personification of the divine and what has been perceived as "irrational" accounts of biblical narrative, as well as of rabbinic lives and practices (e.g., magical acts), are among the difficulties with which later generations had to come to terms. Various strategies were offered and (as one can imagine) each not only expressed the view of an individual thinker but also encapsulated the wider cultural context in which it was written.

For example, Rav Sherira (the Gaon of Pumbedita, 968–1006) writes that the "teachings based upon verses in the Midrash and Aggadah are approximations . . . and therefore we do not depend on teachings of the Aggadah."[9] Similarly, Maimonides (1135–1204) attempted to reconcile Midrash and medieval rational philosophy by describing it as a genre characterized by "poetical conceit." For Maimonides, the Midrash is problematic not only because of objectionable content but also because of its exegetical rhetoric, which misleads a populace "that imagines that the [sages] have said these things in order to *explain* the meaning of the text in question."[10]

Turning to modern scholarship, we find that Midrash has remained puzzling but for slightly different reasons. To the sensibilities of the modern scholar, who may still seek to preserve rabbinic authority (intellectually, if not on strictly religious grounds), Midrash presents itself as a curious exegetical

---

[9] *Sefer Ha-Eshkol*, eds. Shalom and Hanoch Albeck (Jerusalem: Wagshall, 1984), 157 (60a); translated by Joshua Levinson, "Literary Approaches to Midrash," in *Current Trends in the Study of Midrash*, 192–3.

[10] *Guide of the Perplexed*, trans. Shlomo Pines (Chicago: University of Chicago Press, 1974), 572 (Part III, 43). Emphasis added.

discourse. Did the rabbis deliver their exegesis in good faith or did they consciously exploit the biblical text to express whatever preconceived ideas they may have had? Did the rabbis "really" believe that God consulted the Torah in the creation of the world? Or, rather, was it their way to appropriate the text for their own goals and purposes, rendering the Genesis account of Creation a myth that anticipates their own midrashic enterprise (consulting the Torah) in which Torah also serves as the Jewish *Sophia* or *Logos*?

Scholars including Isaac Heinemann (1876–1957), Joseph Heinemann (1915– 1978), and Jonah Fraenkel (b. 1928) provided key insights into the production of Midrash. I. Heinemann not only pointed out basic poetic mechanisms of Midrash in its reading of Scripture but also related what he termed their "creative philology" and "creative historiography" to an underlying pre-rationalist principle of "organic thinking."[11] As Daniel Boyarin observes, for I. Heinemann, the rabbis are the "Goethes of Judaism, who with their gigantic creative abilities understand the 'reality' of the salvation history and communicate this reality with their legends, the agaddah."[12] Whereas this view of Midrash (shared by Fraenkel) seeks and finds transhistorical romantic truths in the rabbinic enterprise, J. Heinemann directs his attention to specific historical and ideological factors that trigger – according to his reading – the different midrashim.[13]

Although at odds regarding Midrash and its historical consciousness, these three influential scholars assume that Midrash is, in fact, *pseudo*-exegesis: its exegetical character being a pretense of sorts, a means to deliver either ahistorical truths or historical and ideologically driven ideas.[14] It is in opposition to this assumption that Boyarin produced his revolutionary study, *Intertextuality and the Reading of Midrash*, which focuses on the *Mekhilta de-Rabbi Ishmael* (i.e., a third-century Palestinian exegetical compilation on the book of Exodus).[15] For Boyarin, Midrash is a valid method of interpretation, assuming that any interpretative discourse involves a meeting point between the interpreter – who is inevitably informed by intellectual desires and ideologies – and a given text. Boyarin claims (and it may be argued that the extremity of his argument impinges on apologetics) that the rabbis are attuned – always – to the poetics of the biblical text, sensitive to its gaps and

[11] Isaac Heinemann, *Darkhe ha-Aggadah* (2nd ed.; Jerusalem: Magnes Press, 1954).
[12] Boyarin, *Intertexuality*, 9.
[13] Joseph Heinemann, *Aggadah and its Development* [in Hebrew] (Jerusalem: Keter, 1974).
[14] On Joseph Heinemann and Jonah Fraenkel, see also Joshua Levinson, *The Twice-Told Tale: A Poetics of the Exegetical Narrative in Rabbinic Midrash* [in Hebrew] (Jerusalem: Magnes Press, 2005), 30–5. For a reading of Joseph and Isaac Heinemann, see Boyarin, *Intertextuality*, 1–11.
[15] Boyarin, *Intertextuality*.

intricate analogies. What Boyarin claims to be the intertextual quality of Midrash resides not only in the explicit double-layeredness of rabbinic commentary and cited Scriptural verses but also the poetics of the Bible itself. The rabbis, although predating Meir Sternberg, Robert Alter, or even Martin Buber, are thus vindicated by modern literary scholars of the Bible.

For I. Heinemann, the midrashic reading of Genesis 1:1, which renders the Torah as the plan without which God could not create the world, would probably be construed to express the eternal power of Scripture. To that end, Midrash employs what he termed "creative philology" attuned to single words: because the word *beginning* appears in both Genesis 1:1 and Proverbs 8:23, it follows that between these verses there is an essential connection and that the latter explains the former (and vice versa). What seems to be missing from this Midrash is an explicit textual analogy between Wisdom and Torah. This is where J. Heinemann would probably step in and argue that it is precisely this absence that indicates the ideological, historical, and extratextual impetus of Midrash: Torah is rendered equivalent to Wisdom in answer to Hellenistic notions of Wisdom as a cosmic underlying principle, but there is no real trace of that equivalence in Scripture itself. Boyarin, conversely, might view the equivalence as an example of an axiomatic interpretative point of departure that is part and parcel of any interpretative system. The notion that Wisdom preceded the creation of the world and that it played a key role in subsequent acts of creation is attested by different sources of the Second Temple period.[16] In this context, the association of Torah (as the book of Divine Wisdom) with Wisdom might not seem an indicator of rabbinic pseudo-exegesis but rather point to the underlying intellectual paradigm of the time.

Second Temple sources provide a necessary background for understanding rabbinic Midrash; they set the stage on which rabbinical exegetical plays are performed and, at times – as in the previous example – provide a repository of paradigms and motifs that may underlie later rabbinic interpretations. Yet, the rabbinical exegetical enterprise was selective not only in its content but also in its style. The rhetoric of Midrash – whereby exegesis is constructed by explicit citations and is presented (as a norm) as contingent on biblical verses – is what sets it apart from earlier interpretations. This rhetoric carries an epistemological position – how one knows what one knows – that is implicated in most forms of rabbinic discourse. Not unlike the European novel that subsumed existing literary forms, Midrash infiltrated most of the literary genres within the rabbinic corpus (e.g., parables, riddles, and tales of the Sages). It also served as an implied model for the Talmudic

---

[16] See Kugel, *Bible As It Was*, 55–6.

explications of the Mishnah, whereby the Talmud – in order to enhance its own reading – cites the Mishnah. The implication of this midrashic thrust cannot be overstated: it provides an epistemological model that resonates in a host of cultural productions – whether the obvious notion of textuality that it entails, or the character of God (who reads Scripture), or (as discussed below), the profile of the human subject that it conjures.

THE SUBJECT OF CREATION: FROM A UNIVERSAL COSMOLOGY TO ABRAHAM

The Mishnah (unique in its character in rabbinic literature because it is not "midrashically" structured) clearly expresses anxiety over the exposition of *Ma'aseh Bereshit*, the account of Creation in the beginning of Genesis, for it states: "One may not expound the Forbidden Degrees before three; nor *Ma'aseh Bereshit* before two; nor the Chariot before one" (m. Ḥagigah 2:1). The categories of kindred and affinity (the "Forbidden Degrees," '*arayot*, as listed in Leviticus 18), the account of the Chariot in Ezekiel 1, and the Creation narrative are considered dangerous topics and thus are put under exegetical constraint. The seeming paradox between the Mishnah's dictums and the abundance of midrashim relating to the mysteries of Creation cannot be easily resolved. As Philip Alexander, who attempted to provide such a resolution, correctly noted, "the doctrine of creation is central to the rabbinic theistic world-view" and it may be that it is this centrality, as well as the threat of competing doctrines (unacceptable in rabbinic eyes), that triggered what he termed "pre-emptive exegesis."[17] It is beyond the scope of this chapter to draw a fuller, if not necessarily more coherent, picture of rabbinic esoteric and mystical beliefs and practices relating to the Genesis Creation narrative. Rather, we follow a slightly less harrowing path, one that involves the first patriarch.

Yet, turning to the patriarch leads us back precisely to the Creation story in Genesis because, counter to what we might think, the particularistic national narrative, according to Midrash, does not begin in Genesis 12 but rather earlier. *Genesis Rabbah* 1:4 lists six things that preceded the creation of the world, some of which were actually created whereas others were merely contemplated. Following the Torah and the Throne of Glory, which were created, we learn that the Patriarchs were among the contemplated things (together with the Temple, Israel, and the name of the messiah) because it is written in Scripture: "Your *fathers* seemed to Me like the *first* (*bᵉrešitah*) fig to ripen on a fig tree"

---

17 Philip S. Alexander, "Pre-Emptive Exegesis: Genesis Rabbah's Reading of the Story of Creation," *Journal of Jewish Studies* 43 (1992), 230–45.

(Hosea 9:10). God, speaking through the mouth of his prophet, associates the fathers with a fig in its beginning – *b^erešitah*, *b^erešit* being the word with which the book of Genesis starts. The rabbis thus read the Hosea verse as an intertext of Genesis 1:1. It is not clear from the rabbinic passage why some items are actual creations whereas others – like the fathers – are defined as potential creations (to be fulfilled later in history). Be that as it may, the list makes clear that what might otherwise be viewed as a universalistic Creation narrative (Genesis 1) already contains a particularistic, Israelite trajectory. Particularizing the Creation story (leaving aside the messiah's name and the Temple) is by no means a rabbinic innovation. We find a similar move alluded to in Scripture itself (e.g., in the Creation language of the tabernacle account) and it is manifested in *Jubilees*. What the rabbis do introduce is their explicit exegetical premise: the authority for inscribing the fathers in the primordial moment is to be found in Scripture itself.

TEXTUAL REFLEXIVITY AND HUMAN REFLECTIVITY: MIDRASH AND ABRAHAM

The "historical" story of Abraham, therefore, is part of a cosmological design rooted in the very beginning of time. Yet, much of the biblical narrative of Abraham (and of the other patriarchs) appears to be anything but an execution of a *linear* divine plan. There is much grief and many detours along the ancestral path, leading to the climactic moment of revelation on Mount Sinai, to mention only one pivotal landmark in the history of the Israelites. Such setbacks are an essential component of any well-formed and meaningful story, which the biblical narrative undoubtedly is and perhaps had to be in order to carry its theological and ideological agendas. The biblical story is also, of course, a story of human beings in their intricate relationships with themselves and with other mortals, as well as with God. Although the poetics of the biblical text may only allude to the inner life of its characters (the famous example that comes to mind is Auerbach's reading of Genesis 22, the binding of Isaac),[18] the rabbis' interest in thoughts and intentions produces what Joshua Levinson terms a "rabbinic literary anthropology."[19]

Abraham's overall piety and obedience make him worthy of his role as the Father of the Nation, to whom God promises fertility and salvation. The recurring hardships that he encounters are taken by Midrash to form

---

[18]   See also Chapter 1 by Robert Alter in this volume.

[19]   Joshua Levinson, "Literary Anthropology in Rabbinic Literature" [in Hebrew], in *Studies in Talmud and Midrashic Literature in Memory of Tirzah Plesser-Lifshitz*, eds. M. Bar-Asher, J. Levinson, and B. Lifshitz (Jerusalem: Bialik Press, 2005), 217–29.

a series of ten trials that God sets before him – thus forming an implicit linear trajectory of the detoured biblical plot – the last of which is the decree to sacrifice his beloved son. The terse, gapped text of Genesis 22 is afforded elaborate interpretations that comprise two entire chapters in *Genesis Rabbah*, attesting to the abundance of material on the subject and to the centrality it held in the eyes of the editor. Shalom Spiegel and many scholars since have compared interpretations of the story in competing Jewish and Christian contexts; indeed, some of the midrashim are polemical in some respects.[20] What I draw attention to here is the explicit reflexivity that characterizes Abraham's devotional act when crafted by rabbinic hands:

> "And He said: 'Take, please, your son,'" etc. (Genesis 22:2)
> Said He to him: "Take, please" – I beg you – "your son."
> "Which son?" He asked
> "Your only son," replied He.
> "But each son is the only one of his mother?"
> "Whom you love."
> "Is there a limit to the affection?'"
> "Isaac," said He. (*Genesis Rabbah* 55:7)

The Midrash addresses the seemingly superfluous repetition in the Genesis verse, "Take, please, your son, your only son, whom you love," because for the literal pragmatic meaning of the text, God could have simply said to Abraham: "Take Isaac and sacrifice him." Yet, assuming that no formulation in Scripture is accidental or arbitrary, the rabbis unpack the verse and introduce a *dialogue* between God and his servant. The immensely charged Scriptural verse is transformed into a (more) explicit psychological portrayal of a father trying to fend off the worst of all possible commands. In a paradoxical move, Midrash explains that this tormenting dialogue is meant to make Isaac "even more beloved in his eyes and reward him for every word spoken." The Midrash thus explains the excruciatingly painful dialogue according to its underlying principle of divine justice (i.e., theodicy).

In so doing, it accentuates the importance of language in a moral universe, for Abraham will be rewarded "for *every word* spoken." It is language that forms the underlying exegetical principle, not only as it expresses itself implicitly in the rabbinic reading of the beginning of verse 2 but also in the comparison it draws between the latter and God's first appeal to Abram in Genesis 12:1. There, God orders Abram: "Go forth from your native land and

---

[20] Shalom Spiegel, *The Last Trial: On the Legends and Lore of the Command to Abraham to Offer Isaac as Sacrifice: The Akedah*, trans. Judah Goldin (New York: Jewish Publication Society, 1967). See also Chapter 10 by John Collins in this volume.

from your father's house to the land that I shall show you." Why, asks the Midrash, did God not just order him to leave? The answer given is similar to the one given regarding Genesis 22:2: "in order to make it more beloved in his eyes and to reward him for every step." The intertext that the Midrash points to draws an implied analogy in Scripture itself between the first and last of Abraham's ten trials, thereby highlighting an underlying and unifying principle – not only theodicy but also the unity of the discrete episodes in the Patriarch's biography.

Another Midrash, which is brought in to elucidate Genesis 12:1, points to further similarities between the two scenes:

> Now what preceded this passage? "And Terah died in Haran" (Genesis 11:31), [which is followed by], "Now YHWH said unto Abram: Go forth (lek l^eka)."
>
> R. Isaac said: "From the point of view of chronology a period of sixty five years is still required." (*Genesis Rabbah* 39:7)

The Midrash alludes to a seeming contradiction in Scripture: if Terah was seventy years old at Abraham's birth (Genesis 11:26), whereas Abraham departed from Haran at the age of seventy-five (12:4), this means that Abraham departed sixty-five years before Terah's death, which occurred when Terah was 205 years old (11:32). Yet, Terah's death is mentioned *before* Abraham's departure. Now, one could argue that there is no contradiction in the text because Genesis 11 provides a genealogy that culminates with Terah, which provides a background for the Abraham narrative in Genesis 12. In other words, chapters 11 and 12 are generically different and, therefore, no contradiction in the biblical narrative need be discerned. However, for the Midrash, there is another issue at stake here:

> For Abraham was afraid, saying: "Shall I go out and bring dishonor upon the Divine Name, as people will say: 'He left his father in his old age and departed?'" Therefore, the Holy One, blessed be He, reassured him: "I exempt you (l^eka) from the duty of honoring your parents, though I exempt no one else from this duty. Moreover, I will record his death before your departure." Hence "and Terah died in Haran" (Genesis 11:31) is stated first and then "Now the Lord said to Abram" etc. (Genesis 12:1)

As in the previous Midrash, in which we are led into a father's dread of hearing what he already knows, this Midrash leads us into Abram's psyche. Abram is hesitant about complying with the decree because he sees the possible contradiction between two sets of duties and values that such a decree involves:

respecting one's father versus obeying God.[21] Having two father figures (however dysfunctional the biological one is, according to Midrash) results in a theological–moral dilemma. Besides the specific import of this Midrash, it is important to note its implicit "rabbinic anthropology": Abram, the father who is about to sacrifice his son, and Abram, the son who is about to leave his father, is a reflective figure whose thoughts, emotions, and intentions constitute his persona.

In both cases, Abraham is represented as a reflective agent, and it is here, I suggest, that the rabbinical exegetical subject – both the rabbis themselves and their projected biblical figures – converge. To be sure, according to the rabbis, when Rebekah sees Isaac praying in the fields or Jacob frequents the house of study, they are clearly dressing the biblical past with their own garb. Similarly, when Moses and Rabbi Akiva are shown to have had similar biographies – both are "late bloomers" (i.e., they only begin studying at the age of forty, study for forty years, and then teach forty years) – the ideological, rabbinically centered motivation is obvious. However, beyond what may be a "rabbinization" of biblical figures on the level of content (e.g., prayer and house of study) or Abraham's awareness of the fifth commandment, "Honor your father and your mother" (Exodus 20:12; Deuteronomy 5:16), it is the very midrashic discourse and the subject that it entails that is staged here. That is, the self-reflexivity that is implied in Midrash as an exegetical discourse reverberates in the representation of its biblical characters.

Midrash is a propagator of reflection, both in itself and as a generative and metonymic model of rabbinic hermeneutical practices. For the sage, who is "inside and outside the text"[22] at the same time – as is Midrash itself – this implies a position of liminality. If we understand self-reflection to be directed at categorical boundaries and at systemic shortcomings, then the source of reflectivity should emerge from those very same ambiguous or liminal categories. Stated differently, it is through liminal states that we come to know ourselves and our world, to know how we know, and to reflect on our own interpretative processes.[23] It is the liminal, betwixt-and-between position of Midrash as a discursive practice that makes it self-reflexive.

There are few instances in which Midrash employs self-reflectivity as an explicit trope – that is, where actual (i.e., visual) reflection takes place. One

[21] Levinson, *Twice-Told Tale*, 184.

[22] As described by Joshua Levinson, "Dialogical Reading in Rabbinic Exegetical Narrative," *Poetics Today* 25 (2004), 524.

[23] As Kenneth Burke writes (*Language as Symbolic Action: Essays on Life, Literature and Method* [Berkeley: University of California Press, 1968], 24), it is through "the reflexive capacity to develop highly complex symbol systems *about* symbol systems that humans act upon themselves and others."

of the rare occurrences of such a trope is found in relation to Abraham where it appears in a crucial point in the unfolding of the biblical plot. The book of Genesis tells us that soon after Abraham reached his destination, the famine in the land of Canaan forced him to leave once again, this time for Egypt (although it is not clear if he should have succumbed to this difficulty). His share of hardships was not yet complete. Crossing the geographical border, Abram was confronted with another set of boundaries – namely, those that define him as a sovereign male vis-à-vis Pharaoh. As the biblical narrative tells it, he decides to give up his wife in order to save his life. Midrash, as one can well imagine, found this point troubling in the father-of-the-nation's biography (as did earlier readers of the text). In turn, Midrash provided its own retold version in which reflection – and self-reflectivity – is granted a pivotal role:

> They (Abram and Sarai) went. As they arrived at the pillars of Egypt and stood at the Nile, Abraham saw the reflection of Sarai in the river, and she was like a radiant sun. From this our sages learned that all women compared to Sarai are like monkeys compared to human beings. He (Abram) said to her: "Now I know that you are a beautiful woman" (Genesis 12:11). From here one learns that prior to that he had not known her as a woman. He said to her: "The Egyptians are immersed in lewdness as it is written 'whose members are like those of asses' (Ezekiel 23:20). Therefore I will put you in a casket and lock it, since I am frightened for myself that the Egyptians will see you." (*Tanḥuma*, printed edition, *Lek lᵉka*, p. 50)

This short narrative is produced to explain the verse in Genesis 12:11: "As he was about to enter Egypt, he said to his wife Sarai, 'Now I know that you are a beautiful woman.'" Surely, having been married to Sarai, he would have noticed her beauty before! The exegetically anchored anecdote addresses this apparent quandary by providing a reflective episode that transforms Abraham's (self) knowledge as well as the ensuing biblical plot. According to this midrashic tale, owing to his piety, Abraham had never actually seen his wife prior to this event, implying that he had also never known her in the biblical sense. Struck by her radiance – and possibly even knowing her (as he states: "now I *know* that you are a beautiful woman") – he immediately understands that her overwhelming beauty may put him in danger because the Egyptians, realizing that she is his wife, will kill him. To be sure, the added tale seeks not only to answer the seemingly odd phrasing, "*Now* I know what a beautiful wife you are," but also to mitigate Abram's dubious act of hiding his marital status. This exegetical move therefore should be seen in the context of an array of exegetical attempts – found in Scripture itself and in early commentaries (including rabbinic) – to answer the questions that the biblical story of Abraham in Egypt leaves open.[24] After all, as Avigdor Shinan and Yair Zakovitch suggest, there are hints in the biblical tale itself that betray a competing tradition, one in which Abram's arguably cowardly conduct resulted in Sarai's becoming Pharaoh's wife.[25]

According to the *Tanḥuma* narrative, it was a moment of transformative epiphany, possibly coupled with shock, that drove Abram to preventive measures – which, according to this retelling – did not result in setting up Sarai as his sister. Here, the reflective moment – Abram literally sees his wife's reflection in the river – implies new awareness on Abram's part, one that informs his next moves. Although Abram does not see his own reflection but rather Sarai's, it is nevertheless a moment of actual reflection that transforms not only her identity (as she is perceived by her husband) but his too. In this sense, it could be said to be self-reflective for it brings about Abraham's new self-perception as a husband of a desirable woman. More than that, however, the reflective gaze evokes the recognition of desire itself: it is when Abram's desire for his wife surfaces that he becomes wary of the lustful Egyptians.

Desire and danger thereby become the rationale that drives the midrashic narrative. Identity, narrative, and – most important – Midrash, as this example teaches us, are inextricably connected to self-reflection. Self-reflectivity, it tells us, informs not only the identity of the figures in the tale but also governs the identity of the text, motivating its chain of events. In the most basic sense, the mirroring moment is a crucial point in the tale on which hang the identities of the evolving figures and the text as a whole. This short tale connects self-reflectivity with Eros, which comprises an animating force that motivates the figure and his actions as well as a force that determines the identity of the figure and the "identity" of the entire tale. Moreover, the actual moment of reflection is coupled here with Abram's citing Ezekiel: reflection and midrashic intertextual hermeneutics (i.e., the textual self-reflexivity) are – as this transformative moment demonstrates – inextricably connected.

The Midrash cited is not unique in its search for a transformative moment in the troubling biblical plot. Let us take a brief look at the *Genesis Apocryphon* – that is, a fragmentary Aramaic text discovered at Qumran, ca. first century

---

[24] See Kugel, *Traditions of the Bible*, 271–2.
[25] Avigdor Shinan and Yair Zakovitch, *That's Not What the Good Book Says* [in Hebrew] (Tel Aviv: Yedioth Ahronoth and Chemed Books, 2004), 205–11.

B.C.E., which consists of first-person narratives by figures from Genesis. The *Apocryphon* suggests that it was a dream that was the transitional point:

> I, Abram, dreamt a dream, on the night of my entry into Egypt. And in my dream I saw a cedar and a palm tree ... [...] Some men arrived intending to cut and uproot the [ce]dar, and to leave the palm-tree by itself. But the palm-tree shouted and said: "Do not hew down the [ce]dar, because both of you are from root ... " And the cedar was saved thanks to the palm-tree, and was not [hewn down.] [*blank*] I woke up from my slumber during the night and said to Sarai, my wife: "I have had a dream [and] I am alarmed [by] this dream." She said to me: "Tell me your dream so that I may know it." And I began to tell her the dream, [and I told her the interpretation] of th[is] dream. [I] sa[id:] " ... they want to kill me and leave you alone. This favor [o]nly [must you do for me]: in every place (we reach, say) about me: 'He is my brother.' And I shall live under your protection and my life will be spared because of you." (1QapGen XX)[26]

The *Apocryphon* belongs to the Second Temple genre of the "rewritten Bible" and, as such, it tells a continuous narrative.[27] That is, even if its underlying exegetical motive is to comment on the existing Scriptural story, it nonetheless presents itself rhetorically as an independent, self-contained tale. In the previous passage, Abraham recounts his story as a first-person narrative. The narrative is thus granted authority by his own first-hand testimony, and it is through revelation – in a dream – that Abram is informed of the impending danger and resorts to extreme measures. It is here that the authority of the narrative and the authorization of its protagonist's acts converge: the narrative is, as it were, directly revealed by a witness, who retells a long, successive narrative, and who in turn is granted a divine revelation via a dream. Unlike the rabbinic Abram, the *Apocryphon*'s Abram does not and cannot (given the epistemology of the narrative) cite verses.

It may be that the peculiar image of the palm and the cedar that appears in the dream alludes to Psalms 92:13, "The righteous bloom like a date-palm; they thrive like a cedar in Lebanon." However, rhetorically, the *Apocryphon* text is devoid of scriptural references. It is not surprising that we find the explicit Scriptural reference in a later rabbinic source, *Genesis Rabbah* (40 [41]: 1), which – when comparing Abram and Sarai with a palm and a cedar – cites the Psalm. This may be a case where rabbinic interpretation makes use of a repository of themes and motifs handed down from earlier times,

[26] *The Dead Sea Scrolls Study Edition*, eds. Florentino García Martinez and Eibert J. C. Tigchelaar (Leiden, the Netherlands: Brill, 1997), vol. 1, 41–2.

[27] The term *rewritten Bible* was coined by Geza Vermes, *Scripture and Tradition in Judaism* (Leiden, the Netherlands: Brill, 1961).

adapting them to a midrashic discourse. The rabbinic tradition may point to the implied exegetical kernel in the earlier *Apocryphon*. However – and this is a key point for understanding the midrashic enterprise – the citational, intertextual rhetoric of Midrash is not to be taken merely as an external device designed to create an impression of pseudo-exegesis. The explicit exegetical marker of Midrash epitomizes a new epistemological premise. Accordingly, Abraham of the Midrash is a reflective figure who echoes the very reflexivity that characterizes Midrash as an exegetical discourse.

The rabbis engaging in Midrash, unlike their predecessors in Scripture itself or in the Second Temple period, present us with a garment whose seams are sewn (at least partly) on the outside: the midrashic Abram is a construct of explicit intertextuality. Just like his makers (i.e., the rabbis), he himself is a reflective figure whose reflectivity involves Midrash (i.e., he cites Ezekiel). That Midrash, a pivotal premise of rabbinic culture, reverberates in its projected image of the forefather should not come as a surprise because consulting the Torah, as discussed previously, was an act of God Himself at the foundational moment of Creation. The deep and by no means cynical (or naïve) understanding of Scripture as an overarching hermeneutical key – which would have been shared by different communities of the Second Temple period – is carried out by Midrash in an explicit form of interpretation. This provides the rabbinic enterprise with a distinctive intertextual rhetoric that stages the rabbis and their biblical protagonist as reflective figures – subjects who are, like Midrash itself, "betwixt and between." They are, *mutatis mutandis*, reenacting the very moment of Creation where it was God who read the Torah in order to create the world. Because the Midrash is also quick to note that the Torah is among the things created before the Creation of the world, it is God Himself who operates "betwixt and between." The self-reflective cosmos that the rabbis imagine – and which they stage in the self-reflexive practice of Midrash – thus stretches out from the divine to the human, from Creation to rabbinic exegesis.

7

Interpretation in the Early Church

Richard A. Layton

What benefit might an interpreter of Genesis obtain from the text's reception by early Christian readers? One would scarcely turn to Christian readers in an effort to reconstitute an original audience of Genesis, given that they were intellectually informed by a Platonist worldview, socially constituted by diverse Gentile communities, and textually dependent on the Septuagint translation. At the same time, early Christian interpreters stand quite distant from the community of contemporary scholarship. As Hans Frei has detailed, almost all interpreters before the modern period understood themselves to participate within "a single cumulative and complex pattern of meaning" that rendered the reality of Scripture concrete and actual for the believer.[1] This precritical stance, as Frei called it, alienates the ancient Christian readers as far from today's scholars as they were from the Jewish readers of Late Antiquity.

This chapter situates the call and migration of Abraham in early Christian interpretation within the horizon of reception criticism. Reception criticism proposes to make interpretive use of all reader experiences, even readers alienated by cultural and temporal distance from the original production of the work. The aim in doing so is to generate an interpretive dialogue that expands the potential range of meaning that a contemporary reader might obtain from a text. This mode of engaging texts bears significant implications for how concepts of text, of reader, and of interpretation might be conceived. Consequently, the effort to expand the interpretive dialogue necessitates reflection on the reading process and the agents involved in that activity.

---

[1] Hans W. Frei, *The Eclipse of Biblical Narrative: A Study in Eighteenth- and Nineteenth-Century Hermeneutics* (New Haven, CT: Yale University Press, 1974), 16–37, quote from p. 33.

THEORIES OF RECEPTION

Reception criticism refers, in general, to an array of reader-oriented interpretive strategies that situate a text's meaning in a dialogue of readers.[2] Concern with the experience of a reader or an audience is not new. The monastic practice of *lectio divina*, for example, aimed to draw the reader through the "lowly" (*humilis*) words of Scripture to its exalted (*sublimis*) meaning. Gregory the Great gave especially concise (and oft-quoted) expression to this theory: Scripture "transforms the heart of the reader from earthly desires to embrace celestial realities." The divine text "assists the soul of the reader by lowly words, lifts it to lofty meanings, [and] in some way grows with those who read it."[3] Didactic theories of poetry abounded through the Renaissance and into the Enlightenment, in which apologists for literature touted the imaginative potency of the "speaking picture of poetry" to clarify the moral vision of the soul.[4] Confidence in the transformative power of literature, whether secular or sacred, sustained attention to both the written effects that might induce such change and the necessary habits that lifted the reader to a higher condition.

Interest in the experience of the reader waned in the modern era, a trend capped by formalist criticism that detached the meaning of a literary work from the effects it had on an audience. A chief concern of the mid-twentieth-century formalist New Criticism was to ground interpretation on objective criteria to ensure validity of literary meaning independent of any particular situation. Within this framework, a critic who confused a poem with its

---

[2] I use the term *reception history* to incorporate perspectives that can originate either from "reader response" (*Wirkungsästhetik*) or "reception" (*Rezeptionsgeschichte* or *Rezeptionsästhetik*) theoretical vantage points. Numerous attempts have been made to identify a secure distinction between the two (for a discussion, see Robert C. Holub, *Reception Theory: A Critical Introduction* [London/New York: Methuen, 1984], x–xiv). For a survey of the diverse forms that reader-oriented theories of interpretation can take, see *The Cambridge History of Literary Criticism, Volume 8: From Formalism to Poststructuralism*, ed. Raman Selden (Cambridge: Cambridge University Press, 1995), 255–403.

[3] Gregory the Great, *Moralia in Job* 20.1.1 (CCSL 143.1003), a passage subsequently quoted by bishop Taio of Caesaraugustana (PL 80.790C) and Smaragdus of Saint-Mihiel, *Diadema monachorum* (PL 102.597). For a similar view of the ability to ascend to celestial realities through the reading of Scripture, see Augustine, *On Christian Doctrine* 2.7.

[4] See Robert L. Montgomery, *The Reader's Eye: Studies in Didactic Literary Theory from Dante to Tasso* (Berkeley: University of California Press, 1979) (quote from Philip Sidney's *Apology for Poetry* on p. 121). For theoretical interest in the mental reactions of the audience in the Enlightenment, see idem, *Terms of Response: Language and Audience in Seventeenth- and Eighteenth-Century Theory* (University Park, PA: The Pennsylvania State University Press, 1992).

results – that is, its impact on the reader – committed the "affective fallacy." The affective fallacy was problematic because it began with an attempt to "derive the standard of criticism from the psychological effects of poem" and ended "in impressionism and relativism."[5] A critic who fell prey to this confusion – or to its companion, the "intentional fallacy" – found that the "poem itself, as an object of specifically critical judgment, tends to disappear."[6] The task of the critic was to produce an interpretation that held persistent and objective meaning across time and culture, independent from the intention of the author or the understanding of any individual reader.

The pivot to the reader in reception theories takes aim at precisely this "platonizing" conception of a poem outside of time, and places temporality at the heart of a text's identity and meaning.[7] In an essay first published in 1970, and which subsequently proved seminal to reception studies, Stanley Fish attacked the "affective fallacy fallacy" by conceiving the text as a temporal rather than a spatial entity. Instead of interpreting a spatial text consisting of marks, units, and patterns that occupy a page, the reception-oriented critic views all of the reader's mental operations (of which Fish provided a long list) as integral to the meaning of a sentence, a verse, or a narrative, "even though they take place in the mind, and not on the page." This type of analysis opposes the notion that "meaning is located (presumed to be imbedded) *in* the utterance, and the apprehension of meaning is an act of extraction." Instead, the nature and location of meaning are both configured as an event: "something that is happening between the words and in the reader's mind, something not visible to the naked eye but which can be made visible (or at least palpable)" to the critic.[8]

Fish's challenge to formalism did not simply put the spotlight on the reader; it also presented the text as an event rather than a static entity. This challenge operates on two axes. The first is defined by how the critic defines the mode of existence one assigns to a text (its "ontology"). The second axis, complementary to and intersecting with the first, is defined hermeneutically: what is the nature of a text's "meaning," where is it located, and how does an interpreter access that meaning? In subsequent decades, Fish probed further along the ontological axis, whereas in Europe, the catalyst for a reader-centered

---

5   W. K. Wimsatt, Jr., *The Verbal Icon: Studies in the Meaning of Poetry* (Lexington: University of Kentucky Press, 1954), 21.

6   Ibid.

7   See "Interview: Hans R. Jauss," *Diacritics* 5 (1975):53–63, p. 53.

8   Stanley Fish, "Literature in the Reader: Affective Stylistics," in idem, *Is There a Text in This Class? The Authority of Interpretive Communities* (Cambridge, MA: Harvard University Press, 1980), 21–67, quotes from pp. 26–8 (emphases in original). The essay, which Fish subsequently described as an "early manifesto," originally appeared in *New Literary History* 1 (1970), 123–62.

model of criticism centered initially on the second hermeneutical axis. In a provocative inaugural address at the University of Constance in 1967, Hans Robert Jauss issued a manifesto charting a new course for literary theory.[9] Proposing a middle way between a historically isolated formalist aesthetic and a historically sensitive but crudely deterministic Marxism, Jauss argued for a literary history that assigned the reader an essential role for critical assessment of a work's aesthetic value and meaning. This "aesthetics of reception" entailed a new "paradigm" in Jauss's estimation by prompting critical attention to center on a realm of experience previously subordinated – if addressed at all – by theorists and historians.[10] Jauss's provocation to literary theory opened new directions, especially in Germany, in the following fifteen years, encouraging the development of historically conscious reader-oriented theories that turned away from formalist modes of analysis.[11] Reception study, however, began to be eclipsed by poststructuralist theories in the 1980s and continued to decline throughout the rest of the twentieth century.[12] The precipitous decline of *Rezeption* as a method in literary theory, nevertheless, only reflects part of the story and not necessarily the most important part. Even if the aesthetics of reception did not represent the new paradigm as Jauss once hoped, the critical questions introduced by reception theorists have spread throughout the disciplines of the humanities and stimulated general attention to the importance of considering the historically situated condition of interpreters and interpretation.[13]

[9] Hans Robert Jauss, "Literaturgeschichte als Provokation der Literaturwissenschaft," in idem, *Literaturgeschichte als Provokation* (Frankfort: Suhrkamp, 1970), 144–207 (translation: Hans Robert Jauss, *Toward an Aesthetic of Reception*, translated by Timothy Bahti [Theory and History of Literature, 2; Minneapolis: University of Minnesota Press, 1982], 3–45).

[10] Hans Robert Jauss, "Paradigmawechsel in der Literaturwissenschaft," *Linguistische Berichte* 3 (1969), 44–56, positioned the emerging *Rezeptionsästhetik* as analogous to a scientific revolution. For a critique of this claim, see Holub, *Reception Theory*, 2–12; Rolf Kloepfer, "Escape into Reception: The Scientist and Hermeneutic Schools of German Literary Theory," *Poetics Today* 3 (1982), 47–75. Jauss defended his view of a paradigm shift in Rien T. Segers, "An Interview with Hans Robert Jauss," *New Literary History* 11 (1979), 83–95.

[11] Robert Holub ("Reception Theory: School of Constance," in *Cambridge History of Literary Criticism, Vol.* 8, 321) judges that Jauss's "Provocation" essay "was certainly the single most important document for the movement which came to be known as reception theory."

[12] See the essays collected in *Zur Reception der Rezeptionstheorie*, eds. Dorothee Kimmich and Bernd Stiegler (Berlin: Berliner Wissenschafts Verlag, 2003), especially Walter Erhart, "Aufstieg und Fall der Rezeptionsästhetik: Skizzenhaftes zu einer Wissenschaftsgeschichte der Literaturtheorie in Deutschland," 19–38, and Rainer Warning, "Von der Rezeptionäshetik zum Dekonstruktivismus," 63–78.

[13] Sven Strasen, *Rezeptionstheorien: Literatur-,sprach-, und kulturwissenschaftliche Ansätze und kulturelle Modelle* (Trier, Germany: Wissenschaftlicher Verlag Trier, 2008) proposes to develop a revised model of reception that incorporates linguistic elements. The contribution of reception to diverse fields is captured by two valuable recently collected studies, *Reception*

Reception criticism intersects, at least potentially, with the interpretation of biblical texts through two separate paths, distinguished by the character and function of the "reader" under investigation. In biblical studies, the primary use of reception has been to place critical attention on the discursive strategies encoded within biblical texts.[14] In this case, the recipient in view is the reader as ideally envisioned by the author, or an "implied reader." Such a reader is a function of the text and is differentiated from the real readers who might subsequently encounter a work. By contrast, the study of actual readers in the "history of exegesis" of biblical texts has primarily been the provenance of the church historian rather than the biblical scholar. Conceived of as the "after-life" (*Nachleben*) of the text – rather than as a constituent element of the text's life – historical exegesis often reflects the concerns of church historians with the development and authority of ecclesiastical institutions and theology. The modern drive to document Christian biblical exegesis began in post–World War II France with Jesuit scholars, most prominently Henri de Lubac and the future cardinal, Jean Daniélou. As part of the revitalizing movement of the *nouvelle theologie*, Lubac and Daniélou were concerned that Catholic thought had become dominated by a theology that emphasized an inherent and universal logic to doctrine over historical development. Lubac and Daniélou spearheaded a reassessment of early Christian hermeneutics – particularly championing the validity of figural interpretive techniques – and also helped to promote the publication of source texts, the *Sources Chrétiennes*, by which secular and ecclesiastical, lay and scholarly readers might encounter early Christian exegesis. For Lubac and Daniélou, the celebration of the achievements of early Christian exegetes was directed toward a spiritual renewal of contemporary Christian life.[15]

In the United States, study of the history of exegesis has branched into several different streams. Elaine Pagels sought to retrieve marginalized readings that challenge the hegemony of ecclesiastical authorities over the theological appropriation of canonical texts.[16] In a somewhat different vein, Elizabeth

---

    Study: From Literary Theory to Cultural Studies, eds. James L. Machor and Philip Goldstein (London: Routledge, 2001), and *Classics and the Uses of Reception*, eds. Charles Martindale and Richard F. Thomas (Oxford, UK: Blackwell Publishing, 2006).

[14] See, e.g., Bernard C. Lategan, "Coming to Grips with the Reader in Biblical Literature," *Semeia* 48 (1989), 3–17.

[15] Charles Kannengiesser, *Handbook of Patristic Exegesis: The Bible in Ancient Christianity*, Vol. 1 (Leiden, the Netherlands: Brill, 2004), 7–15, provides a valuable history of the emergence of exegesis as a field in the study of early Christianity. See ibid. pp. 35–7 for the establishment of *Sources Chrétiennes* and p. 39 for history of the valuable English translation series, *Ancient Christian Writers* and *Father of the Church*.

[16] Elaine Pagels, *Adam, Eve, and the Serpent* (New York: Random House, 1988); "Exegesis of Genesis 1 in the Gospels of Thomas and John," *Journal of Biblical Literature* 118 (1999), 477–96.

Clark brought to view the work that exegesis performed for ascetic Christians in antiquity to produce a meaning of biblical texts that reduced the distance between the injunction to "be fruitful and multiply" and the value that these church leaders placed on renunciation. Beyond documenting this exegetical enterprise, Clark seeks to accord readers a "more positive role in the production of meaning" than previous critical paradigms. In Clark's view, the exegesis of the early church deserves study for its success in creating meanings that "shaped moral and religious values for centuries to come." From this perspective, all exegesis is ideologically inflected, and biblical criticism should expand its scope to include a "sociology of interpretation" that can elucidate the interaction of reading strategies with a wider cultural agenda.[17] As does Clark, Gary Anderson has endeavored to include readers in the production of Scriptural meaning. Anderson protests against the "common modern prejudice" that subsequent elaborations of Genesis are "something like useless clutter in the attic." Critics should instead recognize a proper domain for the traditional readings in Jewish and Christian communities that connect biblical narratives to a lived religious life.[18] As these diverse approaches to reception indicate, including the reader's experience as a constitutive element in the meaning of a text does not result in a single prescription for interpretation. Study of the text's reception can promote an exegetical dialogue of present readers with the past, but that dialogue does not reach a conclusive ending.

Two basic claims underlie the diverse spectrum of reception theories. The first, as discussed previously, is that the impact of a literary work on the reader is an intrinsic part of the text's meaning. The meaning of a work is not contained in either its formal units or the conditions of its production but rather is constituted as an event in its appropriation. The second claim concerns the structure of this event. The act of appropriation between text and recipient does not occur in an unconstrained, random, or speciously subjective manner. A written text anticipates a reader; thus, reading is already prefigured into the production of a text. Reciprocally, the reader responds to the scheme that the texts present. The production of meaning, consequently, is necessarily an intersubjective process. Moreover, readers always encounter a text from a situated perspective that is conditioned socially and linguistically. Any interpretive process takes place embedded within a horizon that contextualizes and limits the experience of reading but also provides the indispensable field

---

[17] Elizabeth A. Clark, *Reading Renunciation: Asceticism and Scripture in Early Christianity* (Princeton, NJ: Princeton University Press, 1999), quotes from pp. 5, 371, 373.

[18] Gary A. Anderson, *The Genesis of Perfection: Adam and Eve in Jewish and Christian Imagination* (Louisville, KY: Westminster John Knox, 2001), 9–18.

in which a reader connects the text to other elements in his or her experience and adjusts that vision in response.

A brief glance at a minor but well-known textual ambiguity can introduce the intersubjective structure that characterizes interpretation. How old is Isaac at the *aqedah*? There is, of course, no explicit designation in Genesis 22. Isaac is referred to as a "boy" (*na'ar*, 22:5), but he is also able to carry the wood for the sacrifice up the mountain (22:6) and to pose an acute question to his father (22:7).[19] Nonetheless, if a reader (or an artist) is to visualize the scene, it is necessary to represent both father and son with specific characteristics (e.g., a gray beard, a careworn visage, a smooth face, youthful limbs, and well-developed muscles) that pertain to males at distinct phases of life. Moreover, how a reader or an artist construes these features subtly influences the broader interpretation of the sacrifice. The typical depiction in ancient iconography of Isaac as significantly smaller than Abraham conveys an impression that the father would have the power to subdue his son (were it necessary). By contrast, Josephus lays it to the son's credit that although he was a full-grown man, he was determined to accede to the will of both God and his father.[20] Josephus bears witness to a long-standing tradition that Isaac's willing acceptance of the divine decree merits God's approval as much as Abraham's readiness to offer his son.[21] At least some medieval mystery plays contradicted this view and cast the victim as a mere child, piteously evoking the compassion of the audience for the innocence of youth.[22]

In whatever manner Isaac is visualized and however that determination might be justified, the mere necessity of this act points to a reciprocal dynamic between the structure of the text and its appropriation by a reader. To employ the terminology of Wolfgang Iser, the absence of an age designation for Isaac points to a narrative "gap" or degree of "indeterminacy" that stimulates the

---

[19] The term *na'ar* covers a wide range of ages: both the infant Moses (Exodus. 2:6) and seventeen-year-old Joseph (Genesis 37:2) are designated by this term.

[20] See, e.g, the fourteenth-century *Egerton Genesis*, f. 13r [12r], in which Isaac is depicted as a young child playing a children's ball-and-stick game (Mary Coker Joslin and Carolyn Coker Joslin Watson, *The Egerton Genesis* [London: British Library, 2001], p. xxv). See, more generally, Isabel Speyart Van Woerden, "The Iconography of the Sacrifice of Abraham," *Vigiliae Christianae* 15 (1961), 214–55; Joseph Gutmann, "The Sacrifice of Isaac in Medieval Jewish Art," *Artibus et Historiae* 8 (1987), 67–89; and E. van den Brink, "Abraham's Sacrifice in Early Jewish and Early Christian Art," in *The Sacrifice of Isaac: The Aqedah (Genesis 22) and its Interpretations*, eds. Ed Noort and Eibert Tigchelaar (Leiden, the Netherlands: Brill, 2002), 140–51.

[21] Josephus, *Ant.* 1, 227 (cf. *Targum Pseudo-Jonathan*, which identifies Isaac as thirty-seven at the *aqedah*). Further examples are provided by James L. Kugel, *The Bible as It Was* (Cambridge, MA: Harvard University Press, 1997), 174–6.

[22] For medieval mystery plays, see Minnie E. Wells, "The Age of Isaac at the Time of the Sacrifice," *Modern Language Notes* 54 (1939), 579–82.

reader to "concretize" the scheme that the text presents.[23] The recognition that texts evince gaps has a long history in literary criticism. Indeed, Erich Auerbach's famous description of the *'aqedah* as "fraught with background" enunciates this same principle as a distinctive aesthetic feature of biblical narrative.[24] Nevertheless, Iser goes beyond the occasional identification of a gap as an interpretive crux or aesthetic device to assign significance to indeterminacy as the "fundamental precondition" for the participation of the reader and, consequently, "the most important link between text and reader."[25]

The phenomenon of textual indeterminacy, in Iser's view, points to the necessity of the reader to constitute the meaning of a text. Is the action of such a reader, however, something like the performance of a musical score, such that the reader enacts the directions offered by the text? If so, how does the reader know how to perform this score? Addressing this underlying issue, Stanley Fish has proposed that an adequate understanding of reading has to consider the social nature of interpretation, which he expresses in terms of the notion of "interpretive communities." Interpretive communities consist of those who share "interpretive strategies," whether or not those members have any other institutional connection. An interpretive community exists prior to the act of reading, and the reader is imprinted with these strategies before encountering a printed page. It is through the constitutive properties set in place by a community that a reader – to continue with the musical analogy – performs the score; or, to adopt Fish's own dictum, knows "how to recognize a poem when you see one." Consequently, Fish dismisses Iser's depiction of the process of reading as an act of "disinterested" perception. He insists that "interpretive strategies are not put into execution after reading" but instead "are the shape of reading, and because they are the shape of reading, they give texts their shape, making them rather than, as it is usually assumed, arising from them."[26] When, for example, Christian preachers in

---

[23] Wolfgang Iser, "Indeterminacy and the Reader's Response in Prose Fiction," in *Aspects of Narrative: Selected Papers from the English Institute*, ed. J. Hillis Miller (New York: Columbia University Press, 1971), 1–45; "The Reading Process: A Phenomenological Approach," in Iser, *The Implied Reader: Patterns of Communication from Bunyon to Beckett* (Baltimore, MD: The Johns Hopkins University Press, 1974), 274–94; idem, *The Act of Reading: A Theory of Aesthetic Response* (Baltimore, MD: The Johns Hopkins University Press, 1978), 180–203.

[24] Erich Auerbach, *Mimesis: The Representation of Reality in Western Literature* (Princeton, NJ: Princeton University Press, 1968), 8–12.

[25] Iser, "Indeterminacy," 14, 43; *Implied Reader*, 279f., *Act of Reading*, 170–9.

[26] Fish, *Is There a Text in This Class*, 168. Fish develops his critique of Iser more extensively in Stanley Fish, "Why No One's Afraid of Wolfgang Iser," *Doing What Comes Naturally: Change, Rhetoric, and the Practice of Theory in Literary and Legal Studies* (Durham, NC: Duke University Press, 1989), 68–86.

antiquity expounded the Creation narrative each year during the Lenten season, they executed an "interpretive strategy" that linked God's sovereignty over the material elements directly to the moral life of their parishioners. The liturgical reading of the "six-days' work" enacted the Creation narrative as a continuing moral reality. If textual meaning is understood as an event, then in these communities the meaning of Genesis 1 was inseparable from this ecclesiastical discipline. The interpretive community gave, as Fish says, the "shape" to the reading of the text; reciprocally, however – as Fish does not seem fully to recognize – the act of reading brought to visibility and defined the interpretive community.

Reception criticism, in summary, examines the experience of the reader in constituting meaning and the "situatedness" of that reader within wider communities. A history of reception traces the indeterminacies readers perceive, on what basis they address them, and how they connect these indeterminacies to other textual features within wider interpretive horizons. Just as no reader exists outside of an interpretive community, so also no gap or indeterminacy is resolved in isolation of other interpretive presuppositions that the reader brings to the experience of the text. The notion of an interpretive "horizon," which Jauss put at the center of his aesthetics of reception, gives interpretive force to this recognition.[27] Horizons of expectation and experience situate the reader concretely within a field of vision that limits the visible terrain but also allows the reader to forge a coherent and unified sense of all the objects within that field. Moreover, just as a horizon moves in tandem with the movement of the viewer, bringing both new objects into view and offering new perspectives on already visible objects, in the same way the interpretive horizon moves along with the interpretive community. A reception history attempts to delineate the emergence, divergence, and joining of interpretive horizons. The case of Abraham's journey to Canaan from Haran illustrates the way such horizons both develop from and help to shape interpretive communities.

THE CALL AND MIGRATION OF ABRAHAM

At the outset of Genesis 12, God instructs Abraham, "Go from your country and your kindred and your father's house to the land that I will show you." The patriarch then departs from Haran "as the Lord had told him" (Genesis 12:1, 4). Several gaps, or indeterminacies, confront a reader who attempts to

---

[27] See, e.g., Hans Robert Jauss, "The Identity of the Poetic Text in the Changing Horizon of Understanding," in *The Identity of the Literary Text*, eds. Mario Valdés and Owen Miller (Toronto: University of Toronto Press, 1985), 146–74; Hans Robert Jauss, "Horizon Structure and Dialogicity," in idem, *Question and Answer: Forms of Dialogic Understanding*, ed. and trans. Michael Hays (Minneapolis: University of Minnesota Press, 1989).

connect this seemingly simple reportage to the preceding narrative. Genesis 11:31 indicates that Abraham's father, Terah, previously moved the clan, including Abraham and his wife, from their homeland in Ur of the Chaldeans (cf. Genesis 11:28) to Haran. Why does God's command intervene only after this first move? If the patriarch's journey from Haran is motivated by divine instruction, what prompted the first migration from the ancestral home? Moreover, is not the command to depart "your country" superfluous because Terah had already made that move at his own initiative? A reader who looks beyond these surface gaps might inquire into the apparent lack of motivation for the call. The narrative provides no previous indication of Abraham's distinction, such as the designation of Noah as "blameless in his generation," who found "favor in the sight of the Lord" (Genesis 6:8f).

These potential indeterminacies provided the basis for the interpretation of the call and migration in both the synagogue and the church in antiquity. These indeterminacies, however, were never addressed in isolation but rather in connection with other thematic elements, from which different horizons of interpretation could emerge. One horizon of reception in antiquity, exemplified by the elaborate expansion of the Genesis narrative in the book of *Jubilees*, emphasized the patriarch as an exemplar of Torah loyalty in the midst of an alien culture. For *Jubilees*, the migration is both a testament to and a consequence of Abraham's monotheistic loyalty to the God of Israel. Even as a boy, in this telling, Abram is sensitive to the damage that idolatry and "pollution" induce in his childhood home of Ur, and he goes so far as to separate from his father to avoid being implicated in idol worship. The boy Abram begins to pray to the "Creator of all" – not known yet by name – to protect him from "errors of mankind" so that he might not "go astray after impurity and wickedness."[28] In a scene widely dispersed throughout Jewish and Christian tradition, *Jubilees* represents Abram's conflict with the false gods as reaching a head when he burns down a local shrine. This incident motivates the first move of the family, from Ur to Haran; however, *Jubilees* does not include another widespread tradition, which held that the residents of Ur attempted reprisals against Abram and his family.[29]

---

[28] *Jubilees* 11.16–17. I quote the translation of James C. Vanderkam, *The Book of Jubilees* (Louvain, Belgium: Peeters, 1989), 67.

[29] See *Jubilees* 12.12–14, with the departure for Haran in 12.15. For the legend of the attempt to burn Abram in reprisal, see *Liber antiquitatum biblicarum*, 6, *Bereshit Rabbah* 38.13. On the place of Abraham in the furnace in Jewish tradition, see Geza Vermes, "The Life of Abraham (I)," in *Scripture and Tradition in Judaism* (Leiden, the Netherlands: Brill, 1973), 67–95. On the transmission of the story in Christian tradition, especially via Jerome, see C. T. R. Hayward, *Saint Jerome's Hebrew Questions on Genesis* (Oxford, UK: Clarendon Press, 1995), 146f. The legend also features in Quranic tradition: 1. Sura 21, verses 51–74, esp. verses 68–70; 2. Sura 29, verses 24–5; and 3. Sura 37, verses 83–98, esp. verses 91–8.

This geographical move spurs on the continued personal theological quest of the patriarch to discover the identity of the creator God. This quest reaches fulfillment in Haran, when during a night vigil, Abram prays for guidance from the "Most High God," asking "shall I return to Ur of the Chaldeans who are looking for me to return to them? Or am I to remain here in this place? Make the path that is straight before you prosper through your servant so that he may do (it)." Immediately, the response from God comes to the patriarch, "Now you, come from your land, your family, and your father's house to the land which I will show you."[30]

This voluminous expansion of the biblical narrative positions the call as the culmination of a struggle on the patriarch's part rather than as the initiation of God's relationship to him. God's call comes only at the end of decades of proven devotion, as Abram demonstrates himself as a loyal monotheist in a land of idolaters.[31] At one level, the elaborate narrative of Abram's youth fills the indeterminacy perceived in the lack of an explicit cause for the migration from Ur to Haran. *Jubilees* instills in the space between the two migrations the revelatory moment that culminates the patriarch's spiritual quest. At a more programmatic level, *Jubilees* situates Abraham within an interpretive horizon that thematically connects the call of the patriarch to an identity that is deeply interwoven with both the land of Israel and Torah observance as constitutive of his identity. He indeed may have arrived in Canaan as an alien but, with his final breath, the dying Abraham praises God Most High, "the Creator of everything who brought me from Ur of the Chaldeans to give me this land in order that I should possess it forever and raise up holy descendants so that they may be blessed forever" (*Jubilees* 25.27). For *Jubilees*, Abram is not simply a recipient of the promises fulfilled in Israel; he is an exemplar of Torah loyalty in the midst of the nations, a point that is further accentuated by having the patriarch revive the language of Hebrew and observe the feast of Booths and the laws of first fruits.[32] Abraham's relationship to the land and to the precepts of the Torah seals his relationship to the "Creator of all" and is therefore the destination and purpose of God's summons to the patriarch.

The horizon of *Jubilees* indissolubly links the patriarch's quest to the national identity of Israel. A second profile emerged that realigned the thematic connections among Abraham's call, the land, and Israel's national

---

[30] *Jubilees* 12.21–22 (trans. Vanderkam, p. 72).

[31] For a similar representation of Abraham's monotheistic piety as resulting in God's call, see Josephus, *Antiquities* 1.154–168, with the nuanced discussion of Annette Yoshiko Reed, "Abraham as Chaldean Scientist and Father of the Jews; Josephus *Ant.* 1.154–168, and the Greco-Roman Discourse about Astronomy/Astrology," *Journal for the Study of Judaism* 35 (2004), 119–58.

[32] *Jubilees* 12.25–27, 15.1, 16.21.

as "righteous" because of the patriarch's belief, even before the circumcision (Genesis 15:6). Abraham, Paul declared, "received the sign of circumcision as a seal of the righteousness that he had by faith while he was still uncircumcised." As a result, the patriarch is "the ancestor of all who believe without being circumcised" and, likewise, "the ancestor of the circumcised . . . who also follow the example of the faith that our ancestor Abraham had before he was circumcised" (Romans 4:11–12). In this way, Paul placed faith as the principle of Abraham's righteousness in tension with the covenant of circumcision.[37]

This contest in the missionary Gentile communities over the inheritance of the promises was not a Jewish–Christian debate; it occurred within the confines of the Church. Paul and his rival Judaizing missionaries both saw themselves as implementing God's promise that in Abraham "all the tribes (*phulai*) of the earth shall be blessed" (Genesis 12:3). The dispute concerned the means by which the covenant established between God and Abraham might be extended to the foreign nations. In this debate, the call did not come explicitly into view, and it was only after Church authorities adopted the Pauline position that the broader Abraham tradition was integrated into Christian thought and literature. Nevertheless, Paul's insistence on "faith" as the defining character of Abraham's "righteousness" (Genesis 15:6) rippled through subsequent Christian interpretation. When the writer of the epistle of James sought to counter potential excesses of Pauline fideism, he did not balance Abraham's faith with the seal of circumcision. He rather argued that the patriarch's obedience to God's command to sacrifice his son demonstrated the perfection of that faith; consequently, "a person is justified by works and not by faith alone" (James 2:14–24).

The inseparable union of faith and obedience is likewise at the center of what might be the earliest Christian document to adduce explicitly Abraham's migration. In a catalogue of the heroes of faith, the writer of the letter to the Hebrews celebrates Abraham's obedience "when he was called to set out for a place that he was to receive as an inheritance; and he set out, not knowing

(Minneapolis, MN: Fortress Press, 1991), 125–46, and idem, *The Theology of Paul's Letter to the Galatians* (Cambridge: Cambridge University Press, 1993), 64–101 (both developing E. P. Sanders' concept of "covenantal nomism"); J. Louis Martyn, "Events in Galatia: Modified Covenantal Nomism versus God's Invasion of the Cosmos in the Singular Gospel: A Response to J. D. G. Dunn and B. R. Gaventa," in *Pauline Theology*, 160–79.

[37] One might contrast Ben Sira 44:19f, which posits a direct continuity among the covenant (Genesis 15), the certifying of the covenant in the flesh (Genesis 17), and the patriarch's faithfulness in testing (Genesis 22).

where he was going" (Hebrews 11:8). The inheritance that the patriarch sought is the same enjoyed by all the saints:

> They confessed that they were strangers and foreigners on earth. . . . If they had been thinking of the land that they had left behind, they would have had opportunity to return. But as it is, they desire a better country, that is, a heavenly one. Therefore God is not ashamed to be called their God; indeed, he has prepared a city for them. (Hebrews 11.13–16)

The patriarch's departure from Haran does not traverse ordinary ground; it is the beginning of an ascent to the heavenly kingdom. Abraham's migration sets the type for all who accept status on earth as an "exile" or "resident alien."[38] *1 Clement*, written (as Hebrews was) before the end of the first century C.E., sounds a similar note: "Abraham, who was called 'the friend,' proved faithful in obeying God's words. It was obedience which led him to quit his country, his kindred, and his father's house, so that, by leaving a paltry country, a mean kindred, and an insignificant house, he might inherit God's promises" (*1 Clement* 10.1f).

For Hebrews and *1 Clement*, as previously for Philo, Abraham's migration becomes a paradigmatic act of renunciation, a moment of detachment from worldly goods that opens the philosopher–saint to celestial benefits. The patriarch becomes less the forerunner of a nation and more the titular saint of a people that eschew nationhood, who claim their foreignness as their distinctive mark.[39] This emerging horizon found expression in both literal and allegorical modes of explication. Preaching on this passage of Hebrews, the Antiochene orator John Chrysostom presented Abraham's departure from Haran as literally accepting exile in this world. "Did they mean only," he asked rhetorically, "that they were strangers from the land that is in Palestine? Not at all! They were strangers in respect to the whole world, and rightly so." God, Chrysostom declared, instructed Abraham, "leave what appears to be your homeland, and go to the one that seems foreign." The patriarch, he continued, "did not cling to possessions, but since he was going to leave the land he regarded as foreign, so also he endured it without attachment."[40]

The Alexandrian exegete, Origen, echoed Philo's allegorical reading of the migration. He filtered his interpretation through Jesus' challenge to his interlocutors in the Gospel of John: "If you are children of Abraham, do the

---

[38] See 1 Peter 1:1, 2:11; *Letter to Diognetus* 5:5.

[39] For a recent discussion of this motif, see Benjamin H. Dunning, *Aliens and Sojourners: Self as Other in Early Christianity* (Philadelphia: University of Pennsylvania Press, 2009), 46–63.

[40] John Chrysostom, *Hom.* 24.2 *in Hebrews* (PG 63.168).

deeds of Abraham!"[41] For Origen, this command represents a challenge to all believers to live up to their Abrahamic heritage. What then are the "deeds of Abraham" that Jesus commands his followers to imitate? The command, Origen holds, to depart from country, kin, and land is

> said not to Abraham alone but to whoever would be his child. For each of us has before the decree of God a certain country and a relative who is not good and a house of our father before the Word of God comes to us, from all of which we must depart, according to the word of God.[42]

By leaving "our land," we will arrive at the "land which God will show us, that land which is truly good and genuinely spacious" (cf. Exodus 3:8), and when we depart from those unworthy relations, "we will become a great people and greater than human fashioning."[43] This people is not defined by a national heritage but rather by their shared renunciation of the temporal benefits of this world – an Israel not of earth but of heaven. Origen's treatment of the "deeds of Abraham," although thoroughly indebted to Philo, goes beyond his predecessor. Where Philo reasoned through the benefits that the one zealous for the philosophical life could anticipate, Origen began with the direct order of Jesus. Grounded on this divine imperative, the migration becomes the *sine qua non* for being a "child of Abraham," and the life of the most authentic type of believer is an existence marked by disruption and renunciation. All other aspects of Abraham's achievement become dependent on the willingness to accept detachment from this world.

This foregrounding of the migration became a prominent interpretive horizon for Christian readers.[44] At the same time, however, the nationalist–monotheistic reading continued to find expression in Christian writers, especially in apologetic contexts. Augustine, for instance, argued that the development within history of the "city of God" obtained a new epoch with the family of Abraham. Noting that Abraham was born in the land of the Chaldeans, a place where "impious superstitions were rife," Augustine held that the family of Terah distinguished itself as the one clan "in which the worship of the one true God persisted." In a speculation that echoed the story of *Jubilees*,

---

[41] Most interpreters and translators construe John 8:39 as an unreal condition: "If you were the children of Abraham, you would do the works of Abraham." The Greek can be read also as an imperative, and Origen construes it as a command.

[42] Origen, *Commentary on John*, 20.10.67–68 (SC 290.190).

[43] Ibid., 20.68-69 (SC 290.190f.).

[44] In addition to Origen's employment of Abraham's migration in his *Commentary on John*, see Gregory of Nyssa, *Contra Eunomium* 2.85–7 (*Opera* 1.251–254); Didymus, *Sur la Genèse*, Vol. 2 (ed. Nautin) (SC 244; Paris: Cerf, 1978), pp. 136–42; Ambrose, *de Abrahamo* I.2.3, II.1.2; John Cassian, *Conl.* 3.6.

Augustine offered that "it is reasonable to suppose that the Hebrew language was preserved" only in Terah's family as well.[45]

In this way, the two horizons that emerged among Jewish readers persisted in the early Church as well; neither were the two horizons fully separated from one another. The horizons of monotheistic resistance and philosophical ascent merge in a fourth-century martyrology that looked back to the Diocletian persecution that preceded Constantine's legitimation of Christianity. The protagonists of the narrative – Agapê, Irene, and Chionê – were three "saintly women" who fled to the mountains from their home city of Thessalonikê after the initial edicts against Christianity. This saintliness is defined in terms of Abraham's renunciation of his homeland to begin his journey to God's Promised Land:

> When the persecution under Maximian had befallen, and these women had adorned themselves with the virtues and were obedient to the evangelical laws, they left their homeland, family, property, and possessions for the sake of their love for God and expectation of heavenly goods, performing deeds worthy of father Abraham.[46]

Having retreated from worldly affairs, they undertook a regime of prayer; although confined in body to the mountaintop, "they had souls that possessed citizenship in heaven."

The introduction of the three women is set against the horizon of Abraham's migration as a spiritual ascent, with an allusion to Origen's call for all believers to imitate the "deeds" of Abraham. This, however, is not the only reference to Abraham as a hero of the faith. At an initial hearing, the women hold resolutely to their monotheistic confession, after which Agapê and Chionê are consigned to the flames. Irene, remanded for a later hearing, returns to reiterate her resistance to the pagan sacrifices and echoes the confession of Abraham in dedicating her loyalty to "God Almighty, who created heaven and earth and sea and everything in them."[47] Irene's truculence merits a more severe punishment, and the prefect Dulcitius condemns her to servitude in a brothel before she, as her sisters before her, is burned alive.

---

[45] Augustine, *City of God* 16.12. I quote the translation of Henry Bettenson, *St. Augustine: City of God* (New York: Penguin Books, 1972), 670f. See also Eusebius, *Demonstration of the Gospel* 1.2 (GCS 23.7–10).

[46] "The Martyrdom of Saints Agapê, Irene, and Chionê at Saloniki," 1, in *The Acts of the Christian Martyrs*, ed. Herbert Musurillo (Oxford, UK: Clarendon Press, 1972), 280. On the dating of the account and the events in view, see the discussion of Musurillo, p. xliif.

[47] "Martyrdom," 5 (Musurillo, p. 288), cf. Genesis 14:22, Psalms 146:6, Exodus 20:11; Nehemiah 9:6; and Acts 4:24.

This martyrology merges the confessional identity of *Jubilees* with the philosophical ascent of Hebrews. The sisters' initial departure from "homeland,
family, and property" occurs within the context of persecution but is directed
toward the attainment of heavenly goods. It is the renunciation not only of
their city but also of all worldly ambitions altogether, and it provides the basis
for ascetic retreat. This migration, however, also strengthens their testimony
to God, identified in the terms of *Jubilees* as the "Creator of All," a title that
situates this as a contest between deities. Finally, we recall that in *Jubilees*,
Abraham provoked the ire of the citizens of Ur by burning their sanctuary –
an act that elsewhere in Jewish tradition was followed by an effort to burn
the patriarch. The martyrdom account of the three sisters might seem to
vary at this point. The narrator's perspective, however, presents the flames of
martyrdom as the culmination of the women's victory. These saintly women
prevailed over "invisible enemies" and the "invisible substance of demons
has been handed over to fire by women, pure and holy, filled with the Holy
Spirit."[48]

The martyrdom of Agapê and her sisters shows that the horizons for appropriating the migration of Abraham were neither fixed nor rigid. With these
fluid horizons in mind, it might be well to conclude this survey by considering
one of the most influential modern readings, that of Gerhard von Rad. Von
Rad's explication of the call centers, as in *Jubilees*, on what we might call the
"motivation gap" – the lack of an explicit reason given for why God summons
this particular individual at this particular moment. For von Rad, the sudden
intervention of God into human affairs defines a critical turning point in
Genesis and in Israel's historical self-understanding. The Yahwistic strand of
the primeval history, according to von Rad, narrates a story of "ever-growing
estrangement of man from God," which culminates in God's silence after the
dispersal of the tower builders (Genesis 11:1–9). This dark history presses an
inescapable question on the reader: does the ominous silence of God point
to a permanent retreat from engagement with humanity? Is that relationship
"now completely broken, and is God's grace finally exhausted?" The reassur-
ing ability of the reader to answer that question in the negative rests on God's
call to Abraham, the summons that simultaneously sets the patriarch on his
journey and breaks the divine silence:

> The end of the biblical primeval history is therefore not the story of the
> Tower of Babel; it is the call of Abraham in Gen. XII.1–3: indeed, because
> of this welding of primeval history and saving history, the whole of Israel's
> saving history is properly to be understood with reference to the unsolved

---

[48] "Martyrdom of Agapê, Irene, and Chionê," 1 (Musurillo, p. 280).

problem of Jahweh's relationship to the nations. . . . Gen. XII.1–3 thus teaches that the primeval history is to be taken as one of the most essential elements in a theological aetiology of Israel.[49]

In his *Old Testament Theology*, from which this quote is taken, von Rad defines the call and migration as the narrative and theological hinge on which turns the dialectic between silence and speech, judgment and grace, and God's universal sovereignty and Israel's particular vocation. In his commentary on Genesis, von Rad reiterates this salvation–historical interpretation and also expands its scope to include a moral vision of Israel's utter dependence on its God. The threefold command to leave country, kindred, and father's house indicates that "Abraham is simply to leave everything behind and entrust himself to God's guidance." In this radical demand and response, Israel recognized "a basic characteristic of her whole existence before God. Taken from the community of nations (cf. Num 23.9) and never truly rooted in Canaan, but even there a stranger (cf. Lev. 25.23; Ps. 39.12), Israel saw herself being led on a special road whose plan and goal lay completely in Yahweh's hand."[50]

This reading is both highly influential and vigorously contested.[51] My concern here is not with the adequacy of von Rad's interpretation but rather how his reading, which is motivated by a particular narrative gap, emerges within the horizons already delineated by early Christian interpreters. Von Rad's reading converges strikingly with the horizon of the migration as detachment and renunciation of Philo, Hebrews, and Origen. In von Rad's view, although Abraham is destined to journey to a new land, neither he nor Israel will ever be "truly rooted in Canaan" but instead live even in their home as a "stranger." The land is not their ultimate goal; indeed, their identity is not bound to place at all and lies only and completely in God's hands. It is true that von Rad specifically confines the existential reading of Abraham to *Israel*'s identity rather than positing a universal self divorced from communal

---

49 Gerhard von Rad, *Old Testament Theology, Vol. 1* (New York: Harper and Row, 1962), 164. Earlier quotes from pp. 160, 163, 164.

50 Gerhard von Rad, *Genesis: A Commentary*, revised edition (Philadelphia, PA: Westminster Press, 1972), 159.

51 See, e.g., E. A. Speiser, *Genesis* (Garden City, NY: Doubleday, 1964), LI, 87f. David J. A. Clines, *The Theme of the Pentateuch* (Sheffield, UK: *Journal for the Study of the Old Testament*, 1978), 77–96, by contrast, although indebted to von Rad, seeks to join the call narrative to other Pentateuchal themes. Other interpreters diverge from von Rad and deny that the dispersion of the tower builders should be read as a judgment that forms the backdrop to the call. See, e.g., Carol M. Kaminski, *From Noah to Israel: Realization of the Primaeval Blessing after the Flood* (London: T&T Clark, 2004), 80–91; and Ellen van Wolde, *Words Become Worlds: Semantic Studies of Genesis 1–11* (Leiden, the Netherlands: Brill, 1994), 104–109.

markers. Nevertheless, von Rad's Israel is one that can exist independently of land and institutions. It is an Israel that is available for appropriation by Christians; its otherness is not so distinct that it cannot be absorbed into the apparently more transcendent categories of the ethics of grace, demand, and response. Von Rad may have had no knowledge of the fluid manner in which Abraham's call could be interwoven by ancient readers into wider narratives of cultural resistance and philosophical ascent. Nevertheless, recognition of the horizonal structure of interpretation – of the extent to which the profiles of the present include the past – can alert us that biblical texts have not existed outside of broader discourses of communities of interpretation. These communities are not static or fixed but instead change over time as they respond to shifting social conditions by foregrounding new elements of their traditions.

CONCLUSION

This chapter explores the basis for regarding early Christian interpretation of Genesis as an integral element in the production of meaning. In this context, meaning is best understood as a dynamic engagement of readers with the text. Although meaning is fluid, it nevertheless persists, and the meanings that Jewish and Christian readers in antiquity identified in the migration of Abraham continue to shape the horizons in which modern readers encounter the text.

The persistence of horizons is not unique to biblical exegesis. It occurs as a function of the relationship between readers and texts. The phenomenon of indeterminacy implies that both the formal patterns encountered on a page and the intentional activities of readers are necessary to constitute a text as an object of interpretation. The readers' activities do not take place in isolation but rather are embedded in preexisting reading strategies that define interpretive communities. Finally, these communities are not static across time and neither are they necessarily unified; rather, they emerge, take shape, and change as they move within varying horizons.

Readers in antiquity responded to indeterminacies that they perceived in Abraham's call. From what "land" was Abram commanded to depart? Why did God address the patriarch only in Haran and not earlier in Ur? For readers such as the *Jubilees* composer and Philo, these narrative gaps afforded glimpses of two different horizons in which individual believers and the whole of Israel itself might obtain identity: one of a covenanted people founded in distinction from an alien culture, and a second in separation from the bondage of materiality itself to facilitate philosophical ascent to a land of contemplative blessings. These two horizons also found expression in the earliest Christian appropriation of the call narrative. Eusebius and Augustine emphasized Abraham as the founder of a monotheistic people, whereas many Christian commentators extended a conception of Abraham as a pilgrim who gave up the benefits of earthly citizenship to obtain the heavenly blessings of the Jerusalem above. Ultimately, these two horizons could be merged, as in the martyrdom of Agapê and her sisters, in which ascetic imitation of the "deeds of Abraham" became the foundation on which to imitate the patriarch's staunch resistance to false gods. As von Rad's exegesis suggests, these horizons continue to inform readers' perception of the meaning and significance of Genesis.

8

~

Translation

Naomi Seidman

The topic of translation might seem an afterthought to any discussion of Genesis, a feature not of the Bible itself but rather of its "afterlife."[1] The book of Genesis, after all, is a record of beginnings; translations, by all appearances, come only later. But Genesis "itself" and its life in translation are not so easily separated. Our understanding of what the Bible is – as a whole and in its smallest details – has been profoundly shaped by translation, even as our experience and understanding of translation owe much to the Bible and its history.

"For Europe," begins the opening essay in a recent collection on *Translating Religious Texts*, "the Bible has always been a translated book."[2] While such a statement mistakenly assumes the equivalence of Europe and Christendom, it remains the case that most of the Bible's readers – in Europe and outside of it, Jewish or Gentile – have known the Bible only in translation. The ramifications of this historical circumstance are hard to overstate. In being translated, the Bible also has been cast and recast, interpreted and rewritten: its obscurities "clarified," its strangeness domesticated, its character transformed. Such transformations, I hasten to add, are inevitable. Even texts that remain in their own languages take on different colors in different contexts and eras as words acquire new meanings and lose old ones. In translation, this process is closer to the surface because two "equivalent" words in different languages rarely overlap precisely in their range of reference. From this perspective, the

---

[1] The terms *Leben* and *Überleben* (life and afterlife) for a text and its translation come from Walter Benjamin's seminal essay on translation, "The Task of the Translator" [*Die Aufgabe des Übersetzers*], trans. Harry Zohn, in Benjamin, *Illuminations*, ed. Hannah Arendt (New York: Schocken Press, 1968), 71.

[2] Stephen Prickett, "The Changing of the Host: Translation, Transgression and Interpretation," in *Translating Religious Texts: Translation, Transgression and Interpretation*, ed. David Jasper (New York: St. Martin's Press, 1993), 4.

narrowest meaning of translation – as interlingual transfer or as the production of a linguistic equivalent – overlaps with the larger sense of translation
as cultural transfer, which encompasses the full range of transformations that
texts undergo in their movement from one cultural context to another.

THE WIND-BREATH-SPIRIT OF GOD

One translational shift that has attracted wide attention is the beautiful and
mysterious image at the end of Genesis 1:2, *wᵉruaḥ 'elohim mᵉraḥepet ʿal pᵉne
hammayim*, which might be tentatively and partially translated as "Elohim's
ruaḥ hovering on the face of the waters." *Ruaḥ* has a range of meanings, from
"wind" to its metaphorical extensions as "breath" and, at a greater distance,
"spirit" (which itself has a range of meanings).[3] Translation into Greek was
not difficult because *pneuma* has a similar range. The Latin *spiritus*, however,
begins to foreground the abstract and immaterial secondary meanings of
the Hebrew term, leaving behind the more tangible significations of wind
and breath; this process was institutionalized and reinforced by Christian
theological developments that – privileging abstraction and "spirituality"
over more concrete imagery – ultimately left behind the meanings of wind
or breath altogether. A modern translator invariably must choose among
"wind," "breath," and "spirit" in the absence of words that mean all these
things. Thus, the King James Version has "And the Spirit of God moved upon
the face of the waters," reflecting the traditional Christian understanding of
ruaḥ 'elohim as a variation of *spiritus sanctus*, evidence for such theologians
as Jerome and Augustine that the "Holy Spirit" – a dimension of the Trinity –
was present at Creation.[4] In many recent Jewish readings, *ruaḥ* is rendered as
wind, with the verb that follows sometimes understood more actively: Harry

---

[3] Harry Orlinsky denies that *ruaḥ* can mean anything other than "wind" and traces the spiri-
     tualizing translation of early Christianity to Philo's allegorical interpretation of the Bible and
     Genesis in particular. See Orlinsky, "The Role of Theology in Christian Mistranslation," in
     Translation of Scripture, ed. David M. Goldenberg (Philadelphia, PA: Annenberg Research
     Institute, 1990), 127–32. However, I am persuaded rather by Buber's formulation of the prob-
     lem, which insists that all three significations for *ruaḥ* are already present in the Bible and
     that *no* translation, Jewish or Christian, can capture the full range of *ruaḥ*. See Buber, "People
     Today and the Jewish Bible," in Martin Buber and Franz Rosenzweig, *Scripture and Trans-
     lation*, eds. Lawrence Rosenwald and Everett Fox (Bloomington: Indiana University Press,
     1994), 16–17.
[4] Jerome insists in his commentary on Genesis that the phrase refers to the Holy Spirit (*Hebrew
     Questions* 1.2). Augustine's meditation on Creation in the last part of his *Confessions* describes
     how he discerned the entire Trinity in Genesis 1:1–2:
        "And under the name of God, I now held the Father, who made these things, and under
     the name of Beginning, the Son, in whom He made these things; and believing, as I did, my
     God as the Trinity, I searched further in His holy words and to, Thy Spirit moved upon the

Orlinsky's Jewish Publication Society (JPS) version has "a wind from God sweeping over the water"; Everett Fox has "breath of God hovering over the face of the waters"; and Robert Alter has "God's breath hovering over the waters."[5]

While Jewish Bible translators have traditionally preferred wind/breath to spirit and Christians have overwhelmingly read *ruaḥ* as spirit, other proclivities have sometimes held sway: modern translators of a variety of affiliations have preferred primal and vivid imagery to established readings. Thus, the Catholic New American Bible of 1970 is perhaps less "Catholic" than "New" in having "but a mighty wind swept over the water," taking *'elohim* as a vivid adjectival intensifier rather than as a name for the divinity. Translations such as this also might be influenced by a desire to render a too-familiar text – as the beginning of Genesis certainly is – more strange. Such translations are often called "foreignizing" in opposition to "domesticating" Bibles that aim to render the text in an easily accessible language. As Friedrich Schleiermacher famously stated, translation could be conceived as working in two possible directions: "Either the translator leaves the author in peace, as much as possible, and moves the reader toward him, or he leaves the reader in peace, as much as possible, and moves the author toward him."[6] While translations that "leave the reader in peace" continue to be produced, the more interesting recent translations follow Schleiermacher's own preference for "difficult" translations that strive not only to reproduce the source language as precisely as possible but also to "move the reader toward" an appreciation for what distinguishes the text's Hebraic roots.

Such a return perhaps begins with the Hebraizing translation of Martin Buber and Franz Rosenzweig, which aimed to produce a Bible as concise and urgent as a modernist poem – or an archaic Hebrew one.[7] For Buber, who resisted the relegation of their German translation to the Jewish camp, the rendering of *ruaḥ* had ramifications that far transcended the Jewish–Christian divide. What was at stake for Buber was not whether a feature of Christian

---

waters. Behold the Trinity, my God, Father, and Son, and Holy Ghost, Creator of all creation." Augustine, *Confessions*, trans. John K. Ryan (Garden City, NY: Image Books, 1960), 339 (13.5).

[5] Harry Orlinsky, *Tanakh* (Philadelphia, PA: Jewish Publication Society, 1985 [*Torah*, 1962]); Everett Fox, *Genesis and Exodus: A New English Rendition with Commentary and Notes* (New York: Schocken, 1983); Robert Alter, *Genesis: Translation and Commentary* (New York: Norton, 1996).

[6] Friedrich Schleiermacher, "On the Different Methods of Translation" (1813), in *Translating Literature: The German Tradition from Luther to Rosenzweig*, ed. Andre Lefevere (Assen, the Netherlands: Van Gorcum, 1977), 74.

[7] Their translation, then, moved in two disparate directions: toward modernism and toward the archaic; this is less of a contradiction than might appear because modernism famously had a fascination with the archaic.

theology could or should be detected at stage-center of the Hebrew Creation narrative; rather, Buber was concerned with the erasure through translation of an ancient and more primal worldview in which "wind," "breath," and "spirit" could be thought together. In Buber's philosophical diagnosis, the translation of *ruaḥ* as spirit was both symptomatic and productive of the modern sundering of body and spirit, the material and spiritual worlds. God's breath, for the narrator of Genesis, *is* the wind, as it is also the air we breathe to live, and all of these are *also* spirit. In losing sight of *ruaḥ*, in dividing it into separate and even antithetical spheres, German (along with a host of other languages) had forgotten a crucial truth about the oneness of the divine and material realms. As Buber writes:

> since the time of Luther, who had to choose between *Geist* and *Wind*, *Geist* has lost its original concreteness – a concreteness it had in company with *ruaḥ*, with *pneuma*, with *spiritus* itself – lost its original sensory character – "a surging and a blowing simultaneously." . . . This splitting of a fundamental word is not merely a process in the history of language but also a process in the history of *Geist* and life, namely the incipient separation between *Geist* and life.[8]

Buber concludes, "I have lingered over this . . . example in order to show what guiding power can lie in a single biblical word if we will only pursue it earnestly and commit ourselves to it."[9] Following the vagaries of translation can not only illuminate the migrations of the Bible through the world but also shed light on the worlds through which the Bible has traveled. The world we live in, in many senses, was created in the image of the Bible, just as the Bible is remade in the shape and image of the world that reads it.

ORIGINALS AND TRANSLATIONS

The Bible has been transformed by its life in translation not only for those who read it in other languages. The title of this collection is evidence that translation has shaped the understanding of the Bible even for those (e.g., contributors to volumes on Bible criticism) who work closely with the Hebrew text: the term *Genesis*, standard in academic literature, is an artifact not of the Hebrew but of the Greek text.[10] "Genesis" is the Greek title of the opening volume of the Pentateuch, found in manuscripts of the translation known as

---

[8] Buber, *Scripture and Translation*, 16–17.
[9] Ibid., 17.
[10] That the traditional Hebrew name for the book *Bereshit* makes reference as well to beginnings is a coincidence – whereas the Greek term describes the content of the book, the Hebrew term is, as with all other books of the Bible, the first word of the book.

the Septuagint (or LXX, for its seventy or seventy-two legendary translators). From these beginnings, it made its way into a host of other translations and into academic terminology. However, it is not only the title of the book that derives from a translation. The very notion of a *book* of Genesis refers to a phrase found only in translation: the LXX rendering of Genesis 2:4, which concludes the story of the Creation, has Αὕτη ἡ βίβλος γενέσεως, "This is the *book* of the genesis of (the heavens and the earth)"; the Hebrew text, by contrast, has *'elleh tol^e dot*, אלה תולדות, "This is the genealogy of." Although it is not always possible to determine why a Hebrew version and a Greek version differ, the consensus view is that the Greek addition of the word *biblos*, or book, in Genesis 2:4 represents an accurate translation of a now-lost ancient Hebrew scribe's "harmonization" of this verse with the Hebrew of Genesis 5:1, which introduces the Adamic genealogy with the phrase *zeh seper tol^e dot 'adam*, "this is the *book* of the genesis/genealogy of Adam."[11] Here, as elsewhere, a copyist made the text more consistent, symmetrical, and "perfect," producing a version of 2:4 that better matched a similar formulation in 5:1. Because this harmonization survived only in its Greek translation, the later Greek (but not the Hebrew) readers of Genesis had before them the very *book* of Creation, and so it has remained in our cultural memory.

Even this brief foray into the territory of what scholars call "ancient versions" has already signaled some of the complexities of the field. In the case of the word "book" (*biblos*) in the LXX Genesis 2:4, the Greek is readily explained as a translation of a secondarily expanded Hebrew text that has not survived. However, this sort of explanation, in which the translation represents a later moment in a text's development, is not always the case. Because any extant manuscript represents a snapshot of a single moment in a continually evolving textual tradition with many branches – some of them now lost or missing at crucial interstices – it is not at all uncommon for biblical scholarship to rely on translations for establishing *earlier* and "more authentic" texts than Jewish tradition has supplied. Thus, the Masoretic text – as the Hebrew text preserved in Jewish circles is known – has an awkward gap in the Cain and Abel story: "And Cain said to Abel his brother and when they were in the field Cain rose up against Abel his brother and slew him" (Genesis 4:8). "And Cain said to Abel his brother" seems to introduce speech – as indeed it does at all other points in the story – but no speech follows. Scholars have filled this lacuna

---

[11] For a discussion of the harmonization in Genesis 2:4, see Ronald S. Hendel, *The Text of Genesis 1–11: Textual Studies and Critical Edition* (New York: Oxford University Press, 1998), 122. On harmonization, see ibid., 81–5, and Emanuel Tov, "The Nature and Background of Harmonizations in Biblical Manuscripts," *Journal of the Study of the Old Testament* 31 (1985), 3–29.

with the help of ancient versions: the Septuagint, the Peshitta, the Palestinian Targums, the Vulgate, and the Samaritan text all supply the words נלכה השדה, "let us go down to the field," with the Samaritan text in Hebrew and the others with Greek, Syriac, Aramaic, and Latin equivalents.[12] In such cases, the overwhelming evidence points to the hypothesis that a portion of the Hebrew text was accidentally omitted at some point in its transmission. Here, textual criticism "corrects" the text, through translations and other ancient versions, toward a more "original" version. This "correction" of the Biblical text, it is worth pointing out, often operates through a kind of reverse translation by which critics attempt to reconstruct the *Vorlage* – the now-lost Hebrew text – that stood before the eyes of the translators. The "original," in such textual reconstruction, emerges from the retroversion, or "back-translation," of a translation or translations. Original and translation, in brief, are not always so easy to distinguish.

The arcane operations of biblical criticism have profound implications for cultural understandings of the Bible. The Bible in Western civilization has a singular force, represented as a book that can be bound and put on a bookshelf, on which an official can place a hand to take the oath of office, and from which a preacher can substantiate theological claims. Even the most superficial acquaintance with its textual history, however, demonstrates that such a notion of "the Bible" is a cultural construction, if a powerful and grounding one. I do not mean merely to insist that all translation is also interpretation or to argue against those who base their authority on "the literal meaning" of the Bible, or on "the Bible itself," while nevertheless reading it only in translation. My point is rather that the Hebrew "original" is, in many senses, *also* a translation, which may be another way of saying that we have no Hebrew original, no single unitary text.[13] There is much evidence that the compilers and the redactors who composed the Bible had little interest in supplying such a unitary text: the text of the Bible as it has come down to us is not only not "an original," it is also evidence of a redactional creed that, as Marc Zvi Brettler has said, "did not create a purely consistent, singular perspective but incorporated a variety of voices and perspectives"[14]; and this is particularly true of the narratives of Genesis. Nevertheless, if the original is also a translation, as I argue, the translation is also in some sense "an

[12] Hendel, *Text*, 46–7.
[13] See Hendel (*Text*, 114) about dating the "original text" of the Pentateuch to its "publication" by Ezra in Nehemiah 8, which interestingly is also the beginning of translation if one reads *mᵉpораš* (Nehemiah 8:8) as translation into Aramaic; see n. 17.
[14] Marc Zvi Brettler, "Introduction," *The Jewish Study Bible*, eds. Adele Berlin and Marc Zvi Brettler (New York: Oxford University Press, 2004), 7.

original." Translators inevitably create new texts in incorporating cultural meanings available in their own language. This, too, is just one aspect of a larger process of "rewriting" that is everywhere present in the biblical corpus.[15] As Robert Alter shows in his contribution to this book, the redaction of the Bible is no simple stitching together of prior texts but rather a thoughtful integration that is sensitive to literary and narrative issues. To the recognition of the role of the redactor in producing the biblical text as we know it we must add an appreciation of the translators who have given us, and continue to give us, the Bible anew. The problem of translation, then, is no modest appendix to the real questions that compel the attention of students of the Bible. Translation, once its kinship with other modes of textual transmission – redaction, "rewriting," and commentary – is recognized, reaches to the very heart of the nature and function of the Bible in Western culture.

Translation is intricately connected to the Bible in a larger, more philo-sophical sense, from the outset to our own day. More than other documents of antiquity, the Bible continues to hold meaning for contemporary readers, maintaining and often increasing its status as sacred text. Its reception, in other words, is critical to its cultural meaning, and translation is a powerful lens for comprehending and appreciating the astonishing reception of the Bible in the world. The international reach of what is, after all, a motley, composite text of a minor group of no great size or importance in either antiquity or the two millennia since has largely depended on translation. Indeed, the history of translation acquires much of its drama and meaning from its involvement with the Bible.[16] The first great translation enterprise of antiquity was the translation of the Bible into Greek, an enterprise whose sacred and even miraculous nature is recorded in countless Late Antique nar-ratives beginning with *The Letter of Aristeas* (second century B.C.E.). Even the Bible seems to view itself, at the moment of its publication in Nehemiah, as bound with its translation. Michael Alpert writes: "The first historical report of translation is in the Bible itself," in the phrase in Nehemiah 8:8 that reports that the Jewish exiles who returned from Babylon in the sixth century B.C.E. "read from the book of the law of God clearly [$m^e poraš$], made its sense plain and gave instruction in what was read" (New English Bible 1970).[17] The JPS

[15] The notion of "rewriting," and of translation as one mode of rewriting, derives from André Lefevere's groundbreaking work, *Translation, Rewriting, and the Manipulation of Literary Fame* (London: Routledge, 1992).

[16] For a theological reading of the "discipline" of translation, on the translator as "empty channel," and translation and taboo, see Douglas Robinson, *The Translator's Turn* (Baltimore, MD: Johns Hopkins University Press, 1991).

[17] Michael Alpert, "Torah Translation," in *Routledge Encyclopedia of Translation Studies*, ed. Mona Baker (London and New York: Routledge, 1998), 269. Alpert does not acknowledge

states this even more bluntly, translating 8:8 as "They read from the scroll of
the Teaching of God, translating it and giving the sense; so they understood
the reading." Whether or not this passage should be understood as describing
an oral Aramaic translation of the Torah, as the Midrash and the JPS do, it is
clear that the fate of the Bible from early in its history – indeed, from before
it reached its canonical form – was bound with translation. Despite his deep
attachment to the Hebrew original, Franz Rosenzweig put it more dramatically when he suggested that the Bible became the Bible only in translation.
As he wrote in a 1917 letter:

> Translating is after all the actual goal of the mind [Geistes]; only when
> something is translated has it become really *audible*, no longer something
> to be disposed of. Not until the Septuagint did revelation become entirely at
> home in the world.[18]

In Rosenzweig's view, translation is not a purely textual operation but rather
a form – perhaps the paradigmatic form – of human speech, partaking of the
openness to another voice, the unpredictable give-and-take, the intimacy and
richness of living conversation. Without translation, texts have no existence,
just as the isolated thought of an individual only begins to mean something
when it is heard. Here, Rosenzweig's view stands in some tension not only
with his own insistence that Jews must encounter the Bible in Hebrew but
also with the views of Buber, his co-translator, who often saw the history of
Bible translation in the West through a rhetoric of loss, in which primary
Hebraic meanings had been buried under theological abstractions and empty
formulations.

The history of Bible translation, as the differences between Buber and
Rosenzweig (and within Rosenzweig's thought, as well), has been a fraught
one – perhaps appropriately, for an enterprise that is inevitably doubled or
split. For all the historical associations of the Bible with translation, the status
of the Bible as a uniquely sacred text has raised questions about the possibility and status of its translation. The very stories that accord the translations
of the Bible sacred status and describe them as perfect also signal an ill-
concealed anxiety on this score. The Bible is the book in which translation
finds its surest and most continual aim, but it is also the book – the exemplary

that his is a midrashic reading of the verse (taken from Babylonian Talmud *Megillah* 3b) and
that few scholars take Nehemiah 8:8 as historical evidence of translation in that period –
the word means "clearly" or "distinctly." See Michael Fishbane, *Biblical Interpretation in
Ancient Israel* (Oxford, UK: Oxford University Press, 1985), 109; and Joseph Blenkinsopp,
Ezra-Nehemiah (London: SCM Press, 1989), 288.

[18] Franz Rosenzweig, Letter of 1 October 1917 to Rudolf Ehrenburg, quoted in Barbara Galli,
Franz Rosenzweig and Jehuda Halevy: Translating Translations and Translators (Montreal:
McGill–Queen's University Press, 1995), 322.

"original" – for which translation represents the greatest loss or embarrass-
ment, potential or actual. If Bible translation is magically perfect in many
legendary formulations, then it is so because it must be; only this peculiar
efficacy of Bible translation ensures that the new forms it takes in translation
will be as authoritative as the old. Translation – fundamental or secondary,
perfect or flawed, miraculous or purely human – lies at the ambivalent heart
of the Bible as we have known it in the world.

IN THE BEGINNING

The tension in biblical studies between an original that is already a translation
and a translation that is (or poses as) an original is already at its most acute in
the very first verses of Genesis. Genesis begins "in the beginning"; in fact, the
opening chapters have commonly been taken as a description of the very first
moments and events of the universe. Such a reading of Genesis as describing
Creation *ex nihilo*, however, is heavily influenced for English speakers by the
famous first line of the best-known English translation. In Hebrew, what Genesis 1:1 is describing has been much more difficult to establish. The translation
of the first verse as "In the beginning God created the heavens and the earth"
reflects what Hendel called "the postbiblical forgetting" of the meaning of
the term, which is not an absolute but rather a construct statement: "in the
beginning of (God created)," or "in the beginning, when (God created)." The
construction may have been misunderstood because of its archaic form. As
Hendel says:

> The classical Hebrew construction, which is attested but rare, has a literary
> effect here, beginning the account in an unusual and seemingly archaic
> register of speech. This colors the account as "above" normal speech – more
> formal, ancient, and authoritative.... The postbiblical "forgetting" of the
> classical Hebrew construction eventually gave rise to the idea of creation out
> of nothing (*creatio ex nihilo*) in Genesis 1.[19]

Not all commentators understood Genesis 1:1 as describing an absolute
beginning. The medieval exegete Abraham ibn Ezra – impelled as much by
contemporary scientific views of an eternal universe as by grammatical sensitivity – indeed understood the biblical Creation story as teaching "the orderly
transformation of preexistent matter into an environment suitable for human
life."[20] Alter's translation follows this understanding: "When God began to

---

[19] Ronald Hendel, *Genesis 1–11: A Commentary* (manuscript in progress).
[20] For a discussion, see Nina Caputo, *Nahmanides in Medieval Catalonia: History, Community,
and Messianism* (Notre Dame, IN: University of Notre Dame, 2007), 61–2.

create heaven and earth, and the earth then was welter and waste." A consensus among scholars and translators has emerged supporting these readings. Genesis as a book that begins "In the beginning" is thus increasingly only a product of translational tradition. In "the original" text, and increasingly in new translations, this absolute beginning is rather more difficult to discern.

The Creation story also has been traditionally understood to be a beginning in another sense, as an original document of Israelite monotheism. Comparative biblical scholarship has upended the notion of this text as itself emerging *ex nihilo*. The Bible openly acknowledges Abraham's Mesopotamian origins, and the text itself attests to the Near Eastern cultural milieu from which it emerged and diverged. As is well known, the Creation story borrows from ancient Near Eastern mythology, and the Garden of Eden and Flood stories have striking parallels with the epic of *Gilgamesh* (elements of the Flood story are found as well in the earlier Mesopotamian *Atrahasis*, parts of which were incorporated into *Gilgamesh*). E. A. Speiser asserted that "on the subject of creation biblical tradition aligned itself with the traditional tenets of Babylonian 'science' . . . [although] since the religion of the Hebrew diverged sharply from Mesopotamian we should expect a corresponding departure in regard to beliefs about creation."[21] The writers of Genesis drew freely, then, from prevailing cultural assumptions while maintaining a separate religious identity. However, in adapting ancient Near Eastern stories and deities into Israelite stories, Genesis provides a narrative of Creation that conceals as much as it hints at its literary precursors. To express this otherwise, the Bible derives literary power from translating the narratives of other (rival) cultures while retaining its formidable status as exemplary *original*. In this regard, the Bible is no different from other translations, and Israelite culture is no different from its precursors and counterparts. While taking the Bible as primary evidence, Willis Barnstone describes this process as an inevitable feature of cultural development:

> The existence of the earlier source is neglected, rejected, or suppressed and, out of apparent void, a fresh god, temple, or scripture appears self-created. Thus translation historically denies itself in order to create originals. In sum, *translation is frequently a historical process for creating originals.*[22]

Barnstone's case may be more difficult to make with the "new gods" and Scriptures of Christianity, in which Jewish precursors are readily acknowledged even as they are reread. For readers of the Hebrew Bible, however, the

[21] E. A. Speiser, *The Anchor Bible Genesis: Introduction, Translation, and Notes* (Garden City, NY: Doubleday, 1964), 11.
[22] Willis Barnstone, *The Poetics of Translation: History, Theory, Practice* (New Haven, CT: Yale University Press, 1993), 141 (emphasis in the original).

emergence of biblical narrative from Mesopotamian literary and religious precursors was not part of the interpretative tradition until recently. As the book
of the Creation and the genealogy of the Israelites and their religion, Genesis
owes more to translation than it or its readers have generally acknowledged.

THE TOWER OF BABEL

Translation is not only inextricable from the book we are referring to as
Genesis, it is also a subject of Genesis. Along with all the other geneses
described in the book – the creation of the universe, the creation of man and
woman, the origins of Israel – is a description of the genesis not of language,
which seems to preexist or accompany God's creation, but rather of languages
in the plural – that is, of the conditions that make translation necessary. It
is no coincidence that the Tower of Babel story provides the titles and cover
illustrations of so many books about translation. The Babel story offers an
explanation for the multiplicity of tongues that makes translation necessary. It
does so, moreover, in the context of a dramatic story of transgression, punishment, and the disastrous effects of the breakdown of communication. It may
thus describe not only translation but also its difficulty or even impossibility:
having deliberately "confused" human languages, God may not care for the
efforts of those attempting to undo the effects of his punishment.

George Steiner, in *After Babel,* takes the story as evidence that the ancient
world recognized and appreciated – much more than moderns do – the sheer
strangeness of the phenomenon it comes to explain, the profligate – and horrifying – overabundance of linguistic diversity. In contrast with the palpable
pleasure taken by the Creation narrative in the diversity and plenitude of
species and other natural phenomena, the abundance of languages is incomprehensible and pointless, even appalling. Speaking of the immense variety
of natural languages, Steiner asks:

> What can possibly explain this crazy quilt? How are we to rationalize the fact
> that human beings of identical ethnic provenance, living on the same terrain,
> under equal climatic and ecological conditions, often organized in the same
> types of communal structure, sharing kinship systems and beliefs, speak
> entirely different languages? What sense can be read into a situation in which
> villages a few miles apart or valleys divided by low, long-eroded hills use
> tongues incomprehensible to each other and morphologically unrelated?[23]

The answer to this question, Steiner writes, can scarcely lie in a Darwinian
scheme of "adaptive variation and selective survival," since the multiplicity

[23] George Steiner, *After Babel: Aspects of Language and Translation* (Oxford, UK: Oxford University Press, 1998 [1975]), 56.

of languages impedes rather than aids survival. "Time and again," he writes, "linguistic differences and the profoundly exasperating inability of human beings to understand each other have bred hatred and reciprocal contempt."[24] Such a bewildering, frustrating multiplicity could only have come about either as tragic accident or intentional punishment, as Steiner categorizes the two strands of the Babel myth ubiquitous in folklore. The Genesis version – appropriately for an Israelite worldview that privileges moral consequences over random fate – takes the second path.

However, Steiner's reading of the myth as a divine punishment for the sin of hubris – a reading held by many ancient and modern commentators – is difficult to square with Genesis 11, in which the intent to storm heaven is at most implied by the description of their desire to build a tower $w^e ro'šo$ $baššamayim$, "whose head is in the heaven," and by God's apprehension that the builders in fact may succeed in this or some other regard. The builders proclaim only, "Come, let us build us a city and a tower, whose top may reach unto heaven; and let us make us a name, lest we be scattered abroad upon the face of the whole earth." *Genesis Rabbah*, perhaps in implicit recognition that the sin of the builders remains curiously unspecified, piles detail onto detail about the precise sin of the builders of the tower. Taking a cue from God's worry that the tower signifies unlimited human capacities, *Genesis Rabbah* describes the builders as opening a war with heaven. It begins, however, by an acknowledgment that the biblical text itself is silent on that score: "Rabbi Eliezer said that the actions of the Generation of the Flood were revealed [to us in the Scriptures], while the actions of the Generation of the Tower of Babel were not." The Midrash goes on to extrapolate these actions from a play on the close associations between $d^e varim$ '$aḥadim$, "uniform words," and $d^e varim$ $ḥadim$, "sharp words":

> "With *uniform* words" – They made *sharp* remarks concerning "The LORD our God, the LORD is one ... " They would say, "Who is he that he chooses the heavens for himself and gives us the earth!? Come, let us build a tower and construct an idol on its top, and place a sword in its hand, so that it appears to be doing battle with him." (*Genesis Rabbah* 38:6)

The sin of Babel is no doubt a terrible one, but in these and other readings, the rabbis acknowledge that the story as it stands fails to provide its own justification for the divine punishment it describes. They do so, moreover, by piling a midrashic wordplay on the phrase $d^e varim$ '$aḥadim$ on top of the biblical wordplay of the name Babel, suggesting that even the initial stage of

---

[24] Ibid., 58.

linguistic uniformity described in Genesis 11 easily gives way to the semantic multiplicity that the Midrash takes as its own shifting foundation.

That the Tower of Babel story is an etiological tale laying out the origins for the multiplicity of languages is clear enough. But is "the confusion of tongues" divine retribution, as many assume, or is it rather divine intervention because the Lord feared that "If, as one people with one language for all, this is how they have begun to act, then nothing that they may propose to do will be out of their reach" (11:6, JPS)? This act of God, whether punishment or preemption, is strangely circular, veering between poetic justice (i.e., seeking to go beyond their proper limits, humans are pushed back) and tautology (i.e., seeking to avoid dispersion, humans are dispersed). The circularity of the events is complicated as well by the verse in the preceding chapter (Genesis 10) that calmly describes the clans and families of Noah's descendents, with their separate tongues, as *already* dispersed. The penultimate line of Genesis 10 reads: "These are the descendants of Shem according to their clans *and languages*, by their lands, according to their nations" (10:31, JPS; emphasis added).

"The City Coat of Arms," Kafka's rewriting of the Babel story, is a close reading of Genesis 10 and 11 in placing interpreters at the beginning of the narrative, before the construction has begun:

> At first all the arrangements for building the Tower of Babel were charac-
> terized by fairly good order; indeed the order was perhaps too perfect, too
> much thought was given to guides, *interpreters*, accommodations for the
> workmen, and roads of communication, as if there were centuries before
> one to do the work in.[25]

Kafka's tone is matter-of-fact here, the very voice of Genesis 10 in recording the existence of multiple tongues before Babel; however, in some ways, this calm vision is darker than the biblical Babel narrative of a primordial unity shattered by transgression and penalty: If the multiplicity of tongues is the preexisting and eternal condition, then hope for its amelioration or reversal may be more difficult to sustain. In this light, divine punishment becomes as much a fantasy or wish as the primordial existence of one shared human language. After all, if the confusion of tongues is God's punishment, we may still repent and find our way back to mutual understanding. In fact, Kafka's story ends with the builders of the city of Babel yearning for a punishment that will signal the existence of a divine overseer and perhaps the rhyme and reason of what they suffer: "All the legends and songs that came to birth in

---

[25] Kafka, *The Complete Stories*, ed. Nahum Glatzer (New York: Schocken Press, 1971), 433 (emphasis mine).

that city are filled with longing for a prophesied day when the city would be destroyed by five successive blows from a gigantic fist."[26]

The reading of Genesis 10 and 11 as a disturbed sequence is not universal. Along with other Bible commentators, Umberto Cassuto insisted that no problem with order should be seen here: Genesis 9 through 11 are thematically and linguistically united in their telling the story of the dispersion of the sons of Noah; the repeated line in Genesis 10, "each with his own language" or "by their languages" (vv. 5, 20, 31), serves "to draw the attention of the reader to the problem [of the multiplicity of languages], and to prepare him to peruse with curiosity what is related in the next chapter."[27] Whether or not one accepts Cassuto's reading, it is nevertheless remarkable that in the very telling of the origins of linguistic multiplicity, a prior origin – in which this multiplicity is *already* there – is offered. The postmodern destabilization of the orderly sequence of "original → translation" reappears here in another form, upending the orderly sequence "one tongue → many tongues" at the very moment that this sequence is first inscribed.

The modern philosopher most responsible for unsettling the stable distinctions between such foundational oppositions as original/translation is, of course, Jacques Derrida, who himself reads the Tower of Babel story, although with a slightly different point in mind. Derrida focuses on the narrative as a performance and enactment of the impossibility of translation, an impossibility parallel to the impossibility of building stable (cultural, philosophical, and political) structures or of establishing for once and for all "a name for oneself," as language forever, and unsuccessfully, attempts to do. Translation is impossible in part because no original exists or rather because the original – the unitary language of Hebrew Genesis, for instance – is already a translation. The weight of Derrida's reading rests heavily on the central word in the narrative, Babel, which means confusion and represents and enacts confusion, as a Babylonian–Hebrew bilingual pun. Derrida cracks open the linguistic scene of Babel by asking, to begin with, "In what tongue was the tower of Babel constructed and deconstructed?" He answers:

> In a tongue within which the proper name of Babel could also, by confusion, be translated by "confusion." The proper name Babel, as a proper name, should remain untranslatable, but, by a kind of associative confusion that

---

[26] Ibid., 434. It is worth noting that the coat-of-arms of Prague, Kafka's hometown, depicts a closed fist, among other images.

[27] Umberto Cassuto, *A Commentary on the Book of Genesis*, trans. Israel Abrahams (Jerusalem: Magnes Press, 1964), 144.

a unique tongue rendered possible, one thought it translated in that very tongue, by a common noun signifying what *we* translated as confusion.[28]

As Derrida later points out, bilingual puns, which already embody an accomplished translation, are themselves resistant to translation. To state this another way, because translation can proceed only from the foundation of a single tongue, multilingual texts – of which this is a prime example – are untranslatable. Unlike common nouns, which are generally seen as translatable from one culture to another, the proper name "retains a singular destiny, since it is not translated in its appearance as a proper name." As such, Derrida notes, a proper name "does not strictly belong . . . to the language, to the system of the language," although proper names are also fundamental to any sense of language. "The Babelian performance," as Derrida refers to the Genesis 11 narrative – in which the central term remains both inside and outside of the structure of translation and meaning – presents the system of language *already* in collapse. As such, it is an accurate description of the human linguistic condition, presenting a chimera of solid construction and the stability of linguistic meaning even as it demonstrates the impossibility of this fantasy. God subjects the people of Babel, Derrida writes, "to the law of a translation both necessary and impossible."[29]

For Derrida, I should point out, the paradoxical nature of translation as necessary and impossible reflects as well on the instability of language in the singular (although Derrida sees linguistic multiplicity as inescapable and the notion of one language as an unrealizable if ever-beckoning ideal). In fact, the vision of a single, primal, shared tongue is as much a legacy of the Babel story as that of a confused and disastrous multiplicity of languages. The prophets spoke of a world in which all humanity worshiped God in a single tongue, reversing the Babel story in a divine prophecy: "For then I will make the peoples pure of speech, So that they invoke the Lord by name, and serve Him with one accord" (Zephaniah 3:9). Acts 2 similarly records a miraculous translation event at Pentecost in which people of different ethnicities could understand each other's speech; patristic writers have described the Pentecost event as a transcendence of the punishment of Babel in the Holy Spirit. Translation, in these intrabiblical readings of Genesis, appears as a miraculous vision, a messianic dream reversing the disaster of Babel.

[28] Jacques Derrida, "Des Tours de Babel," trans. Joseph Graham, in *Difference in Translation*, ed. J. Graham (Ithaca, NY: Cornell University Press, 1985), 166. The English translation of Derrida's essay appears on pp. 165-207; the French original appears on 209–248.

[29] Ibid., 174.

THE LANGUAGE OF JAPHETH

For the rabbis who compiled *Genesis Rabbah* – unlike the prophets, the Church fathers, and modern philosophers – the Tower of Babel story seems to have excited no metaphysical speculation, no messianic visions. The Midrash fills out the comedy of miscommunication that explains just exactly how it is that the confusing of the tongues resulted in the halting of the Babel construction project:

> "Come let us confound their language." When one said to another, "Bring me water," he brought him earth. Whereupon the one cracked the other's skull. When one said to another, "Bring me an ax," he brought him a spade. Whereupon the one cracked open the other's skull.[30]

The story seems to fall, for *Genesis Rabbah*, into farce rather than tragedy, a route Kafka followed in his own reconstruction of the Tower. To the extent that the rabbinic literature of Late Antiquity connects Bible translations with biblical narrative, it does so largely by finding warrant for the Greek translation of Aquila (a translation done under their aegis) in a passage just two chapters earlier than the Babel story – indeed, the first of the three chapters Cassuto reads as part of the narrative unit describing the dispersion of Noah's sons:

> May God enlarge Japheth (*yaft 'elohim l^e-yefet*)
> And may he dwell in the tents of Shem (9:27)

It is Noah's blessing, which the Midrash read as ethnic taxonomy and political prophesy rather than God's curse at Babel, that concerns humankind *in toto*, that elicits the most pointed rabbinic thinking on translation:

> Bar Kappara said: May the words of the Torah be spoken in the language of Japheth in the tents of Shem. R. Judan said: From here we have a biblical source [allowing] for translation [of the Torah].[31]

This same passage was also understood as referring not only to linguistic tent-dwelling but also to the conversion of Greeks to Judaism. Thus, *Targum Pseudo-Jonathan* renders Genesis 9:27 in Aramaic as "May the Lord enlarge the borders of Japheth and they will convert and dwell in the study houses of Shem."[32] Only through proper conversion to rabbinic Judaism (or through

---

[30] *Genesis Rabbah* 38:10 (Theodor-Albeck edition).

[31] *Genesis Rabbah*, 36:26–27 (Theodor-Albeck edition). Although the discussion follows a verse in Nehemiah that seems to permit translation, the Rabbis prefer a verse from the Pentateuch as prooftext in matters of Jewish law.

[32] *Targum Pseudo-Jonathan: Text and Concordance*, ed. E. G. Clark (Hoboken, NJ: KTAV Press, 1984), 10.

the allegory of translation) could such inter-ethnic converse be imagined, either in their time or in some messianic future in which the attractions of Judaism would be widely apparent.

The Babylonian Talmud's discussion of the permissibility of translating the Torah mobilizes the midrashic allegory of Japheth as an embodiment of the beauty of the Greek language:

> Rabban Shimeon ben Gamliel said: The books also may not be written [in any language] other than Greek. R. Abbahu said in the name of R. Yohanan: The law is according to Rabban Shimeon ben Gamliel. R. Yohanan said: What was Rabban Shimeon ben Gamliel's reasoning? It says, "May God enlarge Japheth and he shall dwell in the tents of Shem." But what of Gomer and Magog? R. Hiyya bar Abba said: This is the reason; it says: "May God enlarge Japheth," the beauty of Japheth in the tents of Shem. (Babylonian Talmud *Megillah* 9b, Vilna edition)

The question raised about Gomer and Magog – two children of Japheth other than Javan, who is traditionally seen as the ancestor of the Greeks – is a pertinent one: how do we know that of all the children of Japheth, it is the Greeks who are the reference of Noah's blessing? The response takes its cue from an etymological reading of Japheth and of *yaft*, the verb usually translated as "enlarge," as deriving from the Hebrew word for *beauty*. It must be Greece that is meant because Greece is the possessor of the beauty to which Noah refers.

Commenting on Rabban Shimeon ben Gamliel's ruling on the permissibility of Greek translation, the Palestinian Talmud continues: "They investigated and found that the Torah cannot be adequately translated [*leᵉhitargem kol zorka*] except in Greek." Apparent evidence for this translational adequacy is the version of Aquila:

> R. Yirmeyah in the name of R. Hiyya bar Abba said: Akylas the proselyte translated the Torah before R. Eliezer and R. Yehoshua, and they praised him, and said to him: "You are more beautiful than (all) the children of men [*yofyafita mibbᵉne 'adam*]."(Palestinian Talmud *Megillah* 10a)

The Palestinian Talmud thus weaves together both the midrashic reading of Noah's prophecy – that the Torah will be expressed in the beautiful Greek tongue – and the Targum's understanding of Japheth as a Greek proselyte in the Jewish study-hall – "before R. Eliezer and R. Yehoshua" means also under their tutelage. Aquila's translation is beautiful, then, because it is Greek and because it echoes and fulfills Noah's Hebrew prophetic blessing, to which his teachers append their own. As their punning implies, Aquila is the most

beautiful (*yofyafita*) – that is, the most Japheth-like, as proselyte and translator – of all Adam's (and Noah's) descendants. Whereas the Babel story brings
a Babylonian place-name into Hebrew to denigrate a foreign city, the Palestinian Talmud here brings the biblical name for the Greek nation back to its
Hebrew root in order to praise at least one Greek. The praise, however, is for
a convert from the Greek, just as the Greek language is made to signify, in
this rabbinic wordplay, in the Hebrew target language. The rabbinic embrace
of Aquila was by no means an embrace of translation in general or of Greeks
or even proselytes as a group. Of the Greek translations they knew, the rabbis embraced only Aquila's, which was done "in their tents" under rabbinic
supervision.

A broader rabbinic approach to translation – never systematically provided in the literature – may be only cautiously culled from this material.
Nevertheless, a contrast emerges between the Midrash on Genesis 9 and theological and philosophical approaches that ground themselves in Babel. The
problem of multiple languages – when rooted in "natural" family differences
(Genesis 9) rather than the cosmic breakdown of a mythical, universal, and
anonymous unity (Genesis 11) – manifests itself not as existential impossibility or transgression against God but rather as cross-cultural encounter. In
Aquila, the rabbis linked the possibility of successful translation with that of
religious conversion, in which difference is assumed and recognized. By contrast, Babel-based theories of translation view its operations as linked to the
explosion of a single language or the reversal of this dissolution but, in either
case, as mobilizing the vision of a lost or future unity. Whereas the notion of
translation as necessarily also transformation is a scandal to the aim of perfect
equivalence, translation as transformation (or conversion) is no scandal at
all to the Talmud. By rooting their most pointed thinking on translation in a
story of three brothers, the rabbis who compiled the Midrash in *Genesis Rabbah* and its halakhic extension in both the Palestinian and Babylonian Talmud
also maintained a sense of linguistic difference as inevitable rather than tragic,
a potentially fruitful feature of human diversity rather than glaring evidence
of cosmic disapproval. They did so by reading Noah's blessing as evidence of
a translational triumph, prophesied even before the Babelian blow.

CONCLUSION

In beginning this chapter with an account of Buber's lament over the forgetting of *ruah* in translation, I invited a reading of translation as loss, as a
process of moving away from truth toward something secondary, fallen, and
lesser. Translation, in this familiar scheme, is an erosion that must be reversed,

an accretion that must be scraped away to discover a more authentic original. Each translation seeks to approach anew this original while inevitably representing yet again our ever-increasing distance and dispersion from such an origin. However, there is another vision of the Bible offered by Buber's partner in translation and perhaps also by the midrashists before him, which suggests that the meaning of the Bible is not found at some moment of origin but rather in its movement through time, in its reception by individuals, in its embrace by converts as in its own "conversion" from one tongue to another. In this vision, the Bible is also its afterlife – which is to say, its life.

9

∾

Modern Literature

Ilana Pardes

Generations of readers have thought of Genesis through Milton's *Paradise Lost*, Goethe's *Faust*, Melville's *Moby-Dick*, Kafka's parables, Mann's *Joseph and His Brothers*, Atwood's *The Handmaid's Tale*, Shalev's *Esau*, and Morrison's *Paradise*; yet, literary exegesis has rarely been seen as an integral part of the exegetical history of this founding text. Whereas traditional Judeo–Christian commentary (whether the Midrash or St. Bernard's sermons) and biblical scholarship have held prominent positions in the exegetical canon, literature has been regarded – more often than not – as a separate realm, admirable in its aesthetic power but irrelevant for textual analysis, providing no guidance to deciphering the unformulated meanings and complex links of scriptural texts. Against such mappings of exegesis, I argue that the poetic license of writers does not make their exegetical reflections less earnest or pertinent. Quite the contrary: literary flights of the imagination – despite and, at times, because of their radical departures from the Bible – may entail interpretive insights available to no other exegetical mode. I would go so far as to suggest that the hermeneutic projects of writers are vital to the understanding of Genesis as well as to the exploration of its cultural roles in diverse historical settings.

Genesis is one of the key texts of literary exegesis. The possibility of touching on the beginning of all beginnings – of following the pivotal, primary questions about creation, humanity, language, culture, and life itself – is something few literary exegetes chose to ignore. Of the many writers who have sought to reinvent Genesis, I focus on Melville's *Moby-Dick*, a momentous landmark in the history of the literary reception of the text. To be sure, Melville wanted no less than to reinvent the Bible as a whole – indeed, *Moby-Dick* has acquired the status of a Bible of sorts in American culture and beyond – but Genesis is one of the privileged texts in his grand exegetical voyage through libraries and oceans.

Like his most notable literary precursors – Milton and Goethe – Melville is intrigued by the opening chapters of Genesis. Following Milton's *Paradise Lost*, he too sets out to explore the oscillation between Creation and de-Creation in the biblical representation of primeval history. He too bolsters the half-hidden mythical traces of cosmogonic battles in Genesis 1, giving body and shape to the monsters of the Deep – above all, Leviathan.[1] With Goethe, he probes into the darker aspects of the desire to transgress the limits set on humanity in Eden. Tormented by the restricted contours of his scholarly work, Faust cannot but yield to Mephistopheles' offer and signs a pact that ensures him to be "like God, knowing good and evil" (Genesis 3:5), which means, in this case, to have the devil as his companion and servant. Melville's Faustian Ahab is no less eager to plunge into forbidden zones, venturing as he does to cross all boundaries and chase Moby Dick "round the world," "round perdition's flames," with Fedallah, the Melvillean counterpart to Mephistopheles. Unlike Faust, however, the *Pequod*'s maddened captain is an impatient Adam who remains unredeemed until the very end.

But the renowned scenes of Creation and the Garden of Eden do not suffice for Melville. With characteristic exegetical virtuosity and audacity, he moves beyond the continental scope and positions Ishmael, the outcast, at the center of his reading of Genesis.[2] Although his biblicism is surely indebted to European exegetical traditions, it strives at the same time to be quintessentially American, free of mere imitations: "We want no American Miltons," he declares in "Hawthorne and His Mosses." Ishmael – far more than Adam – allows Melville to translate Genesis into American landscapes and inscapes, to capture the diverse manifestations of the American frontier in big strokes, to envision a biblical scene no European could have imagined. What would happen, Melville ventures to ask, if we were to transfer Ishmael from biblical times onto a nineteenth-century American whaling ship? What new insights would emerge once Ishmael is set within the context of modern outcasts and renegades?

---

[1] Teasing out mythical elements in the Bible is a common strategy in literary exegesis. See Robert Alter's discussion of Bialik's "Dead of the Desert," in *Canon and Creativity: Modern Writing and the Authority of the Canon* (New Haven, CT: Yale University Press, 2000), 97–149. For more on Milton's use of the Bible, see Regina Schwartz, *Remembering and Repeating: Biblical Creation in Paradise Lost* (Cambridge: Cambridge University Press, 1998) and Harold Fisch, *The Biblical Presence in Shakespeare, Milton, and Blake: A Comparative Study* (Oxford: Clarendon Press, 1999).

[2] Ishmael serves as a key model for the adventurous wandering outcast in many of Melville's books – from *Redburn* and *Mardi* to *Pierre*, *Israel Potter*, and *Clarel*. Nathalia Wright regards Ishmael as one of Melville's central "types"; *Melville's Use of the Bible* (Durham, NC: Duke University Press, 1949), 46–59.

Melville's departure from European traditions is bound up with his challenge to the all-too-common tendency to mitigate the radicality of the biblical
text. His Bible is not meant for those who would "[dodge] hospitals and jails,
and [walk] fast crossing grave-yards, and would rather talk of operas than
hell" (424). He foregrounds the anomalies and oddities of the Hebrew canon,
counter-traditions such as Job, Jonah, and Ecclesiastes that challenge the central presuppositions of biblical belief. Even when Melville selects stories that
are set within major biblical texts – such as Genesis – he reads them against
the grain, highlighting the fragility of concepts such as "chosenness" and
"promise" and focusing on the outcast Ishmael rather than on the chosen
Isaac.

My contextualization of Melville's reading of biblical texts focuses on antebellum American culture, but his dark prophecy on the disastrous route of
the American ship of state is by no means relevant only to America a decade
before the Civil War. Rendering a new poetically inspired Bible for Melville
ultimately means to acquire the position of the original Book of Books: to
compose a formative text for a particular community in a particular place
in time that would nonetheless transcend its national and temporal borders,
touching the lives of readers in other cultural contexts as well. Indeed, I
venture to suggest that if *Moby-Dick* was largely misunderstood or ignored
at the time of its publication in 1851 and discovered only in the 1920s (and
more substantively in the 1940s), it was in part because Melville's exegetical
imagination was in many ways ahead of its time.[3]

MELVILLE'S ISHMAELS

There are many Ishmaels on the *Pequod*.[4] Melville's primary aesthetic–
hermeneutic strategy in *Moby-Dick* is to split or duplicate biblical characters
among the different crew members of the *Pequod*. The key to understanding
this strategy lies in a passage from *The Confidence-Man*:

Upon the whole, it might rather be thought, that he, who, in view of its
inconsistencies, says of human nature the same that, in view of its contrasts,
is said of the divine nature, that it is past finding out, thereby evinces a better

---

[3] For a consideration of the mixed reviews that *Moby-Dick* received on its publication, see
Herman Melville: The Contemporary Reviews, eds. Brian Higgins and Hershel Parker (New
York: Cambridge University Press, 1995) and Hershel Parker, *Herman Melville: A Biography*,
Vol. II (Baltimore and London: Johns Hopkins University Press, 2002), 1–30.

[4] The following reading of Melville's Ishmaels is a revised version of Chapter 3 in my *Melville's
Bibles* (Berkeley: University of California Press, 2008), 73–97.

appreciation of it than he who, by always representing it in a clear light, leaves it to be inferred that he clearly knows all about it.[5]

To represent human character as consistent means to smooth out the incomprehensibility of human nature, the prevalent lack of coherence that characterizes human life. In a playful iconoclastic move, Melville demands that the same attention that is given to divine inconsistencies (all the more so since the rise of biblical scholarship) should be given to human ones. This *ars poetic*/hermeneutic passage on the mysteries of character sheds light on the numerous splittings or duplications of the confidence man, but is as relevant to the splittings and merging of biblical characters in *Moby-Dick*. In *Moby-Dick*, however, such inconsistencies are all the more breathtaking given that they are the hallmark of several characters at once.

Exegesis, for Melville, means above all to open up potentialities, to take typology beyond its limits, to experiment with the possibility of thinking that any crew member could be an Ishmael of sorts, each rendition highlighting different aspects of his cryptic tale. That such a study of biblical texts and characters is always on the verge of admitting – through its unparalleled exegetical excess – that hermeneutic enigmas are "past finding out" does not make it less alluring. Somehow it is the impossibility of fathoming divine and human character and the vanity of all knowledge that seems to propel Melville with an ever-growing drive to continue the search.

I begin with the narrator, the most prominent Ishmael of the *Pequod*, the one who actually bears the name. "Call me Ishmael," the famous opening words of "Loomings," the first chapter of *Moby-Dick*, call us out of nowhere to consider the story of Ishmael, the quintessential biblical outcast. The narrator, who was anonymous in the preliminary "Extracts" on whales, now erupts unexpectedly with a name and asks to be heard. There may not be a God to hearken to his plight, but we are required to listen, to listen and respond to his address; to call him, as if one could cross the boundaries between the real and the fictional and enter the space of literature from where his call is delivered – or as if he could find a way to enter our world and make us hear his voice as a real voice calling in the wilderness. Unlike Genesis 16, no angel commands that he be called "Ishmael." It is he who chooses to assume this name as a point of departure for his tale. Whatever his given name may be, it is not a predetermined name that marks his life from the outset. Likewise, his typological penname is anything but fixed. In saying "Call me Ishmael" rather than "I am Ishmael," the narrator implies that he could, as it

---

[5] Herman Melville, *The Confidence-Man: His Masquerade*, ed. Hershel Parker, Norton Critical edition (New York: Norton, 1971), 59.

were, be called Jonah or Job or any other biblical name under other circumstances, within other tales. Indeed, in the course of the voyage, he does merge
with other biblical outcasts, although his primary identification remains
Ishmael.

Ishmael's initial call is followed by a preliminary attempt to carve out a
narrative that would serve as homage to his namesake. If the biblical outcast
was destined to be a "wild man" whose "hand will be against every man,
and every man's hand against him" (Genesis 16:11–12), Ishmael, the narrator,
wonders what such wildness might mean for both his literal and literary
hand.[6]

> Call me Ishmael. Some years ago – never mind how long precisely – having
> little or no money in my purse, and nothing particular to interest me on
> shore, I thought I would sail about a little and see the watery part of the world.
> It is a way I have of driving off the spleen, and regulating the circulation.
> Whenever I find myself growing grim about the mouth; whenever it is a
> damp, drizzly November in my soul; whenever I find myself involuntarily
> pausing before coffin warehouses, and bringing up the rear of every funeral
> I meet; and especially whenever my hypos get such an upper hand of me,
> that it requires a strong moral principle to prevent me from deliberately
> stepping into the street, and methodically knocking people's hats off – then,
> I account it high time to get to sea as soon as I can. This is my substitute for
> pistol and ball. With a philosophical flourish Cato throws himself upon his
> sword; I quietly take to the ship. There is nothing surprising in this. If they
> but knew it, almost all men in their degree, some time or other, cherish very
> nearly the same feelings towards the ocean with me.[7]

Breaking with normative narrative exposition, Ishmael discloses no bio-
graphical background and no date. The usual calendar with its set order of
months is of no interest to him. He goes to sea whenever there is a "damp,
drizzly November in his soul," whenever his own inner climate demands that
he leave the melancholy suffocating city streets where one cannot but suc-
cumb to the spleen, ending up at the rear of funerals, behind coffins, or on
one's sword, like Cato. Ishmael's wild hand and wild imagination – craving
to "knock people's hats off," to use "pistol and ball" – requires the open vast
horizons of the wilderness. His wilderness, however, is not an arid one –
like that of the biblical Ishmael – but rather a watery wilderness, where the

---

[6] Citations to the Bible are to the King James Version, the translation Melville used.
[7] Herman Melville, *Moby-Dick; or, The Whale*, Vol. 6 of *The Writings of Herman Melville*,
     eds. Harrison Hayford, Hershel Parker, and G. Thomas Tanselle (1851; Evanston and Chicago:
     Northwestern University Press and the Newberry Library, 2001), "Loomings," p. 3. Subsequent
     references to the Northwestern–Newberry edition are made in parentheses in the text.

ocean determines the beat of life, and words – be it "growing grim" or "damp drizzly" – however somber, are set free to become sounds.

BIBLICAL ETHNOGRAPHIES: ORIENTAL GUIDES

Melville's commentary is forever embedded in meta-commentary. He engages in a vast dialogue with a whole array of interpretive discourses – from literary renditions of the biblical text to traditional commentary, biblical scholarship, and political sermons – always attentive to the ways in which his own biblical obsessions may intersect with those of other commentators. I read Melville's positioning of Ishmael as narrator and exegetical guide in *Moby-Dick* not only as a token of his admiration for the biblical Ishmael but also as a comment on the ever-growing perception in nineteenth-century America of the Bible as the product of Oriental imagination and the concomitant construction of the Orient and its inhabitants, the so-called descendants of Ishmael, as indispensable keys to understanding Scriptural truths. For many Americans in the nineteenth century, the only way to capture the "true" significance of biblical figures and biblical scenes was to tour the new frontier in the Holy Land and observe the customs of the contemporary Easterners. Numerous Holy Land travel narratives flooded the American literary market, becoming one of the most popular exegetical genres of nineteenth-century America.

References to Arabs as Ishmaels, stamped by their ancestor's character, were common in Holy Land travel literature. In *Incidents of Travel in Egypt, Arabia Petraea and the Holy Land* (1837), John Lloyd Stephens reflects on the Bedouins whom he had encountered at the foothills of Mount Sinai, defining them as the "sons of Ishmael."

> The sons of Ishmael have ever been the same, inhabitants of the desert, despising the dwellers under roof, wanderers and wild men from their birth, with their hands against every man, and every man's hand against them. . . . These principal and distinguishing traits of Bedouin character have long been known; but as I had now been with them ten days, and expected to be with them a month longer . . . I was curious to know something of the lighter shades, the details of their lives and habits; and I listened with exceeding interest while the young Bedouin, with his eyes constantly fixed upon it, told me that for more than four hundred years the tent of his fathers had been in that mountain. Wild and unsettled, robbers and plunderers as they are, they have laws which are as sacred as our own; and the tent, and the garden, and the little pasture-ground are transmitted from father to son for centuries.[8]

---

[8] Stephens, *Incidents of Travel*, ed. Victor Wolfgang von Hagen (Norman: University of Oklahoma Press, 1970), 174–5.

Stephens's ethnography, like that of many American nineteenth-century travelers to the Holy Land, is based on the biblical text. He reads the customs of the Bedouins in light of the biblical verses on Ishmael, with the assumption that ethnic character, regardless of the chasms of time, remains the same: the sons of Ishmael, just like their ancestor, are wanderers and wild men who cannot but despise "dwellers under roof."

The most influential advocate of such biblical ethnography, one with whom Stephens maintained an intricate dialogue, was the Scottish divine, Alexander Keith, whose book *The Evidence of Prophecy* (1823) set out to map the literal fulfillment of biblical prophecies in the Holy Land. Among the bearers of such prophecies, according to Keith, were the Arabs, the living embodiment of what "was prophesied concerning Ishmael: – 'He will be a wild man; his hand will be against every man; and every man's hand will be against him.'"[9] Keith relied on several accounts in defining the character of "The Arabs" (as the chapter is titled), among them the account of a "recent traveler" and "eye-witness," R. K. Porter, whose premises confirm his own:

> that an acute and active people, surrounded for ages by polished and luxurious nations, should, from their earliest to their latest times, be still found a wild people, dwelling in the presence of all their brethren, (as we may call these nations,) unsubdued and unchangeable, is indeed a standing miracle, – one of those mysterious facts which establish the truth of prophecy.[10]

The miracle of unchanging ethnic character is all the more remarkable for Keith, given that the Arabs are unwitting bearers of such prophecies. On describing, at an earlier point in the book, a particularly violent Arab tribe that dwells on the border of the land of Edom (a land that was cursed in the Bible and whose unending desolation and inaccessibility to travelers is regarded by Keith as further evidence of prophetic truth), Keith comments: "And hence, while they used unconsciously the very words of one prophecy, their universal character, as well as their conduct, bear witness to another, 'It shall be called the border of wickedness.'" In attacking all those who venture to set foot in the land of Edom, this tribe "unconsciously" fulfills both the "universal character" of Ishmael and the prophecies of doom concerning Edom (primarily Isaiah 34:5, 10–17; Ezekiel 35:7).

---

[9] Alexander Keith, *Evidence of the Christian Religion Derived from the Literal Fulfillment of Prophecy; Particularly as Illustrated by the History of the Jews, and by the Discoveries of Recent Travelers* (Edinburgh: William Whyte & Co., 1823), 384. The Jews too are construed by Keith as a living prophecy, given that their wandering is compatible with prophetic warnings. Keith and his theories regarding Edom are ridiculed in Melville's *Clarel: A Poem and Pilgrimage in the Holy Land* 2.29. 99–107.

[10] Keith, *Evidence of Prophecy*, 386.

For Stephens, however, Keith's literal exegesis holds only up to a point. Stephens's insistence on traveling through the land of Edom to Petra – dressed in Oriental clothes and disguised as a merchant from Cairo – is undoubtedly his most provocative challenge to Keith (138–9), but his critique is also evident in his reflections on the sons of Ishmael where, careful not to undermine the validity of the biblical prophecy concerning Ishmael, he suggests that in addition to the well-known traits of this people there are unknown ones that need to be explored. The sons of Ishmael may be wild robbers, but they have sets of laws and customs that are no less respectable than those known within the so-called civilized world.

An adventurous traveler who was inspired by American frontier literature, Stephens was also seeking something other than evidence of fulfilled biblical prophecies. He was eager to engage in long conversations with the Bedouins of Sinai, to learn about the "lighter shades" of their habits of life. Sisters, he learns, remain with their brothers until they are married; and, "if the brothers did not choose to keep a sister with them, what became of her?," asks Stephens, only to find that his question is absolutely incomprehensible within the moral framework of that Bedouin tribe. "It is impossible – she is his own blood," the young Bedouin claimed repeatedly. Even plunder has its rules. To the question of whether they paid tribute to the pasha (given that they regard God alone as their governor), the Bedouin answered, "No, we take tribute from him. . . . We plunder his caravans."[11]

The attempt to reinterpret Ishmael's role is carried on in later American travel narratives such as William Prime's renowned *Tent Life in the Holy Land* (1857). "I have traveled seven months among Mussulman people of every name and shade," writes Prime:

> I had carried large sums of money, some of the time in open baskets. . . . [and] had left my boat or my tents often without other guard than my Arab servants . . . and have never lost a farthing by the dishonesty of a follower of Mohammed. . . . An Arab, finding you traveling through his country as a stranger, without having applied to his tribe for permission and protection, regards you as an enemy, open to plunder. Such is the law of his fathers, even to Ishmael. But once having placed yourself under his protection, or confided in his honor, you are safer than in your own house in New York.[12]

---

[11] Stephens, *Incidents of Travel*, 176. For more on John Lloyd Stephens, see John Davis, *Landscape of Belief: Encountering the Holy Land in Nineteenth-Century America* (Princeton, NJ: Princeton University Press, 1996), 32–7, and Hilton Obenzinger, *American Palestine: Melville, Twain, and the Holy Land Mania* (Princeton, NJ: Princeton University Press, 1999), 46–9.

[12] William Prime, *Tent Life in the Holy Land* (New York: Arno Press, 1857, 1977), 479.

Here, too, the biblical assertion regarding Ishmael is not refuted, although the experience of traveling in Palestine generates new possibilities of defining the conditions under which Genesis is valid, especially for those who are capable of drawing fresh analogies between tent life in Palestine and everyday life in New York.

In addition to their exegetical role, Arabs often were guides in the literal sense of the word. Pilgrims rarely traveled on their own; dragomans in Oriental costume, turbans, and rifles led the way from Jaffa to Jerusalem, the Dead Sea, and other popular pilgrim sites. At times, the dragomans themselves were perceived as taking part in the sacred theater of the Holy Land. Prime's dragoman, who falls ill by the side of the road, reminds him of a picture of the Good Samaritan. Stephens goes so far as to rely on his Bedouin guide Toualeb in attempting to find the authentic site of the crossing of the Red Sea. Toualeb, he recounts with some amusement, was as sure of his identification of the site as if he were there when it happened and could see, till this very day, on still nights, the "ghost of Pharaoh himself, with the crown upon his head, flying with his chariot and horses over the face of the deep."[13]

DISLOCATING ISHMAEL

Combining the two grand passions of his life – travel and exegesis – Melville could not but welcome Holy Land travel literature. Like Stephens and Prime, he never ceases to be compelled by the unique pleasures of traveling in an exegetical landscape. What could be more intriguing than to explore hermeneutic problems through travel? What could be more excitingly intense (especially for a writer) than to travel in a Book whose characters unfold before the eyes of the voyagers as they, in their turn, become characters in it?

Yet, his admiration was not uncritical. Melville would have probably endorsed current critiques of Western pilgrimages for overlooking the contemporary Orient in their quest of the ancient layers of biblical realities. He complicates the matter, however, by suggesting that such blindness often prevails in a culture's interpretation of itself as well. By juxtaposing the exegetical

---

[13] Stephens, *Incidents of Travel*, 164. For more on nineteenth-century American travel to Palestine, see Yehoshua Ben Aryeh, *The Rediscovery of the Holy Land in the Nineteenth Century* (Jerusalem: Magnes Press, 1979); Robert T. Handy, ed., *The Holy Land in American Protestant Life 1800–1948* (New York: Arno Press, 1981); Lester I Vogel, *To See a Promised Land: Americans and the Holy Land in the Nineteenth Century* (University Park: The Pennsylvania State University Press, 1993); Obenzinger, *American Palestine*; Milette Shamir, "'Our Jerusalem: Americans in the Holy Land and Protestant Narratives of National Entitlement," *American Quarterly* (2003) 55:1, 29–60. Eitan Bar-Yosef's study on English Holy Land travel literature is most relevant as well: *The Holy Land in English Culture 1799–1917: Palestine and the Question of Orientalism* (Oxford, UK: Oxford University Press, 2005).

practices of Holy Land travel literature with those of traditional American typology, he seems to intimate that both the projection of biblical dramas on Bedouins in Palestine and the glorification of figures in American history through their identification with cherished biblical characters (never with biblical sinners or outcasts) are equally detached from reality.

In a move that questions both of these modes of exegetical projection with their respective constructions of biblical lineage (one based on ethnic continuity, the other on spiritual parallels), *Moby-Dick*'s Ishmael is not an Oriental who wanders about in the plains of the East but rather a white American whaler. As the name of a biblical outcast and one that became part and parcel of the definition of the Islamic Orient, "Ishmael" could not be used – as "Abraham" and "Isaac" could – to corroborate the image of America as a New Israel. Wearing Oriental costumes – as American travelers to the Holy Land often did (Bayard Taylor, author of *The Land of the Saracen*, went so far as to give lectures on his return from the Holy Land in full Arab dress) – was a daring yet acceptable cross-dressing, but bearing the name "Ishmael" would have been perceived as endangering the very core of American identity (there is no instance of the name in the *Nantucket Vital Records*). For Melville, however, who believes in no consistency whatsoever in individual character let alone in collective character, "Ishmael" is a vital name and a text that needs to be regarded differently in both the context of American typology and Holy Land travel literature.

Dislocating Ishmael, Melville attempts to go further than Stephens in correcting the all-too-common unfavorable readings of Ishmael in Holy Land travel literature and beyond.[14] He does not merely provide a respectful account of the untamed customs of Ishmael's sons but rather calls upon us to see wild life on the outskirts of civilization as superior to any settled mode of living. Melville's Ishmael in *Moby-Dick* is by no means an unconscious bearer of biblical prophecies or an unwitting exegetical guide, but rather a narrator–commentator who adopts "Ishmael" as namesake in an attempt to explicate life in the oceanic wilderness. "But as in landlessness alone," claims Ishmael, "resides the highest truth, shoreless, indefinite as God – so, better is it to perish in that howling infinite, than be ingloriously dashed upon the lee, even if that

---

[14] Note that Ishmael becomes a far more negative figure in Christian and Jewish exegesis after he is adopted as an ancestor of Islam; see Carol Bakhos, *Ishmael on the Border: Rabbinic Portrayals of the First Arab* (New York: SUNY Press, 2006). Christian exegesis, one should remember, relies not only on Genesis but also on Galatians 4:21–31. For more on the New Testament's version of the story of Hagar and Ishmael, see Elizabeth A. Castelli, "Allegories of Hagar: Reading Galatians 4: 21–31 with Postmodern Feminist Eyes," in *The New Literary Criticism and the New Testament*, 228–50. On American perceptions of Islam, see Timothy Marr, *The Cultural Roots of American Islamicism* (New York: Cambridge University Press, 2006).

were safety!"(107). To be a wanderer in the "howling infinite" of the ocean – a play on the definition of the wilderness in Deuteronomy 32:10 as a "howling wilderness" – means to be closer to the "shoreless" truth of divine infinity precisely because of the indefinite, ever-changing nature of seascapes.

Moby-Dick is a counter-pilgrimage that calls for a voyage whose purpose is not to visit the well-known sacred sites of Palestine, Sinai, and Arabia Petra but rather to seek revelation in what remains uncharted in Holy Land travel narratives: the "wild and distant seas," where the "portentous and mysterious" (7) White Whale roams about. Instead of following in the footsteps of Abraham or Jesus in Jerusalem or the Galilee, Melville's counter-pilgrimage calls for a whaling voyage that begins with the dramatic opening of the "great flood-gates of the wonder-world" and sets out to follow "endless processions of the whale, and, midmost of them all, one grand hooded phantom, like a snow hill in the air" (7).

To pursue the "grand hooded phantom" of an inscrutable White Whale, although analogous to a wild goose chase, seems to be the ultimate way to approach the inner voyage that all pilgrims attempt to realize, albeit in different ways. As Ishmael opens the great floodgates to the sea, he opens at the same time the gates to an internal wonder world, allowing endless processions of whales to float two by two into his "inmost soul." Ishmael's soul is a gigantic boundless Noah's ark, or a vast inner sea, or perhaps something of Milton's Leviathan, "Hugest of living creatures, on the deep" that "seems a moving land; and at his gills/ Draws in, and at his trunk spouts out a sea."[15] These are "wild conceits," Ishmael admits, but they are the kind of wild imaginings that make Ishmael worthy of his penname and of his role as guide to the deep.

THE EVERYDAY LIFE OF WHALERS

With a keen ethnographic eye, Ishmael is eager to consider what being a "wild man" may mean through ongoing meditations on his fellow wandering whalers. To explore Ishmael's character, we discover, one need not necessarily travel to the Orient to study the customs of Bedouins or Arab peasants. Ishmaels of diverse ethnic backgrounds and religious persuasions may be found on whalers in the oceans of the world. The wonder at the base of Ishmael's biblical ethnography is not the "miracle" of unchanged ethnic character but rather the ever-surprising possibilities of tracing biblical dramas in the daily lives of whalers of every imaginable origin – be they American, Polynesian, Chinese, or European.[16]

---

[15] These lines from *Paradise Lost* are quoted in the opening "Extracts" of *Moby-Dick*, xxii.
[16] Timothy Marr regards Melville's ethnography as cosmopolitan. His observations are relevant to Melville's biblical ethnographies. See "Without the Pale: Melville and Ethnic

As an observer–participant, Ishmael sets out to interpret both the Ishmael-like inclinations of others and his own. His biblical ethnography, in other words, has a pronounced self-reflexive dimension. Consider Ishmael's first impressions of the Polynesian Queequeg:

> No more my splintered heart and maddened hand were turned against the wolfish world. This soothing savage had redeemed it. There he sat, his very indifference speaking a nature in which there lurked no civilized hypocrisies and bland deceits. Wild he was; a very sight of sights to see; yet I began to feel myself mysteriously drawn towards him. And those same things that would have repelled most others, they were the very magnets that thus drew me. I'll try a pagan friend, thought I, since Christian kindness has proved but hollow courtesy. (51)

Something in the palpably wild appearance and conduct of Queequeg frees Ishmael from his tendency to turn his "maddened hand" against the "wolfish" world, a melancholy variation on "his hand will be against every man and every man's hand against him" (Genesis 16:12). Sitting calmly, "a sight of sights," Queequeg reveals a different mode of becoming an Ishmael. He opens up the possibility of opposing "civilized hypocrisies" without a "splintered heart" and without relinquishing the gift of friendship, especially the kind of unconventional friendship that is to be an ongoing celebration of the wild side of life.[17]

Or consider Tashtego, the "wild Indian" harpooner from Gay Head, the heir of "proud warrior hunters" who had scoured "bow in hand, the aboriginal forests of the main." In shaping Tashtego as an Ishmael, Melville may be alluding in particular to the common conflation of Arabs and Indians in Holy Land travel literature – "The Bedouin roams over [the desert of Idumea] like the Indian on our native prairies," writes Stephens – as well as to the common identification of Native Americans as the descendants of the lost tribes of Israel.[18] Above all, Tashtego is another distinct embodiment of a "wild man." No longer "snuffing in the trail of the wild beasts of the woodland, Tashtego now hunted in the wake of the great whales of the sea; the unerring harpoon of the son fitly replacing the infallible arrow of the sires" (120). Moving from land to sea, from bow to harpoon, Tashtego underscores the lure of the ocean

---

Cosmopolitanism," in *A Historical Guide to Herman Melville*, ed. Giles Gunn (New York: Oxford University Press, 2005), 133–66.

[17] In *The Sign of the Cannibal*, Geoffrey Sanborn reads this passage as a point of transition in which Ishmael shifts away from the normative relation to savages, "governed by the logic of spectacle," and discovers the possibility of an "open dialogue" (Durham, NC: Duke University Press, 1998), 136. See also Sanborn, "Whence Come You, Queequeg?," *American Literature* 77:2 (June 2005), 227–56.

[18] On the conflation of Arabs and Native Americans in Holy Land travel literature, see Vogel, *To See a Promised Land*, 77–85; and Obenzinger, *American Palestine*.

for those whose hunt of beasts is as wild as their target. Always attuned to the aesthetic potential of being wild, Ishmael is drawn to the musicality of Tashtego's hunt, to his capacity to turn the conventional whaler alert on spying whales – "There she blows" – into a wild rhythmic cry – "There she blows! there! there! there! she blows! she blows!" (215).

Everyday life on a whaling ship seems to be particularly relevant to an understanding of Ishmael given that the biblical Ishmael is not only an untamed wanderer but also a hunter. In Genesis 21, Hagar and Ishmael, then but a child, are forced to leave Abraham's household. Wandering in the wilderness of Beersheba, left with no water, the desperate Hagar "cast the child under one of the shrubs" and sat

> over against him a good way off, as it were a bowshot: for she said, Let me not see the death of the child. And she sat over against him, and lift up her voice, and wept. And God heard the voice of the lad; and the angel of God called to Hagar out of heaven, and said unto her, What aileth thee, Hagar? fear not; for God hath heard the voice of the lad where he is. Arise, lift up the lad, and hold him in thine hand; for I will make him a great nation.... And God was with the lad; and he grew, and dwelt in the wilderness, and became an archer. (Genesis 21:15–20)

Ishmael's vocation as archer captures his misery as a castaway whose weeping mother sat a "bowshot" away, unwilling to witness his death, yet unable to leave. It entails a continuation of the death risk of the plight in the wilderness. His bow also serves as a mark of divine protection – an endowment of power, indicating that although God has assigned Isaac the privileged position of the chosen son of Abraham, Ishmael too is destined to become a great resilient nation.

Whereas the Bible provides no account of Ishmael's adventures as archer, *Moby-Dick* abounds in detailed depictions of the sorrows and pleasures of the minutest moments in the life of a whale hunter. To come close to losing one's life, to approach "the jaws of death," is a daily experience in the whaling world, where whales are chased in the midst of squalls and whalers are left soaking wet in their small leaking boats, never certain that they will be able to find their way back to the ship or that their fellow mariners will make an effort to rescue them.

The *Pequod*'s whalers are at once wild hunters and adamant pilgrims. Undermining the customary demarcation in Holy Land travel literature between pilgrims and indigenous populations, Melville fashions an exegetical voyage in which the ordinary hunting practices of his Ishmael-like whalers are part and parcel of a metaphysical search for the inscrutable White Whale,

Moby Dick. In thinking of ways to ensure his crew's ongoing commitment to the chase of the White Whale, Ahab realizes (or so Ishmael surmises) that even "the high lifted and chivalric Crusaders of old times were not content to traverse two thousands miles of land to fight for their holy sepulcher, without committing burglaries, picking pockets, and gaining other pious perquisites by the way" (212). Ahab's equivalent for the Crusaders' "pious" burglaries is the normative chase of whales as commodities that he maintains at least in the initial stages of the voyage. But the crew's double quest – both whale hunt and pilgrimage – is not only a result of Ahab's manipulations and obsessions. Haunted by obsessions of their own, the daily lives of the *Pequod*'s whalers continuously oscillate between the two quests. Any lowering of the boats can potentially lead not only to more blubber but also to the sought-for White Whale whose lure, it seems, is far greater than that of the Holy Sepulcher in Jerusalem.

FOLLOWING THE TURBANED FEDALLAH: "THE SPIRIT-SPOUT"

There is one Oriental Ishmael aboard the *Pequod*: Fedallah the Parsee. Ascending at night to the top of the masthead (i.e., the oceanic equivalent of the camel), the turbaned Fedallah becomes, in the course of the journey, the *Pequod*'s Oriental guide to the celestial traces of spirit spouts in the sea:

> It was while gliding through these latter waters that one serene and moonlight night, when all the waves rolled by like scrolls of silver; and, by their soft, suffusing seethings, made what seemed a silvery silence, not a solitude: on such a silent night a silvery jet was seen far in advance of the white bubbles at the bow. Lit up by the moon, it seemed celestial; seemed some plumed and glittering god uprising from the sea. Fedallah first descried this jet. For of these moonlight nights, it was his wont to mount to the main-mast head, and stand a look-out there, with the same precision as if it had been day. And yet, though herds of whales were seen by night, not one whaleman in a hundred would venture a lowering for them. You may think with what emotions, then, the seamen beheld this old Oriental perched aloft at such unusual hours; his turban and the moon, companions in one sky. But when, after spending his uniform interval there for several successive nights without uttering a single sound; when, after all this silence, his unearthly voice was heard announcing that silvery, moon-lit jet, every reclining mariner started to his feet as if some winged spirit had lighted in the rigging, and hailed the mortal crew. "There she blows!" Had the trump of judgment blown, they could not have quivered more. (232–33)

A dreamy exegetical scene unfolds during this "moonlight night," in which the sea is a "silvery scroll" that awaits interpretation. Fedallah, whose turban blends with the moon, is the first to detect the sudden silvery jet and cry out "There she blows!" The customary whaler cry sounds on this occasion like the blowing of the "trump of judgment" in messianic times. Chasing the ungraspable phantom of Moby Dick by day is reckless enough; doing so at night is sheer madness, a lowering not "one whaleman in a hundred" would venture to do. But the sheer madness of this somnambulist wild search makes it all the more alluring – "almost every soul on board instinctively desired a lowering."

Half celestial, half demonic, the "old Oriental" spurs the *Pequod*'s crew to venture a lowering, but the silvery jet vanishes. Fedallah's cry turns out to be a delusional cry that leads nowhere. The midnight spout is sighted yet again on the following nights but remains ungraspable. Although there were seamen

> who swore that whenever and wherever descried; at however remote times, or in however far apart latitudes and longitudes, that unnearable spout was cast by one self-same whale; and that whale, Moby Dick. For a time there reigned too, a sense of peculiar dread at this flitting apparition, as if it were treacherously beckoning us on and on.

Should Fedallah's misleading exegetical practices be seen as an expression of Melville's refusal to regard Orientals as privileged exegetical guides?[19] This is, it seems to me, a plausible reading of the "Spirit-Spout," although one should bear in mind that to begin with, Fedallah is not quite the exegetical guide whose goal is to illuminate Christian truths. Fedallah, whose Arabic name means "The Sacrifice (or Ransom) of God," has been associated with Islamic mysticism, primarily Ismailism.[20] Named after Ishmael, Ismailism speaks of a series of Imams (i.e., the revealed prophets of Islam who followed Mohammed) that would end with the climactic appearance of the seventh Imam, "the hidden prophet," Ishmael.[21] In one of the branches of the Ismailiya, the devotees were called "Fedais" for their willingness to sacrifice themselves for the sake of religious duty. Whether or not Fedallah's religion

[19] The question of exegetical guidance is a central question in *Clarel* and is by no means confined to Oriental guides. The young divinity student, Clarel, follows several potential spiritual guides but finds no exemplary mentor. See Walter E. Bezanson, "Historical and Critical Note," in *Clarel: A Poem and Pilgrimage in the Holy Land* (The Northwestern–Newberry Edition), 552–66.

[20] Dorothee Metlitsky Finkelstein, *Melville's Orienda* (New Haven, CT: Yale University Press, 1961), 229.

[21] Already in the Koran, Ishmael is defined as prophet. Ismailism offered a substantive elaboration on this title.

bears resemblance to Ismailism, the spirit spouts he discovers seem far closer to treacherous demonic apparitions than to the spirit of the gospels.[22]

While pointing to the delusional qualities of Fedallah's reading of the silvery sea scrolls, Ishmael is at the same time wholly mesmerized by this exotic Oriental exegetical scene on a moonlit night and by the risky routes it displays. True or false, there is magic in Fedallah that inspires Ishmael to merge his own gaze with that of the old Parsee – much as the latter's turban unites with the moon – and turn his narrative into a spellbinding chain of "s" sounds – "silvery scrolls, "soft, suffusing seethings," "silvery silence," "solitude" – all adding resonance to the double "s-p-t" of the "spirit-spout."

INTERTWINED DESTINIES AND DOOMS

The quest for the White Whale ends with the tragic sinking of the *Pequod*. Tashtego's red hand, holding a hammer, is the very last sign of life to emerge from the doomed whaling ship. Although death is inescapable, the hand of this Native American Ishmael is still out there against all, against all odds, trying to nail the flag to a subsiding spar, ending up nailing to the flag a sky hawk that "chanced to intercept its broad fluttering wing between the hammer and the wood" (572). That the final moment of the *Pequod* is devoted to Tashtego's defiant hand is a reminder that the ship is named after a "celebrated tribe of Massachusetts Indians, now extinct like the ancient Medes" (69).[23] Although Melville sets out to record the plight of all outcasts, he undoubtedly has a special need to bear witness to the cry of the Ishmaels of America. For Melville, the dispossession of Native Americans is one of the darker moments in American history, a moment that is relived in antebellum America through the horrors of slavery and the reinforcement of the Fugitive Slave Law.[24]

Whereas most American travelers to Palestine were proud to post the American flag on their tents or caravans and happy to reaffirm America's Manifest Destiny through their encounter with the Land of the Bible (Stephens

---

[22] Fedallah's religious practices have been read in different ways. In addition to Ismailism, Fedallah has been associated with the religions of the Far East (India and Japan in particular). See James Baird, *Ishmael* (Baltimore, MD: The Johns Hopkins Press, 1956).

[23] The Pequots were not extinct but were nearly annihilated in 1637. Melville read about the war against the Pequot Indians in Benjamin Trumbull's *A Complete History of Connecticut*. See *Moby-Dick*, Norton Critical Edition (2002), 69. For more on the Pequod war and Melville's response to it, see Rogin, *Subversive Genealogy: The Politics and Art of Herman Melville*. (Berkeley: University of California Press, 1979), 122–4.

[24] Michael Rogin offers an illuminating discussion of Melville's critique of the use of the story of Ishmael to legitimate American dispossessions in the political discourse of his time (*Subversive Genealogy*, 141).

discovers on Mount Sinai, of all places, a Greek monk who sings the praises
of America), the *Pequod* offers a far more somber flag, one in which the
American eagle and the sky hawk of Native American culture seem to be
nailed together.[25] To be sure, Melville lacks no passion in his preoccupation
with American destiny, but he is, at the same time, a harsh critic of his
contemporaries' understanding of the term and its so-called manifestations.
If America will continue to turn a deaf ear to the afflictions of the dispossessed,
the only end Melville can envision for it is as dark as that of the *Pequod*.[26]

He thus ventures to lay bare what American travelers failed to chart in
their readings of Genesis: the fragile distinctions between Isaac and Ishmael,
the interconnectedness of their lives. There are striking similarities between
the story of the plight of Hagar and Ishmael in the wilderness (Genesis 21)
and the following chapter on the binding of Isaac (Genesis 22). Both stories
revolve around a child on the verge of death whose demise is prevented at the
very last moment through the intervention of an angel. Both stories end with
a divine promise of future prosperity.

Melville's exegetical imagination offers a decisive reminder of the insights
and foresights of writers. In his underscoring of antithetical trends in the
Bible, in providing outcasts and renegades with a stage, and in questioning
the boundary between the chosen and the nonchosen, Melville brilliantly
anticipates some of the predominant trends in twentieth-century biblical
scholarship. The affinities between Ishmael and Isaac in Genesis, as Phyllis
Trible and Yair Zakovitch have noted, resurge in the lives of their descendants
in Exodus and Numbers.[27] There are numerous textual links between the
tale of Hagar and Ishmael and the history of ancient Israel. If Hagar, the

---

[25] On the use of the American flag in Holy Land travels, see Davis, *Landscape of Belief*, 33.

[26] In *Empire for Liberty* (Princeton NJ: Princeton University Press, 1989, 109–39), Wai Chee
Dimock points to the striking similarities between the representation of Ahab and the prevalent American ethnographic accounts of Native Americans in antebellum America. Both are
depicted as savages, both are doomed to extinction from the very outset: Ahab, as one who
bears a name of a king whose body was dismembered, and the Indians due to what the
American school of ethnography defined as an incapacity to change and adjust to modern
civilization. Dimock sees the similarities as resulting from a shared antebellum discourse of
Manifest Destiny in which fates are sealed by Scriptural paradigms. However, Dimock does
not see that Melville's insistence on the fragility of the boundaries between the possessors
and the dispossessed is indebted to the critical position of the Bible in this connection.

[27] Phyllis Trible, *Texts of Terror: Literary Feminist Readings of Biblical Narratives* (Philadelphia,
PA: Fortress Press, 1984), 9–36; Yair Zakovitch, "*And You Shall Tell Your Son . . .* ": *The Concept of
the Exodus in the Bible* (Jerusalem: Magnes Press, 1991), 26–30. For more on the interrelations
of the stories of Isaac and Ishmael, see Ronald Hendel, *Remembering Abraham: Culture,
Memory, and History in the Hebrew Bible* (New York: Oxford University Press, 2005). On
the evasiveness of promises in Genesis, see Chana Kronfeld, "Theories of Allusion and
Imagist Intertextuality: When Iconoclasts Read the Bible," in *On the Margins of Modernism:
Decentering Literary Dynamics* (Berkeley: University of California Press, 1996).

Egyptian bondwoman, was oppressed by her mistress, Sarah, the Israelites, in an inverted scene of affliction, are oppressed as slaves in Egypt. Hagar runs off to the desert and so do the Israelites. Indeed, the wandering Israelites will cross her track on passing through the wilderness of Shur, and they too will find the desert not only a place of acute thirst but also one of divine revelation and intervention.[28]

The boundaries between the chosen and the nonchosen in the biblical text are never as stable and decisive as the discourse of Manifest Destiny would have it.[29] From the very first vision of the nation to be, even before its emergence on the stage of history, it is doomed to exile and slavery. In the "Covenant between the Parts," God tells Abraham: "Know of a surety that thy seed shall be a stranger in a land that is not theirs, and shall serve them, and they shall afflict them four hundred years.... But in the fourth generation they shall come hither again: for the iniquity of the Amorites is not yet full" (Genesis 15:13–15). The fate of the Israelites is not radically different from other nations. Their chosenness does not exempt them from spending many years in the lowly position of oppressed exiles; neither does it assure their unconditional possession of the Promised Land. The divine plan takes into account other peoples as well, which is why the return of Israel to its land will depend, among other things, on the moral conduct of the Amorites. The Amorites have the right to reside in Canaan until their "iniquity" is "full." Only then will God deliver Abraham's descendants out of bondage and lead them back to Canaan.

Melville returns to the question of chosenness and the Abraham cycle in *Billy Budd*. We are told that Captain Vere, the "austere devotee of military duty, letting himself melt back into what remains primeval in our formalized humanity, may in the end have caught Billy to his heart, even as Abraham

---

[28] In Islamic exegesis, the interconnectedness of the two stories was taken a step further in renditions of Ishmael as the intended victim of the binding. According to Al-Tabarsī, Abraham had a vision regarding the sacrifice of Ishmael right after Sarah demanded the expulsion of Hagar and Ishmael. In this vision, he was asked to sacrifice Ishmael during the pilgrimage month in Mecca. With phenomenal devotion, Abraham brought Ishmael with him to perform the Hajj and informed him of the divine decree. He then lay him down for the Sacrifice at al-Jamra al Wustā. This is but one of many Islamic commentaries that sought to shape a story of the Sacrifice of Ishmael and to turn Mecca into the center of Islamic sacred geographies (the biblical Temple, as one recalls, was constructed on Mount Moriah, where the binding of Isaac took place). See Reuven Firestone, *Journeys in Holy Lands: The Evolution of the Abraham–Ishmael Legends in Islamic Exegesis* (New York: State University of New York Press, 1990), 148–51.

[29] I provide an extensive consideration of the fragility of the biblical concept of chosenness in *The Biography of Ancient Israel: National Narratives in the Bible* (Berkeley: California University Press, 2000). Another pertinent book in this connection is Regina Schwartz's *The Curse of Cain: The Violent Legacy of Monotheism* (Chicago: Chicago University Press, 1997).

may have caught young Isaac on the brink of resolutely offering him up in obedience to the exacting behest."[30] Through this hypothetical typology, Billy is likened to Isaac, a moment before the sacrifice. However, he is also an untamed Ishmael, whose arm flies swiftly at those who infuriate him. The "binding" of Billy may thus be construed as yet another commentary on the interrelated lives of Abraham's sons. Whether an Isaac or an Ishmael, Billy – the chosen "Handsome Sailor," the center of attention and admiration – is not spared.[31] Captain Vere cherishes Billy's "Primary Nature," to use Deleuze's terms, but he can neither save the innocent, lawless sailor whom he loves nor avoid "the sacrifice of Abraham."[32]

THE FINAL SHOT

No God rescues the *Pequod*. There is but one wild whaler who has the privilege of being delivered like his biblical precursor: Ishmael, the narrator. As the ship sinks down and the "great shroud of the sea" (572) rolls over it, the coffin Queequeg had built is "liberated by reason of its cunning spring, and, owing to its great buoyancy, rising with great force, the coffin life-buoy shot lengthwise from the sea, fell over, and floated by [his] side" (573). Queequeg's coffin seems to embody its maker's remarkable hunting skills, shot out of the closing vortex like an arrow or a grand harpoon, hitting its mark, floating by Ishmael as an unexpected gift of life. Ishmael, who in "Loomings" speaks of his tendency to follow funerals and "pause before coffin warehouses," now finds himself floating on a coffin, trying to spring back to life after the catastrophe.

In the closing scene of Ishmael's deliverance, the ship *Rachel* appears out of nowhere and picks up the floating castaway: "It was the devious-cruising Rachel, that in her retracing search after her missing children, only found another orphan" (573). That the *Rachel* adopts the son of the rival nation – Ishmael – rather than her own children is Melville's final bold comment on the intertwined destinies of the chosen and the nonchosen. Here, in the final line of the book, he ventures to move beyond visions of doom and to imagine a strikingly benevolent bond. The *Rachel*'s merging with Hagar and

[30] Herman Melville, *Billy Budd, Sailor and Selected Tales* (Oxford, UK: Oxford University Press, 1998), 346.

[31] To complicate the typological reading of Billy even further, note that in the opening section, the "Handsome Sailor" is represented as an idol, a sacred "grand sculptured Bull," calling to mind the Golden Calf. What is more, Melville – as many critics have noted – also follows the normative Christian reading of the binding of Isaac as a prefiguration of the crucifixion. Billy, in fact, is one of Melville's most prominent Christ figures.

[32] Gilles Deleuze, "Bartleby; or, the Formula," in *Essays Critical and Clinical*, trans. Daniel W. Smith and Michael A. Greco (Minneapolis: University of Minnesota Press, 1997), 80–1.

Ishmael's merging with the exiled Israelites of Jeremiah's Rachel (Jeremiah 31:15) introduce the possibility of remodeling relations between nations and religions, of inventing a new ship of state where untamed "orphans" would have the freedom to break with previous genealogies and traditions.

But the *Rachel* offers only a fragmentary, fleeting consolatory image whose power lies in the very refusal to endorse too facile a notion of salvation. The consoling *Rachel* remains inconsolable even as she rescues Ishmael. Her "devious cruising" in the "Epilogue" continues her earlier woeful winding, making clear that the crying over what has been lost and the crying for what will be lost never really stops. Cruising between possible and impossible worlds, between the redeemable and the irredeemable, the *Rachel*, above all, sketches a wondrous dreamy potentiality, a dim glittering beginning of another pilgrimage, no less unknown and no less evasive than the quest for the inscrutable White Whale.[33]

[33] I provide an elaborate reading of Melville's Rachel in *Melville's Bibles*, chapter 5.

10

Modern Theology

John J. Collins

WHAT IS THEOLOGICAL INTERPRETATION?

Theological interpretation of the Bible is a contested concept.[1] Even those who engage in the practice disagree among themselves as to what constitutes a theological reading. Many biblical scholars regard anything labeled "theological" as an enterprise of doubtful legitimacy in an academic context. Such skepticism is not without reason, but whether it is justified will depend, naturally enough, on the brand of theological interpretation that is proposed.

As New Testament scholar Richard Hays has recently argued, theological exegesis is not a "method" like, say, redaction criticism. Rather, he describes it as a practice, a way of approaching Scripture.[2] Hays, like many theologically oriented exegetes, stands in a distinctly Protestant tradition inspired by Karl Barth's famous commentary on the Epistle to the Romans. Barth conceived of theological exegesis as making the text speak directly to the present:

> By genuine understanding and interpretation, I mean that creative energy which Luther exercised with intuitive certainty in his exegesis . . . how energetically Calvin, having first established what stands in the text, sets himself to re-think the whole material and to wrestle with it, till the walls which separate the sixteenth century from the first become transparent! Paul speaks, and the man of the sixteenth century hears. The conversation between the original record and the reader moves round the subject-matter, until a distinction between yesterday and today becomes impossible. . . . Criticism (*krinein*) applied to historical documents means for me the measuring of

[1] Cf. James Barr on biblical theology as "a *contested* concept," in *The Concept of Biblical Theology: An Old Testament Perspective* (Minneapolis, MN: Fortress Press, 1999), 605.
[2] Richard Hays, "Reading the Bible with Eyes of Faith: The Practice of Theological Exegesis," *Journal of Theological Interpretation* 1 (2007), 11.

words and phrases by the standard of that about which the documents are speaking – unless, indeed, the whole is nonsense.[3]

Of course, "that about which the documents are speaking" is a good deal more elusive than Barth supposed, and many scholars would argue that maintaining a distance between past and present is of the essence of criticism. As John Barton stated, "some distancing of theology from biblical study is essential if the Bible is to be properly interpreted."[4] Krister Stendahl, reacting in part against Barth, drew a famous distinction between "what it meant" and "what it means" and insisted on the priority of the former.[5] Nonetheless, few would dispute the rather minimal formulation of Rudolf Bultmann: theological interpretation of biblical writings operates "under the presupposition that they have something to say to the modern world."[6] Theological interpretation, then, cannot be content with describing "the world behind the text" or its literary stylistics, but rather must address the implications of the text for the modern reader.

Of course, any classic writing, theological or not, has something to say to the modern world, and most theological interpreters mean something much more specific than that. For Hays, theological interpretation is a matter of "seeing with the eyes of faith" and is performed in the service of the church. On that understanding, it would be difficult to justify its place in the university (except in the case of Church-run schools). Personally, I incline more to the view of the Finnish New Testament scholar, Heikki Räisänen, that a scholar who works for the Church is like a scientist who works for the government.[7] I would add that both government and Church ultimately are better served if the scholar and scientist are not constrained by their wishes.

Nonetheless, the theological interpreter inevitably stands in some relation-ship to a religious tradition. It is often pointed out that the Bible is a construct of religious communities. If it were not for the place assigned to this col-lection in Judaism and Christianity, the study of these ancient texts would be construed quite differently.[8] Theological interpretation usually assumes

---

[3] Karl Barth, *The Epistle to the Romans* (translated from 6th German edition; Oxford, UK: Oxford University Press, 1968), 6, 7, 8.

[4] John Barton, "James Barr as Critic and Theologian," in *Language, Theology, and the Bible: Essays in Honour of James Barr*, eds. Samuel E. Balentine and John Barton (Oxford, UK: Clarendon Press, 1994), 19.

[5] Krister Stendahl, "Biblical Theology, Contemporary," *Interpreter's Dictionary of the Bible*, ed. G. A. Buttrick (Nashville, TN: Abingdon Press, 1962), Vol. 1, 418–32.

[6] Rudolf Bultmann, *Theology of the New Testament* (New York: Scribner's, 1955), Vol. 2, 251.

[7] Heikki Räisänen, *Beyond New Testament Theology* (2nd ed.; London: SCM Press, 2000).

[8] R. W. L. Moberly, *The Bible, Theology, and Faith: A Study of Abraham and Jesus* (Cambridge: Cambridge University Press, 2000), 11–14.

that the biblical text is authoritative or normative in some way, and this assumption also presupposes an ecclesial or synagogal context. Scriptural authority, however, can be construed in different ways. Protestant Christians traditionally profess a doctrine of *sola scriptura*, whereas Catholics and Jews profess to read Scripture through the lens of a tradition. However, Protestant scholars too have increasingly come to realize that the role of tradition is inevitable in interpretation. In this respect, even Stendahl's famous distinction between "what it meant" and "what it means" is difficult to maintain. George Lindbeck, for example, argues that "the descriptive task is also a normative one; theologians seek to describe speech and conduct that make sense in terms of a given religion's standards."[9] Even the description of "what it meant" inevitably is colored by the presuppositions the interpreter brings to the task.

Some Christian theologians argue that a Christian theological interpretation of the Old Testament must read it through the lens of the New Testament, or that the two must be conceived as a unity.[10] There is a renewed fashion in some circles of "finding Christ in the Old Testament"[11] or, in some cases, even "finding Mary" there.[12] British New Testament scholar Francis Watson goes so far as to say that the books of the Old Testament can be meaningful for Christians only in the full (Christian) canonical context.[13] This brings to mind the notorious remark of Walther Eichrodt that Judaism has only "a torso-like appearance . . . in separation from Christianity,"[14] which Jon Levenson cited as one of the reasons why Jews are not interested in Christian theology.[15] (I doubt that Watson was thinking of Judaism at all.) However, this is a peculiarly narrow view of Christian theology. Even Brevard Childs, whose canonical approach was similar to that of Watson in many ways, wrote that "the task of Old Testament theology is . . . not to Christianize the Old Testament by identifying it with the New Testament witness, but to hear its

9   George Lindbeck, "Towards a Postliberal Theology," in *The Return to Scripture in Judaism and Christianity: Essays in Postcritical Scriptural Interpretation*, ed. Peter Ochs (New York: Paulist Press, 1993), 94.
10 German biblical theology often sees a typological relationship between the Testaments; e.g., Hartmut Gese, *Essays on Biblical Theology* (Minneapolis, MN: Augsburg, 1981).
11 R. W. L. Moberly, "Christ in All the Scriptures? The Challenge of Reading the Old Testament as Christian Scripture," *Journal of Theological Interpretation* 1 (2007), 79–100.
12 Gary A. Anderson, "Mary in the Old Testament," *Pro Ecclesia* 16 (2008), 33–55.
13 Francis Watson, *Text and Truth: Redefining Biblical Theology* (Grand Rapids, MI: Eerdmans, 1997), 181.
14 Walther Eichrodt, *Theology of the Old Testament* (Philadelphia, PA: Westminster Press, 1961), Vol. 1, 26.
15 Jon D. Levenson, *The Hebrew Bible, the Old Testament, and Historical Criticism* (Louisville, KY: Westminster John Knox Press, 1993), 19.

own theological testimony to the God of Israel."[16] Theological interpretation, however, quite commonly assumes that both the canonical context and also later tradition (whether Jewish or Christian) must be taken into account.

Some theological interpreters, like Hays, assume that theological interpretation requires "the eyes of faith." They actually believe that the biblical text is a message addressed to them by God, even if they do not say so explicitly. According to the "Introduction" to the *Dictionary of Theological Interpretation*:

> Those who seek to interpret Scripture theologically want to hear the word of God in Scripture and hence to be transformed by the renewing of their minds.... God is not simply a function of a certain community's interpretative interest; instead God is prior to both the community and the biblical texts themselves.[17]

Such a belief renders any negative criticism of the biblical text out of the question. However, it is also possible to read a text – asking what it has to say to the present and being mindful of its role in Jewish or Christian tradition – without any such presupposition of faith. Divine inspiration is not a subject that can be debated with any profit. Scholars can establish what a given author or text says about God, but to say that the text is divinely inspired goes beyond the limits of rational argument.[18]

It is apparent from the discussion so far that biblical interpretation can be a problematic enterprise in an academic, university setting because it often relies on the faith assumptions of a particular religious community, which are not shared by academia at large. Theological interpreters often respond that academia too has its faith commitments. In this respect, they eagerly welcome postmodern relativism:

> Postmodern readers come to Scripture with a plurality of interpretative interests, including (perhaps) the theological, though no one interest may claim more authority than any other: Biblical interpretation in postmodernity means that there are no independent standards or universal criteria·

[16] Brevard S. Childs, *Old Testament Theology in a Canonical Context* (Philadelphia, PA: Fortress Press, 1986), 9.
[17] Kevin J. Vanhoozer, "Introduction: What Is Theological Interpretation of the Bible?," in *Dictionary for Theological Interpretation of the Bible*, ed. K. J. Vanhoozer (Grand Rapids, MI: Baker Books, 2005), 22.
[18] Compare James Barr's distinction between descriptive theology and assertions of belief, in "Does Biblical Study Still Belong to Theology," in idem, *The Scope and Authority of the Bible* (Philadelphia, PA: Westminster Press, 1980), 22.

for determining which of many rival interpretations is the "right" or "true" one.[19]

Although the postmodern critique of modernity can be adapted for apologetic purposes, the adaptation is disingenuous because most theological interpreters strongly believe that their interpretation *is* the right and true one. While academia has traditions, they are, in principle, open to critique in a way that religious traditions are not – at least in conservative theology. They do not have the status of divine revelation.

Nonetheless, it remains true that most people who read the Bible read it with theological interests in the expectation that it has something to say to the present. Biblical scholarship needs to address these interests and to find a way to do so responsibly.

READING GENESIS 22

There has been no lack of theological readings of Genesis. Readings of Genesis 1–3 have perhaps been the most influential and controversial in this regard because they deal with the constitution of humanity and the world, and especially with issues of gender. For my test case, however, I turn to the story of the sacrifice of Isaac in Genesis 22 because of the inherent interest of the story and because it has been given extended treatment by several major theological interpreters in recent times. I review four such readings by Gerhard von Rad, Brevard Childs, Walter Moberly, and Jon Levenson and conclude with comments on the problems and possibilities of theological reading.[20]

Gerhard von Rad

For Gerhard von Rad, as a Christian, Lutheran, biblical theologian, "all exegesis of the Old Testament depends on whom one thinks Jesus Christ to be."[21] The patriarchal narratives, to be sure, precede the revelation in Christ, but "what we are told here of the trials of a God who hides himself and whose promise is delayed, and yet of his comfort and support, can readily be read

---

[19] Vanhoozer, "What Is Theological Interpretation of the Bible?," 20–1.
[20] See my own previous treatment, "Faith Without Works: Biblical Ethics and the Sacrifice of Isaac," in J. J. Collins, *Encounters with Biblical Theology* (Minneapolis, MN: Fortress Press, 2005), 47–58.
[21] Von Rad, *Genesis: A Commentary* (3rd ed.; London: SCM, 1972; original German edition, 1952), 43.

into God's revelation of himself in Jesus Christ."[22] The understanding, then, is typological. The Old Testament is thought to anticipate what is revealed more fully (from a Christian perspective) in the New. In practice, the New Testament provides the lens through which the Old is interpreted.

Biblical theology has often been conceived as a systematizing enterprise that organizes its material under doctrinal categories. Von Rad objected to this procedure and emphasized instead what he saw as the predominant form of the biblical material: "The Old Testament writings confine themselves to representing Jahweh's relationship to Israel and the world in one aspect only, namely as a continuing divine activity in history."[23] The concept of "revelation in history" was notoriously problematic, and von Rad later acknowledged that it did not fit all the Old Testament in any case. In the context of Genesis, however, it led him to focus on the narrative and resist any attempt to distill universal doctrines from the text. (He did not make any attempt to show that the Genesis narratives were historical by modern standards.) Von Rad acknowledged that the story had gone through many stages of revision and suggested that it had originated as a cult saga of a sanctuary, which legitimated the substitution of an animal for child sacrifice. His main focus, however, was on the text as found in Genesis. This story, he argued, could not be restricted to one valid meaning. Rather, it was open to interpretation, as long as it was not interpreted as "a general unhistorical religious truth."[24] Accordingly, he argued that "it is impossible to suspect it of so theoretical an occupation with the phenomenon of child sacrifice as such" or of being programmatic in character.[25]

Von Rad accepted the opening redactional statement that "God tested Abraham" as definitive; it is not to be undermined by a psychologizing explanation. "The story concerns a temptation given by God, a demand which God did not intend to take seriously"[26]; Abraham, of course, is unaware of this. While von Rad acknowledges the spare, nonpsychological prose, which "refrains from giving us an insight into Abraham's inner self," he cannot refrain from filling in Abraham's thoughts:

> For Abraham, God's command is completely incomprehensible: the child, given by God after long delay, the only link that can lead to the promised greatness of Abraham's seed, is to be given back to God in sacrifice.[27]

[22] Ibid.
[23] Von Rad, *Old Testament Theology*, Vol. 1, 106.
[24] Von Rad, *Genesis*, 243.
[25] Ibid., 244.
[26] Ibid., 239.
[27] Ibid.

Having already been cut off from his past, Abraham is now cut off from his future. Therefore, says von Rad, "the story concerns something much more frightful than child sacrifice. It has to do with a road out into Godforsakenness, a road on which Abraham does not know that God is only testing him."[28] Any Christian reader will catch here an echo of the words of Christ on the cross: "My God, my God, why hast thou forsaken me?" Abraham has become a type of Christ. (In Christian theology, Isaac was more often cast in that role.[29]) The story is read as a radical test of obedience, which underlines that God can freely take away what he has freely given and that human beings can claim no entitlement with God.

This interpretation has overtones of the Lutheran theology of the cross but also of existentialist philosophy, which was popular when von Rad wrote. Both the theology and the existentialism have heuristic value. They lead von Rad to formulate an interpretation to which a modern person can relate. Many people have found it profound and moving. Von Rad, I think, would not have claimed that it was the only way to read the text. Although he says that Isaac is not a mere foil for Abraham, he pays little attention to him; the same could be said of the biblical text. The most questionable aspect of the interpretation, by which von Rad claims to know the mind of Abraham (so to speak), is also what gives it its power.

Yet, for a modern non-Lutheran, what is most striking about this interpretation is its *a priori* acceptance of the divine demand for child sacrifice. To be sure, we are assured that God did not intend to follow through with it, but Abraham does not know this, and he is commended for his willingness to obey. There is an acute moral problem here (to which we subsequently return), but von Rad's theological reading, which is profoundly humane in other respects, does not acknowledge it at all. Presumably, this is because it would put the moral lesson of the story and, therefore, the word of God, in question.

Brevard Childs

The distinctive contribution of Brevard Childs to theological interpretation was to emphasize the importance of the canonical context. In accordance with the German tradition in which he was trained, Childs distinguishes layers in the text with the aid of form and redaction criticism. For Childs, in contrast to most historical critics, the contributions of the redactor were especially

---

[28] Ibid., 244.
[29] See, e.g., James Swetnam S.J., *Jesus and Isaac: A Study of the Epistle to the Hebrews in the Light of the Aqedah* (Rome: Biblical Institute Press, 1981).

important because they are decisive in the "canonical shaping" of the text. So, the initial statement that "God tested Abraham" is a "canonical feature," which provides normative guidance for the interpretation of the story.[30] Also, the use of the verb "to see" at crucial points in the story points to the centrality of divine revelation. For Childs, it is axiomatic that the larger context in the book of Genesis be borne in mind. Three of the keywords in the chapter – *ram, burnt-offering*, and *appear* – are also found in Leviticus 8–9 and 16:

> The effect for the informed reader is that the story of Abraham's uniquely private experience is thus linked to Israel's collective public worship, and conversely Israel's sacrifice is drawn into the theological orbit of Abraham's offering.

Genesis 22 and Leviticus "are not diverse ideologies but diverse witnesses to the same gracious ways of God with Israel."[31]

These canonical observations, however, do not get to the heart of the matter. Childs is emphatic that echoes of ancient Near Eastern custom are mere background and

> do not function in the text as the bearers of the essential testimony. Rather, the command is presented in Gen. 22.2 as a direct imperative of God to Abraham. To raise the psychological question as to how Abraham knew it was from God, or the historical question as to whether the sacrifice of children was once a part of Hebrew religion, is to distract the interpreter from the witness of this text.[32]

For Childs,

> the theological issue at stake is that God's command to slay the heir stands in direct conflict with his promise of salvation through this very child. . . . The Old Testament bears witness that God was faithful to his promise and confirmed his word by providing his own sacrifice instead of the child.[33]

Moreover, the editors did not let the witness become tied to the past. The same God lets himself be known in Israel's public worship. The same emphasis on the faithfulness of God is found in the New Testament, where Paul says that "God did not spare his own son but gave him up for us all" (Romans 8:32). The parallel is with the behavior of Abraham rather than that of Isaac. Genesis witnesses to Abraham's faith in God's promises, even when God

---

[30] Childs provides a substantial discussion of Genesis 22 in his *Biblical Theology of the Old and New Testaments* (Minneapolis, MN: Fortress Press, 1992), 325–36.

[31] Ibid., 327–8.

[32] Ibid., 334.

[33] Ibid.

seems to contradict himself. This too is picked up in the New Testament, in the Epistle to the Hebrews, chapter 11:17–19, although the New Testament text anachronistically attributes to Abraham a belief in the resurrection of the dead. Childs is wary, however, of much typological interpretation, based on superficial analogies such as the fact that both Isaac and Jesus are said to carry the wood that is to be the instrument of their execution. "It belongs to the basic theological task to pursue exegetically how the uniqueness of each text is preserved."[34]

In fact, however, Childs preserves much less of the uniqueness of Genesis 22 than did von Rad. He scarcely deals at all with the text as narrative. Rather than preserve the unique specificity of the text, he draws from it abstract principles, such as the faithfulness of God and the necessity of belief in the promises. The canonical observations tend to lead the interpreter away from Genesis, to very different texts like Leviticus, to which it is related only tangentially at best. Although von Rad may have gone beyond the text in imagining the anguish of Abraham, he at least brought the text to life. On Childs's reading, the text is removed from its historical or literary specificity already by the editors (or canonical shapers) and is reduced to being an illustration of a rather abstract and formal principle.

Childs simply dismisses questions that arise from psychological or even historical considerations as distractions. However, a reading that has to rule out questions of basic human interest is not very satisfactory. Even apart from whether one shares Childs's view of the biblical text as word of God, his reading does not adequately address the problems raised by the text.

Walter Moberly

An extensive recent treatment of Genesis 22, somewhat in the spirit of Childs, has been offered by Walter Moberly.[35] Like Childs, Moberly does not offer a narrative exposition as much as a contextualization that largely depends on his analysis of key Hebrew terms in the story: "test," "fear God," "provide/see" (the verb *ra'ah*), and "bless." His method is to examine how these terms are used elsewhere in the Hebrew Bible and interpret their use in Genesis 22 in light of that usage. So, for example, he concludes that whereas "fear of God" entails obedience, it should not be associated with religious awe, in the sense associated with Rudolf Otto, or with fear of unpleasant consequences.

---

[34] Ibid., 336.
[35] Moberly, *Bible, Theology, and Faith*, 71–183.

Rather, we are told, "the term depicts human integrity . . . rooted in responsive recognition of God."[36] He adds:

> Abraham's embodiment of this appropriate human response to God is also enriched in content through its links, tacit within Genesis 22 itself but clearer in a canonical context, with God's election of Israel and the covenant of Sinai.

From my perspective, all of this smacks of *eisegesis* – that is, a flattening harmonization of the diversity of biblical traditions – of which even Childs would not approve. Whether "fear of God" bespeaks "human integrity" is a value judgment and depends on a circular argument. It requires considerable exegetical freedom to read an allusion to the Sinai covenant into Genesis 22.

To Moberly's credit, he at least acknowledges the moral problem that some modern scholars have with the sacrifice of Isaac. "Is this not a story which, unless subverted and read 'against the grain,' could lead people to believe in a cruel and capricious God and perhaps to suppose that they themselves might be justified in abusing or killing a child?"[37] However, he quickly dismisses this as "a more or less artificial problem" because he finds no evidence in the history of interpretation that these fears were ever realized. I am not reassured.

Carol Delaney has described a modern case in California in which a man obeyed a supposed divine voice and killed his beloved daughter.[38] He did not cite Genesis 22 as justification, but he was a convert to evangelical Christianity, and it is difficult not to suspect a connection. More important, however, the influence of a text like this need not manifest itself in direct imitation. The problem lies in the attitude it imparts. There is an analogy here with the ḥerem, or ban, in the Conquest stories: the command to commit genocide against the Canaanites in the Promised Land. Again, a biblical command that is offensive to modern sensibilities – and was carefully relativized in both Jewish and Christian tradition – has remained "on the books," so to speak. In that case, there is ample evidence that it has been used repeatedly as a paradigm to legitimate violence, by Christians and Jews alike, from the Maccabees to modern Israel.[39]

What defines a theological reading for Moberly is that the text is read "within a wider scriptural and communal context which provided guidelines and constraints for understanding and appropriating the story."[40] In this

---

[36] Ibid., 96–7.
[37] Ibid., 128.
[38] Carol Delaney, *Abraham on Trial* (Princeton, NJ: Princeton University Press, 1998).
[39] John J. Collins, *Does the Bible Justify Violence?* (Minneapolis, MN: Fortress Press, 2004).
[40] Moberly, *Bible, Theology, and Faith*, 129.

respect, he seems to move away from the traditional Protestant principle of
sola scriptura and endorses the Jewish and Catholic emphasis on tradition as
the context for interpretation. In this context, he claims, "the metaphorical
significance of the text was taken for granted" and this "enabled the meaningful preservation of a story about child sacrifice."[41] There is, of course, a
long tradition of allegorical interpretation, dating back to Philo of Alexandria, which seeks to save the appearances of the text by claiming that it means
something other than what it seems to say. That tradition has largely lost its
persuasiveness in the modern world. Moberly's "metaphorical" understanding of the *aqedah* is not quite the same as allegory, but it moves in a similar
direction. It is essentially an apologetic strategy that seeks a way to affirm a
text that would be quite problematic if read literally.

Jon Levenson

Jon Levenson has famously and persuasively explained why Jews are not
interested in biblical theology, but he must be considered an exception to his
own rule. Like Moberly, Levenson insists on the priority of tradition. Jews
and Christians can work together on many aspects of the biblical text,

> but when we come to "the final literary setting" and even more so to "the con-
> text of the canon," we must part company, for *there is no non-particularistic
> access to these larger contexts*, and no decision on these issues, even when made
> for secular purposes, can be neutral between Judaism and Christianity.[42]

He has addressed the sacrifice of Isaac at some length in his book on *The
Death and Resurrection of the Beloved Son*[43] and again in a more overtly theo-
logical article in the journal *Judaism*, entitled "Abusing Abraham: Traditions,
Religious Histories and Modern Misinterpretations."[44]

Despite his insistence on the theological inadequacy of historical criticism,
Levenson takes the ancient Near Eastern context of the story more seriously
than any of the Christian interpreters considered previously. One common
interpretation of the story, among Jews as well as Christians, is that its real
purpose was to explain that God did not want human sacrifice. So, for example, Shalom Spiegel wrote: "the primary purpose of the Akedah story may

---

[41] Ibid.
[42] Levenson, *Hebrew Bible, Old Testament, and Historical Criticism*, 80.
[43] New Haven, CT: Yale University Press, 1993.
[44] *Judaism* 47 (1998), 259–77.

have been only this: to attach to a real pillar of the folk and a revered reputation the new norm – abolish human sacrifice, substitute animals instead."[45] Levenson finds this etiological explanation ineffective:

> ... it is passing strange to condemn child sacrifice through a narrative in which a father is richly rewarded for his willingness to carry out that very practice. If the point of the aqedah is "abolish human sacrifice, substitute animals instead," then Abraham cannot be regarded as having passed the test.[46]

Moreover, he refuses to dismiss child sacrifice as a "pagan" practice, as many theological interpreters do too readily. After all, the demand for child sacrifice is still "on the books" in Exodus 22:28: "You shall give me the first-born among your sons," even though it is later countermanded in Exodus 34:19–20. To be sure, child sacrifice cannot have been standard practice, but, Levenson argues, it could be required in special cases: "Most fathers did not have to carry out this hideous demand. But some did. Abraham knew it was his turn when he heard God in his own voice, ordering the immolation of Isaac."[47]

Levenson also refuses to dilute the seriousness of the story by saying that it was *only* a test:

> Nothing in the verb used (*nissah*) implies that the act commanded will not be carried to completion, that Isaac will be only bound and not sacrificed.... This being the case, Abraham's willingness to heed the frightful command may or may not demonstrate faith in the promise that is invested in Isaac, but it surely and abundantly demonstrates his putting obedience to God ahead of every possible competitor.[48]

By these incisive observations, Levenson deflates much of the Lutheran line of interpretation, which focuses on the faith of Abraham:

> To say, with Kierkegaard and von Rad, that he is prepared so to do because through faith he expects to receive Isaac anew (as indeed happens) is to minimize the frightfulness of what Abraham is commanded to do. It is also ... to miss one of the key ambiguities and energizing tensions of the story.[49]

---

[45] Shalom Spiegel, *The Last Trial* (New York: Behrman, 1967), 64.
[46] Levenson, *Death and Resurrection*, 13.
[47] Ibid., 17.
[48] Ibid., 126.
[49] Ibid.

The Kantian Critique

But is obedience to a divine voice that makes a serious demand for human sacrifice a good thing? The classic objection was raised by Immanuel Kant:

> There are certain cases in which a man can be convinced that it cannot be God whose voice he thinks he hears; when the voice commands him to do what is opposed to the moral law, though the phenomenon seem to him ever so majestic and surpassing the whole of nature, he must count it a deception.

Kant cited the case of Abraham as a specific example:

> The myth of the sacrifice of Abraham can serve as an example: Abraham, at God's command was going to slaughter his own son – the poor child in his ignorance even carried the wood. Abraham should have said to this supposed divine voice: that I am not to kill my beloved son is quite certain; that you who appear to me are God, I am not certain, nor can I ever be, even if the voice thunders from the sky.[50]

This passage is often cited by theological commentators only to be quickly dismissed. (An exception is provided by Martin Buber, who allows that the identity of the divine voice would have been clear to Abraham, but insists that for the rest of humanity "the question that takes precedence over every other is: Are you really addressed by the Absolute or by one of his apes?"[51]) Childs, for example, would simply say that it is inappropriate to question the authenticity of the revelation. For Moberly, such a suspicious approach to the text shows "a reluctance to enter into the narrative world in its own right and to take the irreducibility of the narrative with full seriousness."[52] This, I think, is a valid objection if the goal is a literary appreciation of the text. However, Moberly also views the text as "the vehicle of moral and theological discourse" as being in some sense normative for the community. In that case, we are obliged to ask how the narrative world of the text relates to the world as we otherwise know it. When Moberly speaks of taking the narrative with full seriousness, he means simply, "believe that God actually spoke to Abraham." Claus Westermann responds to Kant by arguing that he fails to appreciate the context in which the story is set:

---

[50] Immanuel Kant, *The Conflict of the Faculties* (New York: Orbis Books, 1979), 115 (original publication 1798).
[51] Martin Buber, "The Suspension of Ethics," in *Four Existentialist Theologians*, ed. Will Herberg (Garden City, NY: Doubleday, 1958), 251–2.
[52] Moberly, *Bible, Theology, and Faith*, 179.

the command is spoken out of this context of familiar mutual trust. Horrible, inhuman, it is nevertheless the word of his trusted God. . . . This is the reason Kant was unable to understand what is meant here . . . for him, it is possible to abstract the word as "that which is said," from the speaker.[53]

But trust in the speaker is hardly a sufficient ethical warrant for obedience if that which is commanded is clearly morally wrong.

Some scholars seek to evade the force of Kant's argument by arguing that we cannot judge an ancient character by modern criteria. Moberly, for example, says:

> There is a modern tendency, encouraged (in different ways) by people of the stature of Kant and Kierkegaard, to suppose that this modern moral judgment must also apply to the story in its ancient context. Yet such an approach is a classic example of anachronism. . . . Our first point, about the nature of the testing, indicates that the story is to be seen as a positive moral example.[54]

A positive moral example for whom? Ancient people? Or modern Jews and Christians? Anachronism is a double-edged sword. It defends the story from criticism in a different historical context but does so at the price of rendering it irrelevant to modern concerns.

Levenson engages Kant's position at some length in his essay "Abusing Abraham." He focuses on Kant's view of a universal moral law, which is a good deal more problematic in the age of postmodernism than it was at the height of the Enlightenment. Levenson focuses his critique precisely on the conflict between the universal and the particular:

> The implications of Kant's view are profound: Any community that elects "rational theology" over "biblical theology," as Kant argues all should, will necessarily surrender its distinctive norms and the identity that adhering to them creates and sustains.[55]

There is a legitimate concern here. Kant notoriously and chillingly wrote that "the euthanasia of Judaism is pure moral religion, freed from all the ancient statutory teachings, some of which were bound to be retained in Christianity."[56] Therefore, concludes Levenson,

> His indictment of Abraham is thus more than an attack on one man's misjudgment: it is an indictment of Judaism itself and (though perhaps to a

---

[53] Claus Westermann, *Genesis 12–36* (Minneapolis, MN: Augsburg, 1985), 356–7.
[54] R. W. L. Moberly, *Genesis 12–50* (Sheffield, UK: Sheffield Academic Press, 1992), 43.
[55] Levenson, "Abusing Abraham," 261.
[56] Kant, *Conflict*, 95.

lesser degree) of Christianity as well. It is a call for the end of the religion of the commandment, the *mitzvah*, altogether.[57]

Levenson does not directly address the most fundamental question raised by Kant, and echoed by Buber, which is the epistemological one. How does one recognize whether a commandment is from God? His answer is clearly implied. One knows if the tradition tells one so. In this respect, Levenson's position is similar to the cultural–linguistic model of theology proposed by the Christian theologian George Lindbeck.[58] There is no position of pure reason – independent of all tradition – from which moral judgments can be made. Theological interpretation presupposes trust in a particular tradition. Similarly, for Moberly,

> ... the question of the truth, or otherwise, of the story cannot be answered except by engaging with the beliefs and values that the story portrays. Is it true to the character of God, and is it true to the nature of human life? ... those who stand in some kind of continuity with the ancient community of faith which cherished and wrote the story, and who themselves cherish it as part of scripture will be inclined to affirm that the story is true.[59]

But one need not subscribe in full to Kant's idea of the moral law – or to the possibility of pure moral religion – to regard child sacrifice as morally wrong. Even in a postmodern age, there is increasing recognition that crimes against humanity exist. When I was writing this chapter, I happened to watch the 2004 Israeli movie, *God's Sandbox* (a.k.a. *Tahara*), in which a Western woman falls in love with the son of a Bedouin sheikh and is forced to submit to female circumcision, which traumatizes her for life. At one point, her beloved tries to assure her: "This is something my people do; it is okay." It obviously is not okay and was not okay for Bedouin women either. Respect for particularistic traditions cannot excuse everything that is done in their name.

Moreover, in this case, it is not necessary to appeal to universal criteria. The practice of child sacrifice is almost universally condemned within Jewish and Christian tradition, at least from the time of Josiah's reform and the prophet Jeremiah, who declares in the name of the Lord that human sacrifice was something that "I did not decree nor did it enter my mind."[60] Ezekiel, intriguingly, says:

---

[57] Levenson, "Abusing Abraham," 262.
[58] George Lindbeck, *The Nature of Doctrine: Religion and Theology in a Postliberal Age* (Philadelphia, PA: Westminster Press, 1984).
[59] Moberly, *Genesis 12–50*, 56.
[60] Jeremiah 19:4–6. See further Collins, "Faith without Works," 51–2.

I gave them statutes that were not good, and ordinances by which they could not live. I defiled them through all their very gifts, in their offering up all their firstborn, in order that I might horrify them, so that they might know that I am the LORD. (Ezekiel 20:25–26)

The anomaly of Genesis 22 is that it glorifies Abraham for being willing to do something that even the prophets considered an abomination.

Kierkegaard

Perhaps the most famous attempt to overcome this problem was that of Søren Kierkegaard, the nineteenth-century Danish philosopher and theologian who is often regarded as a forerunner of existentialism. Kierkegaard drew a sharp antithesis between ethics and faith:

> The ethical expression for what Abraham did is that he would murder Isaac; the religious expression is that he would sacrifice Isaac; but precisely in this consists the dread which can well make a man sleepless, and yet Abraham is not what he is without this dread.... For when faith is eliminated by becoming null or nothing, then there only remains the crude fact that Abraham wanted to murder Isaac – which is easy enough for anyone to imitate who has not faith, the faith, that is to say, which makes it hard for him.[61]

Levenson comments sympathetically:

> To imitate Abraham's deed alone, abstracted from the love, the promise, and the faith, is grossly to misinterpret him. That such a misinterpretation can arise is clear.... By restoring the *aqedah* to its context in Genesis, Kierkegaard has profoundly undercut the analogy between Abraham and the violent fathers of his day and ours.[62]

It is certainly true that Genesis 22 would be a very different story if Abraham were not said to love Isaac. However, attempted murder is not excused by the fact that the person who attempts it loves the victim. The real force of Kierkegaard's argument is that faith requires "the teleological suspension of the ethical." Ethics are based on universal laws, but in faith, an individual isolates himself as higher than the universal.[63] The Finnish scholar Timo Veijola stated the issue clearly:

---

[61] Kierkegaard, *Fear and Trembling and the Sickness unto Death* (Garden City, NY: Doubleday, 1954), 41.

[62] "Abusing Abraham," 269.

[63] *Fear and Trembling*, 65–6. See Jerome I. Gellman, *The Fear, the Trembling, and the Fire: Kierkegaard and Hasidic Masters on the Binding of Isaac* (Lanham, MD: University Press of

It is of the essence of religious statements that one cannot evaluate their ultimate claim to truth by objective standards. Rather, one is convinced on the basis of one's own experience – or not. Abraham had the firm unshakeable certainty that this God would prove himself to be the true God even when he demanded from humans that which made no sense.[64]

Every fanatic has the unshakable certainty that his or her conviction is right. The comment of Martin Buber, that "ours is an age in which the suspension of the ethical conscience fills the world in a caricatured form,"[65] is true in any age. The fact that a conviction is conceived of as a divine command is no safeguard against fanaticism.

CONCLUSION

My objective in this chapter, however, is not to pronounce on the ethics of Genesis 22 but rather to illustrate some of the ways of reading Genesis theologically. On the basis of the examples considered here, a tendency to apologetics seems to be ingrained in the enterprise. If theological interpretation is thought to presuppose a belief that the biblical text is the word of God, addressed to the reader across the centuries, then it is hardly conceivable that the text could be judged to be wrong. Many theological interpreters obscure – if they do not deny – the human origin of scripture. In this respect, it is well to remember the warning of Wilfred Cantwell Smith, in his comparative study of Scripture: "Scripture is a human activity. . . . No doubt, their scripture to a mighty extent makes a people what they are. Yet one must not lose sight of the point that it is the people who make it, keep it, scripture."[66]

Most theological interpreters, except for Fundamentalists, have come to terms with the fact that biblical texts are not necessarily historically reliable. There is a far greater reluctance to accept the idea that they may not be ethically reliable or even dangerous and malignant. Genesis 22 is not the only or the gravest illustration of this problem. The view of gender promulgated in Genesis as the order of Creation has become highly controversial in recent decades. Outside of Genesis, scholars have become increasingly aware of the moral problem of the violent conquest of Canaan – ordered in Deuteronomy

America, 1994), 1–22. Gellman (45–71) compares the teleological suspension of the ethical to the Hasidic idea of "sinning for the sake of heaven."

[64] Timo Veijola, "Das Opfer des Abraham – Paradigma des Glaubens aus dem nachexilischen Zeitalter," *Zeitschrift für Theologie und Kirche* 85 (1988), 129–30.

[65] Buber, "The Suspension of Ethics," 252.

[66] Wilfred Cantwell Smith, *What Is Scripture? A Comparative Approach* (Minneapolis, MN: Fortress Press, 1993), 18.

and implemented in Joshua – and its use as a paradigm in both Christian and Jewish history.[67]

Admittedly, the apologetic cast of modern biblical interpretation may be somewhat exaggerated by the particular examples I have chosen. There also exist more liberal theological interpreters, who are criticized at length by Levenson and Moberly.[68] For example, Terence Fretheim cites the concerns of psychoanalyst Alice Miller that Genesis 22 may have contributed to an atmosphere that makes it possible to justify the abuse of children.[69] Whereas Fretheim insists that "we may not simply dismiss the possible negative impact of this text," his own emphasis is on Abraham's trust in God, which he does not question at all. Walter Brueggemann, in his *Theology of the Old Testament*, acknowledges "counter-traditions" in the Bible that question the dominant emphases in the text. Like Childs, he speaks of the "witness" and "testimony" of the text and allows that "in any serious court room trial, testimony is challenged by other, competing testimony."[70] However, he also says that the biblical testimony "will not submit to any other warrant,"[71] and it is not clear how far he is willing to question the values of the text.[72] Even the feminist critic Phyllis Trible has typically directed her fire at the biases of male critics, or those of ancient Israelites, rather than at the text itself: "[T]he intentionality of biblical faith, as distinguished from a general description of biblical religion, is neither to create nor to perpetuate patriarchy but rather to function as salvation for both women and men."[73] Fretheim, Brueggemann, and Trible are all less inhibited in acknowledging problems in the text than Childs or Moberly, but even they are not free of the apologetic tendency that characterizes so much of theological interpretation.

It seems to me, however, that one does not have to be a believer to appreciate that the biblical texts have important things to say to the present, by way of

---

[67] Keith Whitelam, *The Invention of Ancient Israel: The Silencing of Palestinian History* (London: Routledge, 1996); Collins, *Does the Bible Justify Violence?*

[68] Levenson ("Abusing Abraham," 262–8) singles out Burton Visotzky, a Jewish professor of Midrash, and Ted Peters, a Christian theologian. Moberly takes issue with Terence Fretheim (*Bible, Theology, and Faith*, 129) and Phyllis Trible (ibid., 163–8). Moberly's other examples of the hermeneutics of suspicion are not attempting to do theological interpretation.

[69] Terence E. Fretheim, "The Book of Genesis," in *The New Interpreter's Bible*, eds. Leander Keck, et al. (Nashville, TN: Abingdon Press, 1994), Vol. 1, 499.

[70] Walter Brueggemann, *Theology of the Old Testament: Testimony, Dispute, Advocacy* (Minneapolis, MN: Fortress Press, 1997), 715.

[71] Ibid., 714.

[72] See my discussion of Brueggemann in my book, *The Bible after Babel: Historical Criticism in a Postmodern Age* (Grand Rapids, MI: Eerdmans, 2005), 142–8.

[73] Phyllis Trible, "Depatriarchalizing in Biblical Interpretation," *Journal of the American Academy of Religion* 41 (1973), 34. For further discussion of Trible, see Collins, *Bible after Babel*, 78–9, 86–96.

both insight into human nature – as is true of any great literature – and raising moral issues. As James Barr observed, "empathy and personal involvement are not to be identified with the acceptance of the theological or ideological position of the matter studied. If this were so, it would lead to an impossibly solipsistic position."[74] As John Barton put it, "One cannot establish what the Bible means if one insists on reading it as necessarily conforming to what one already believes to be true."[75] Barton may go too far when he adds "which is what a theological reading amounts to." I do not believe that a theological reading *must* subordinate exegesis to belief in this way, but it is a fair characterization of much of what has passed for theological reading hitherto.

Insofar as the Bible functions as normative literature for religious communities, I suggest that it should do so more by providing a fund of common stories and examples that provide a context for ongoing discussion and debate than by providing prescriptive solutions. It is difficult for anyone nourished in either Jewish or Christian tradition to regard Genesis 22 as a positive moral example, unless one subordinates the text to a later tradition that either allegorizes it or suppresses some aspects of it. The text poses basic questions about the nature of moral obligation and of priorities between different commitments, and it provides a wonderful focus for discussion. I also suggest that religious communities would be better served by a question-oriented exegesis that is uninhibited in raising and confronting the problems that arise from the text than by the apologetic attempt to smooth over the problems or by insistence on deference to tradition. Many of the greatest figures in the Bible itself (e.g., the prophets, Job, and Jesus) were fiercely critical of their tradition. Modern theological interpreters, in contrast, seem too willing to "lie for God" like the friends of Job, and theological interpretation has suffered as a result.

---

[74] Barr, "Does Biblical Study Still Belong to Theology?" 26.
[75] John Barton, *The Nature of Biblical Criticism* (Louisville, KY: Westminster John Knox Press, 2007), 164.

Index of Biblical Citations

This index includes citations to specific verses. For complete coverage of a particular story, see the name of the story in the general index (e.g., "Creation story").

General Index

Abel and Cain, 58, 60n36, 68n59
Abraham story
  and blessings of younger son in post-biblical
    literature, 117
  call and migration of, 144–55
  expression of hospitality by, 78
  genealogy of preserved in place names, 41
  in *Genesis Apocryphon*, 134
  inner life of, 128, 130
  in J source, 59
  in Midrash, 128–35
  and national identity of Israel, 146–47
  in P source, 56, 58
  in Philo, 147–48
  and representation of Sarah as his sister, 90,
    132–33, 134
  sacrifice of Isaac. (*See* Binding of Isaac
    (*aqedah*))
  as type of Christ, 201–2, 203–4
  as universal model for spiritual quest,
    147–48, 150–51, 156
Abrahamic covenant
  continuity with Jacob's covenant, 37–38, 39
  and Israel as oppressed exile, 193
  in J source, 60
  theological interpretation of, 203
  See also patriarchal promises
Ackerman, Susan, 75
Adam and Eve
  Beauvoir on, 71, 72n7
  in Garden of Eden, 11–12
  in P source, 56, 57, 60
  See also Garden of Eden
advocacy readings, 7
aesthetic qualities of biblical literature, 15
aesthetics of reception theory, 139

affective fallacy, 138
afterlife of texts
  and reception criticism, 140
  theological exegesis and implication of the
    text for the modern reader, 197
  as transformation of text, 6
  and translation, 157, 157n1, 175
Agapê, Irene, and Chionê story, 152–53, 156
agency
  and forbidden sexual relations, 83
  and male power to offer hospitality, 78–79
  reversal of Lot's roles, 89
  by women in sexual relations, 90–91
aggadah
  and clash between authority and
    sensibilities, 124–25
  interpretation of biblical texts in, 94
  on Torah, 97–98
aggression, male-male penetration as, 83–84
Ahab (captain in *Moby-Dick*), 177, 189
Akiva, Rabbi, 131
Albright, William F., 41
Alexander, Philip, 127
allegorical interpretation
  of binding of Isaac, 206, 214
  in early Christian writers, 150
  in Midrash, 172
  in Philo, 123, 147, 158n3, 206
allusions to biblical events, 92
Alter, Robert
  on criticism *vs.* interpretation, 48
  as modern approach to literary criticism,
    53n22, 61
  on poetics of memory, 33
  on Sodomites' violation of social norms,
    81